Contemporary Chief Information Officers:

Management Experiences

M. Gordon Hunter
University of Lethbridge, Canada

IGI PUBLISHING
Hershey • New York

Acquisition Editor:	Kristin Klinger
Senior Managing Editor:	Jennifer Neidig
Managing Editor:	Sara Reed
Assistant Managing Editor:	Sharon Berger
Development Editor:	Kristin Roth
Copy Editor:	Lanette Ehrhardt
Typesetter:	Michael Brehm
Cover Design:	Lisa Tosheff
Printed at:	Yurchak Printing Inc.

Published in the United States of America by
IGI Publishing (an imprint of IGI Global)
701 E. Chocolate Avenue
Hershey PA 17033
Tel: 717-533-8845
Fax: 717-533-8661
E-mail: cust@igi-pub.com
Web site: http://www.igi-pub.com

and in the United Kingdom by
IGI Publishing (an imprint of IGI Global)
3 Henrietta Street
Covent Garden
London WC2E 8LU
Tel: 44 20 7240 0856
Fax: 44 20 7379 0609
Web site: http://www.eurospanonline.com

Library of Congress Cataloging-in-Publication Data

Hunter, M. Gordon.
Contemporary chief information officers : management experiences / M. Gordon Hunter.
p. cm.
Summary: "This book explores the experiences of the contemporary Chief Information Officer in the United States, Taiwan, and New Zealand. This role is now more of the management role with focus on employing technology to address business goals. CIO must know the expectations of senior management and everyone must concur on how they will meet corporate objectives"--Provided by publisher.
Includes bibliographical references and index.
ISBN 978-1-59904-078-3 (hardcover) -- ISBN 978-1-59904-080-6 (ebook)
1. Chief information officers--Interviews. 2. Chief information officers--Biography. 3. Information technology--Management. 4. Information resources management. 5. Business planning. I. Title.
HD30.2.H863 2007
658.4'038--dc22
2007007269

British Cataloguing in Publication Data
A Cataloguing in Publication record for this book is available from the British Library.

Contemporary Chief Information Officers:

Management Experiences

Table of Contents

Foreword

I am excited to have the opportunity to write the Forward to this book, as it provides honest insights into the role of the contemporary CIO in modern business from the personal experiences of the technology leaders who are either currently performing or have performed as chief information officers. This book also explores the role on a global scale through interviews with CIOs based in Taiwan, New Zealand, and the United States. I believe that this book has significant value to a number of groups/stakeholders including those in academia and in industry.

Students of business, both undergraduate and graduate, will gain an advantage from the introduction to the strategic issues of managing IT effectively within an organizational context. Identification of CIO issues and the innovative approach to conducting research into aspects of senior management will fascinate business researchers. The CIO and those pursuing this career path will benefit from the insights and identification of important issues to be considered. The CEO and other C-level executives can profit from the information and better leverage this area that is growing rapidly in its importance as a strategic enabler.

This book combines personal knowledge with academic analysis. The numerous studies and research referenced provide historical and current perspective on the role of the CIO. From the creation of the role in the mid1980s, this book provides an impressive context on how contemporary CIO experiences and views compare and contrast to previous work over time. Those reading this book will benefit from understanding the CIO role and how it has evolved in today's environment, and how to apply it to their business needs.

In this forward, I would like to add some brief comments about NetJets Inc. and my experiences, which I think contributes further to the aspects discussed in this book. In my role as chief information officer and senior vice president of NetJets Inc., a Berkshire Hathaway

Company, I have seen firsthand how technology, in collaboration with business leaders, can transform processes and enable a degree of optimization beyond business intelligence that cannot be achieved by any other means. We have reached a point where technology and advanced mathematics can be cost effectively directed to provide tremendous returns and competitive advantage. Business leaders that recognize this will quickly outpace their competitors.

NetJets Inc. provides the safest and most secure private aviation solutions in the world. NetJets fractional aircraft ownership allows individuals and companies to buy a share of a private business jet at a fraction of the cost of whole aircraft ownership, and guarantees availability 365 days a year with just a few hours' notice. The NetJets programs worldwide offer the largest and most diversified fleet in private aviation, which includes 14 of the most popular business jets in the world. With 665 aircraft under management worldwide, NetJets fleet size equals the second largest airline. Access to the NetJets fleet is also available in the form of a short-term lease, sold on an all-inclusive, prepaid basis in 25-hour increments, through an exclusive alliance with Marquis Jet Partners. NetJets Inc. also offers aircraft management, charter management, and on-demand charter services through its subsidiary, Executive Jet Management. NetJets flies to over 140 countries and has operations in United States, Europe, and the Middle East.

I have a passion for continual improvement and have been fortunate to have worked with many talented technologists and business leaders in several industries, including financial services, manufacturing, aviation, hospitality, and technology services. Technology properly applied to any business model is a very powerful driver of top-line and bottom-line performance. Reading this book reemphasized how much of my success is owed to the business executives, those in the business, and the technologists, whose hard work collectively delivered tremendous results.

This book highlights many similarities to those I have seen in regard to culture. I have managed technology delivery in more than 100 countries across six continents, and have a great respect for cultural differences and their impact on effective communications, internally and externally. This book does an excellent job of exploring cultural differences, which I think is a key factor to the success of any business regardless of size or target market, as leveraging skill sets globally can provide advantages in whatever market a business operates.

The role of the chief information officer is very challenging because one must be comfortable with many managerial styles, interpersonal, informational, and decisional. From business knowledge, change management, and interpersonal skills to technologist, all are discussed in this book. The CIO interviews are summarized and compared for common themes and against previous studies, including Mintzberg's framework of Managerial Roles.

I am pleased to recommend this book to all of the stakeholders I have referenced above. The issues presented are current and important to the evolving role of the CIO. Working with the CIO to effectively adopt and employ IT will continue to grow in its importance and differentiate successful firms. I wish each of you all the very best in this endeavor.

Alan S. Cullop

Chief Information Officer & Senior Vice President

NetJets Inc.

Preface

This book is about the experiences of contemporary chief information officers (CIO). CIOs in New Zealand, Taiwan, and the United States of America agreed to participate. They also agreed to be identified along with the name of their company. They provided their interpretation of issues that have been dealt with and those they anticipate having to deal with in the foreseeable future. The results of the interviews allowed the identification of emerging themes related to management and technological aspects. Another important result is the identification of an alignment issue. That is, it is important to ensure that the interpretation of the CIO role is clearly and explicitly agreed upon by both the chief executive officer (CEO) and the CIO.

As senior management address the importance of information technology to the functioning of an organization, the formally recognized role performed by a CIO emerges (Kishore & McLean, 2002). The emergence of this role can take on many forms and is contingent upon many factors. Some of the major factors may relate to some of the following items. First, the CIO role may be affected by environmental factors such as size, industry, or organizational structure. A second factor may relate to the level of maturity of the CIO role. Thus, the role in one firm may be contributing more to a firm's competitive advantage. Along with this factor is also the aspect of senior management's interpretation of the value of information technology to the overall operation of the firm. A third factor relates to industry-based government regulations that may exist and perhaps influence the role performed by the CIO in relation to processes of gathering, retaining, and distributing information.

Recent research projects that have directly investigated CIO perspectives include the following. Seddon, Graeser, and Willcocks (2002) surveyed 80 senior IT managers about the benefits for their organizations from various approaches to evaluating IT projects and the IT function. Kishore and McLean (2002) documented the discussion of a CIO panel of nine senior executives and their opinions about the future of virtual organizations.

While the above projects are elucidating, they do not provide an in-depth and comparative perspective to the emerging CIO role. This book identifies the emerging aspects of the CIO role. In-depth interviews were employed to attempt to develop a better understanding of this role. The results of this investigation expand our understanding in this area through a discussion of the emerging roles of the CIO.

An interview protocol served as a discussion guide for the conversations with each CIO. The personal and family history, as well as the background material of the company, provided some context within which to view the CIO comments about their management experiences. The remainder of the interview protocol attempted to document CIO comments about issues the CIO felt were significant. The questions include the following:

- Personal and family history
- Company background
- Why the current position was accepted
- Issues
  - Initial
  - Current
  - Future
- Dealing with users
- Deciding on investments
- General comments about being a CIO

The book is organized into five sections.

The first section of the book provides an overview of the book project, an historical perspective to the role of the CIO, and background discussion of the interviews which generated the CIO comments.

Chapter I presents an overview of this book. Reasons for writing the book are discussed along with expected findings. This chapter concludes with a presentation of the format for the remainder of the book.

The historical presentation is in **Chapter II**. The CIO role within organizations is relatively new. This chapter presents a general discussion of the perspective of the role of the CIO. Comments are included from researchers, CIOs, and other senior managers.

Chapter III describes an overview of the process for conducting the interviews, including some of the issues that were addressed during the process of gathering the CIO comments about their experiences and the issues they addressed.

The second section of the book presents chapters about the CIOs from New Zealand. The following CIOs agreed to participate in this project and interviews have been conducted with them.

Chapter IV is about Wendy Bussen, director of information technology, Auckland University of Technology (AUT). Wendy was born and grew up in Huntly, New Zealand. She has a

Bachelor of Science in mathematics from Waikato University and a Master of Philosophy in information systems from Auckland University. She joined AUT in 1996. AUT is New Zealand's newest university, although it opened its doors as a postsecondary institution in 1895. The goal of AUT is to produce excellent, capable graduates in relevant fields.

Chapter V is about George Elder, information and supply chain manager, Tait Electronics Limited. George was born in Dunedin, New Zealand and grew up in Motueka, New Zealand. He has a CPIM certification from the American Production and Inventory Control Society and an MBA from the University of Canterbury. He joined Tait in 1997. Tait was established in 1969 with head offices in Christchurch, New Zealand. The company supplies world class radio communications equipment.

Chapter VI is about Rhys Gould, group manager of information systems, Fulton Hogan. Rhys was born and grew up in Dunedin, New Zealand. He studied accounting at Otago University in Dunedin. His first job after university was with Fulton Hogan. Fulton Hogan was founded in 1933 as a contracting company specializing in road works, quarrying, and civil construction.

Chapter VII is about Zarina Thesing, general manager of information technology, Pumpkin Patch. Zarina was born and grew up in Auckland, New Zealand. Pumpkin Patch was founded in 1990 to provide quality children's fashion.

Chapter VIII is about Russell Turner, chief information officer, MetService. Russell was born in Gisborn and grew up in Wellington, both in New Zealand. MetService was formed in 1992 to provide weather forecasting service in New Zealand.

The third section of the book presents chapters about the CIOs from Taiwan. The following CIOs agreed to participate in this project and interviews have been conducted with them.

Chapter IX is about Lucas Chuang, chief information officer, EVA Airways. Mr. Chuang was born and grew up in Madou, Taiwan. He has a Bachelor of Science in mathematical sciences from National Chenghi University. He joined EVA Airways in 1988. EVA was formed in 1988 as part of Evergreen Marine Corporation the world's largest company for shipping containers and container vessels. EVA is currently the second largest airline in Taiwan providing international passenger and freight service.

Chapter X is about C. M. Ko, section manager, MIS Department, Compostar Technology Corporation. Mr. Ko was born and grew up in Kaohsiung, Taiwan. He studied industrial management at a junior college. He joined Compostar soon after it was formed in 1998. Compostar is a manufacturer and worldwide exporter of resistors and capacitors.

Chapter XI is about James Lin, vice president in charge of information technology, Taiwan Fixed Network Company (TFN). Mr. Lin was born near Sun Moon Lake in Taiwan. He grew up in Taipei, Taiwan. He has a degree in from Tamsui Oxford University majoring in accounting and statistics with a minor in information systems. He joined TFN in 2003. In 2001, Taiwan Fixed Network Company was granted an integrated network license. Since 1991, the company had operated as part of various organizations within Taiwan. The mission of Taiwan Fixed Network is to provide back end (that part of the network that does not move) connections for all international carriers and mobile phone services.

Chapter XII is about C. K. Tsai, deputy director, Information Technology Division, Chi Mei Optoelectronics (CMO) Corporation. Mr. Tsai was born and grew up in Tainan, Taiwan.

He has a Bachelor of Science with a major in geology from National Taiwan University in Taipei. He joined CMO in 1998 when the company was formed. CMO, formed in 1998, is headquartered in Tainan Science Park just south of Kaohsiung, where they are the world leading manufacturer of thin film transistor liquid crystal display products, which are the major components of computer monitors and television screens.

Chapter XIII is about D. I. Wang, chief information officer, Lite-On Technology Corporation. Dr. Wang was born and grew up in Tainan, Taiwan. He has a bachelor's degree in mathematics from a university in Taiwan, and a master's degree in computer science and a PhD in applied mathematics, both from Northern University, Boston, USA. He joined Lite-On in 1998. In 2002, Lite-On Technology Corporation became part of the Lite-On Group. Lite-On Technology has a vision to be a world class producer of light emitting diodes, power supplies, wireless devices, liquid crystal display computer monitors, PDAs, and printers.

Chapter XIV is about M. P. Wang, general manager, Information Systems Department, China Steel. Mr. Wang was born and grew up in Tainan, Taiwan. He has a bachelor's degree in computer science from National Taiwan University in Taipei. He started working for China Steel in 1975. China Steel is an integrated steel mill formed in 1971. With 50% of the Taiwan steel market, the company employs a state of the art computerized continuous casting production process.

The fourth section of the book presents chapters about the CIOs from the United States of America. The following CIOs agreed to participate in this project and interviews have been conducted with them.

Chapter XV is about Jonathan Dove, chief information officer, Worthington Industries. Jonathan was born in Pasadena, California. When he was eight, the family moved to a farm just outside of Pocahontas, Missouri, where he grew up. He has a bachelor's degree in computer science from Coe College in Cedar Rapids, Iowa. He joined Worthington Industries in 1998. Formed in 1955, Worthington Industries is a diversified custom metal processing company and manufacturer of metal related products.

Chapter XVI is about Gary Houk, vice president of Corporate Information Technology and Business Integration, Online Computer Library Center (OCLC). Gary was born in Akron, Ohio. He lived in a lot of different places growing up. He has a bachelor's degree in computer science and an MBA, both from Ohio State University. He joined OCLC in 1974. OCLC was established in 1970 as a nonprofit member-run organization using computers to improve library productivity by creating and maintaining a shared catalogue database. OCLC also owns and maintains the Dewey Decimal Classification System.

Chapter XVII is about Marty Luffy, chief information officer, Installed Building Products. Marty was born and grew up in Pittsburgh, Pennsylvania. He has a Bachelor of Science in industrial management from Purdue University and an MBA from the University of Dayton. Marty is also a certified public accountant. Formed in 1991, Installed Building Products provides commercial and residential construction services such as insulation, waterproofing, gutters, shower doors, shelving, and mirrors.

Chapter XVIII is about Angelo Mazzocco, vice president and chief information officer, The Dispatch Companies. Angelo was born and raised in New Castle, Pennsylvania. He has a Bachelor of Science in mathematics and computer science from Indiana University of Pennsylvania, and an MBA in marketing and information systems from the University of Dayton. He joined the Dispatch Companies in 1998. In 1871, the Columbus Dispatch began printing and selling a daily newspaper. The company currently comprises 14 different entities in television, radio, newspaper, real estate, aviation, magazine, direct marketing, and professional sports.

Chapter XIX is about Cindy Sheets, senior vice president and chief information officer, Mount Carmel Health System. Cindy was born and grew up in Columbus, Ohio. She has a bachelor's degree in medical technology from Ohio State University and an MBA from the University of Dayton. She joined Mount Carmel Health System in 1989. Mount Carmel was formed over 120 years ago by the Sisters of the Holy Cross. Today, it is a leading provider of general health care services in Ohio.

Chapter XX is about Kathleen Starkoff, chief technology officer and group vice president, Limited Brands. Kathleen was born and grew up in Port Clinton, Ohio. She has a Bachelor of Science in mathematics with minors in chemistry and business from Kent State University, and an MBA from Case Western Reserve with a major in policy. She joined Limited Brands in the late 1990s. Formed in 1963, Limited Brands has over 3,800 retail stores carrying six retail fashion brands, including apparel and fragrance.

Chapter XXI is about John Zarb, chief information officer, Libbey. John was born and grew up in Highland Park near Detroit, Michigan. He has a bachelor's degree from Eastern Michigan University and an MBA from Michigan State University. He joined Libbey in 1996. Libbey is the leading producer of glass tableware in North America. Formed over 185 years ago the company produces glass tableware, ceramic dinnerware, metal flatware, and various plastic utensils.

The fifth section consists of three chapters which describe how the results of the interviews were determined and analyzed. There is also a discussion of the content of the themes that were identified.

Chapter XXII (Reviewing CIO Comments) presents a discussion of the content of the comments offered by each CIO in response to the general categories of questions in the interviews. To begin, the first section presents summary data about what the participants did before they became a CIO. This section discusses their early life and education, provides an overview of the types of positions held before the participant became a CIO, and outlines some of the comments made about why the participant accepted the position of CIO. Following this initial discussion, the chapter presents sections related to the major category of questions asked during the interviews. These major categories are as follows:

- Dealing with Users
  - How the CIO interacts with various levels of users within the organization
- Deciding on the Technology
  - What aspects surround the decisions about the acquisition of technology for the corporation
- Initial Issues
  - Categories of issues that required the CIO to take action upon assuming the CIO role
- Current Issues
  - Issues the CIO is dealing with now (or at the time of the interview)

- Future Issues
    - These are issues the CIO foresees having to deal with in the future

In **Chapter XXIII** (Analyzing CIO Comments), an analysis of the comments is presented. Mintzberg's managerial roles framework is introduced and the components are described. The themes identified within each of the major categories of the CIO interviews are then mapped onto the roles described in the framework. This process supports a discussion of the analysis of the CIO role. The final section of the chapter presents some concluding remarks.

While the development of an interview protocol was important to provide consistency across a number of interviews, it was also important to allow the CIO to pursue aspects of their comments about their own experiences that are central to their story. This tension between structure and flexibility requires the interviewer to "walk a thin line." Also, the collection of qualitative interview data takes time. It takes a lot of time and effort to read and reread transcripts, and in this case, then, to develop a chapter based upon a series of transcripts from interviews with the CIO. This approach adds richness and allows insights of the research participant to be gathered. The details of the stories provide a glimpse of insight into the real world of the CIO.

Then, **Chapter XXIV** (Final CIO Comments) presents an overview of the final comments made by the CIOs. At the end of each interview the CIO was asked to provide an overall comment from a general perspective about how they interpret their role within the context of their company. These interpretive comments are divided into three main categories. The first category presented here includes comments about the internal operations of the CIO's business unit. The second category relates to the CIO's interpretation of how the information systems business unit should relate to the corporate user community. The third category discusses how the CIOs view their role in relation to senior management. Then, some final comments are presented about the changing role of CIOs. A brief conclusion section ends this chapter.

Each CIO seemed to really enjoy what they were doing. There was an excitement in their voice when they described how their role was unfolding and how recognition was emerging for their contribution to the company goals and objectives. They are the types of individuals who like the challenge of identifying and understanding an issue, and overseeing its resolution. Finally, ever the optimists, they look forward with anticipation to a future where new technology may be employed in a novel way to benefit their company.

Conclusion

The following chapters document the project and the comments of 18 CIOs about their experiences. Emerging themes are identified relative to both management and technological aspects. In general, it is noted that the CIO role is now emphasizing more of the management aspects than the technological aspects. It remains part of the CIO role that they are knowledgeable about technology. But more often the CIO is looked upon as a leader from a business perspective in the appropriate application of information technology. Thus, the focus is on employing technology to address business goals. It is important that the individual who fulfills this role knows the expectations of the company as expressed by fellow members of the senior management team. It is even more important that the members of the senior management team also understand what role is to be played by them and the CIO, and that they concur with how the role will facilitate attaining corporate objectives.

This book provides valuable insights into the role of the CIO and the necessary interaction with other parts of the organization and external relationships with vendors and suppliers. These insights have been gained through in-depth discussions with currently practicing CIOs. Their comments will prove valuable to both currently practicing CIOs and those who aspire to this challenging role.

References

Kishore, R., & McLean, E.R. (2002). The next generation enterprise: A CIO perspective on the vision, its impacts, and implementation challenges. *Information Systems Frontiers, 4*(1), 121-138.

Seddon, P.B., Graeser, V., & Willcocks, L.P. (2002). Measuring organizational IS effectiveness: An overview and update of senior management perspectives. *Database for Advances in Information Systems, 33*(2), 11-28.

Acknowledgment

There have been very many people involved directly and indirectly in the development of this book. Originally, I discussed the idea of writing this book with scores of people. Some were interested and provided valuable comments and suggestions. Others responded with the glassy-eyed stare reminiscent of "deer in the headlights." It was this latter herd whose nonverbal critique led me to consider a more interesting presentation, which I undertook to the best of my ability. To everyone, even the glassy-eyed deer, I am indebted.

First, and most important, I appreciate the involvement of the CIOs. I realize you are all very busy. Once you committed to participate in the book project you were all very accommodating in arranging your time to talk with me. You were all very forthcoming with insightful and erudite comments about your personal lives, careers, and roles performed as CIOs.

I also want to acknowledge the contributions of sponsors. Initially, the Taipei Economic and Cultural Office (TECO), Canada, contributed funds for me to travel to Taiwan to conduct interviews with CIOs in Kaohsiung and Taipei. TECO, Canada, is an agency of the Ministry of Education of Taiwan, R.O.C. TECO, Canada, also sponsored my attendance at two conferences. One conference was in Ottawa in 2003 and was organized jointly by the University of Ottawa and TECO, Canada. The second conference was in Calgary in 2004 and was jointly organized by the Canadian Asian Studies Association and TECO, Canada. At both conferences, I was able to present my ideas for the book, and obtain valuable feedback from fellow research colleagues. I appreciate the initial contacts for potential participants in the Columbus, Ohio area by Dr. Kay Nelson, Director of the Center for Information Technologies in Management at the Fisher College of Business at Ohio State University. Further, I acknowledge the contribution of the University of Canterbury in Christchurch, New Zealand. During July and August of 2005, I was a visiting Erskine fellow. At that time,

I was able to make contact with potential participants in New Zealand. Finally, Dr. Dennis Fitzpatrick, vice president of research at the University of Lethbridge, provided funds for interview transcription services. This service was expertly provided by Mrs. Judy Jones.

While many people have been very helpful in contributing to the development of my book, I feel it is incumbent upon me to specifically recognize the following individuals. Mr. Angelo Mazzocco, vice president and chief information officer at the Dispatch Printing Company and Affiliates in Columbus, Ohio, not only participated in the project but also was helpful in convincing his fellow colleagues, through the CIO Council in Columbus, Ohio to participate. Mr. Doug Casement, managing editor and publisher at Computer World and CIO IDG Communications, New Zealand, made valuable contacts with potential participants in New Zealand. Further, potential participants were also identified by Dr. Paul Cragg in the Accounting Finance and Information Systems Department of the Business School at the University of Canterbury in Christchurch, New Zealand. I am very indebted to Mr. Flandy Su, chairman of the Bank of Kaohsiung. Mr. Su also made valuable contacts with CIOs in Taiwan. Further, he was instrumental in providing local arrangements in both Kaohsiung and Taipei. In both cities, he provided me with the use of his car and driver. I also appreciate the assistance in Taipei of Mr. Chuck W. L. Chen, senior vice president and general manager of the Taipei Branch and Corporate Banking Department, Bank of Kaohsiung.

I have worked in the past with IGI Global in the production of various edited books. In this, my first authored book, the folks at IGI Global have again been very helpful with all the necessary arrangements associated with the production of the book. I hasten to add that any errors which remain in the final version of the book are entirely my own. I worked directly with Kristin Roth, development editor, who was able to very politely ask the right questions to steer me back on course, or to prod me to ensure that I met a scheduled completion date. Also, as usual, Jan Travers provided valuable guidance in the overall approach to writing this book.

Finally, I include here an acknowledgement of a personal nature. My wife, Shirley, far beyond this project, invariably has been helpful in so many ways. Indeed, it is my opinion that I am her long term "project." I certainly appreciate her persistence! Thank you for always helping me. I appreciated your comments and questions about the book. I appreciated being taken away from the book when the manuscript needed to mature. We are partners in our journey through life. I will be forever grateful that we have been able to do so many exciting things together.

M. Gordon Hunter
October 2006

Section I

Introduction

This book documents an exploratory investigation of the role of the chief information officer (CIO). Participants reside and work in New Zealand, Taiwan, and the United States of America. They agreed to be identified along with the name of their company. Throughout the interviews, the CIOs offered comments about their management experiences. They provided their interpretation of issues that have been dealt with and those they anticipate having to deal with in the foreseeable future. The results of the interviews with each CIO, presented in later chapters, support the identification of the themes related to management and technological aspects.

This section of the book provides an overview of the book project, an historical perspective to the role of the CIO, and some background discussion of the interview process which generated the CIO comments included in their respective chapters.

Chapter I presents an overview of this book. Reasons for writing the book are discussed along with expected findings. This chapter concludes with a presentation of the format for the remainder of the book.

The historical perspective of the CIO role is presented in **Chapter II**. The CIO role within organizations is relatively new. This chapter presents a general discussion of the perspective of the role of the CIO. Comments are included from researchers, CIOs, and other senior managers. This chapter sets the stage for the presentation of the project which investigated the management experiences of chief information officers. The historical perspective of this chapter starts with a brief discussion of the history of the emergence of the CIO role in organizations. The chapter then discusses some of the current research about the role of the CIO. This part of the chapter is divided into a discussion of research which has investigated corporate level factors and research that has investigated unit level factors. Corporate level factors are those aspects in the environment that may serve to facilitate successful performance by the CIO. Unit level factors are those aspects within the area of responsibility of the CIO within the organization. Finally, conclusions are presented which outline how the interview comments reported in this book are beneficial to both academics and those practitioners who may be CIOs or who may be considering working toward becoming a CIO. This chapter presents an historical perspective to the role of the CIO. The focus of the chapter is on the emergence of the role and aspects of the role as identified in current research projects.

Chapter III presents an overview and introduction to the data gathering part of the project conducted to develop this book. It describes an overview of the project, including some of the issues that were addressed during the process of gathering the CIO comments. The objective of this investigation was to document the comments of a CIO within their specific organization about their management experiences. Thus, a Narrative Inquiry approach was taken to conducting one-on-one interviews. This chapter presents an overview of this project regarding the initial phase of gathering comments from the CIOs who decided to participate. To begin, some background information is presented which serves to place the book project within a contextual framework. This background information is employed to facilitate the development of a research question and the consequent adoption of an appropriate research method. Appendix A includes the Interview Protocol. Appendix B contains the Informed Consent Form. The chapter also introduces the specific CIOs who participated, along with their respective organizations at the time of the interviews. The chapter concludes with a brief discussion of some issues that were addressed and resolved during the initial data gathering process.

Chapter I

Overview

Introduction

This book contains the stories of the personal management experiences of individuals performing the role of the chief information officer (CIO). The goal in carrying out the interviews and writing the book was to document and explore those issues, which are considered significant by practicing CIOs. Firms are recognizing the importance of business processes associated with gathering, processing, and disseminating information. The formal establishment of a CIO role is evidence of this recognition.

A new breed of manager, the chief information officer (CIO), became recognized in the late 1980s. This new position was established to provide a link between the data processing department and the company's senior managers. Thus, the data processing manager position was becoming recognized as a CIO in a similar manner as 20 years before, when accountants were elevated to the chief financial officer (CFO) position. The emergence of the CIO role suggests that companies were recognizing the strategic importance of information and its supporting technology.

The CIO role emerged so that one senior executive could be assigned the overall corporate responsibility for an organization's information processing needs. As this role is elevated to senior management involvement, the corporate expectations are being revised. Thus, rather than simply supervising the information technology

(IT) function, the CIO is expected to understand the business and to work toward ensuring that IT supports those initiatives that contribute to establishing and maintaining the firm's competitive advantage. The management of the IT function relates directly to the bottom line. The role of the CIO is to ensure appropriate activities are carried out. It is considered important both for survival and to attain competitive advantage that the business goals are reflected in the actions of the information technology function.

Writing the Book

Before the interviews for this book could be conducted, it was necessary to find individuals who were interested in the idea of the book and who would be willing to volunteer to participate. Through various personal contacts, individuals were sent information about the book. Those who responded as expressing an interest in the project were contacted and provided further information. Eventually, CIOs from New Zealand, Taiwan, and the United States of America agreed to participate. They were not chosen. They volunteered. The interviews and resulting chapter represent the CIO's opportunity to tell his or her story. The stories provide an interesting perspective on the personal management experiences of practicing CIOs in various industries in three diverse countries. Individual interviews were scheduled with each CIO who volunteered. Some were conducted face-to-face, while others were carried out via the telephone. In all cases the interviews were audio taped. Transcripts were prepared from the audio tapes and sent to the respective participant for review. The approved transcripts formed the basis for the chapters included later in this book. While the author developed each chapter, the respective CIO retained the final editorial rights to their own chapter.

In order to ground the discussion in the CIO's personal management experiences, an interview protocol was developed which guided a chronological discussion of the CIO's personal work experience. Questions were posed regarding the CIO's past career and personal experiences. A chronological process was followed from early life, through formal education, and into the various positions held throughout their career up until the current position. Then the detailed specific issues of the current position were investigated. Questions were asked about initial, current, and future issues. The questions about issues were nondirective in nature. Thus, the CIO was able to decide which issues they considered important enough for them to raise the item and expound upon it. This approach supports the idea that important issues will come to mind first during a specific conversation.

Interviews were conducted either face to face or via the telephone. It is important to adopt a data gathering approach which ensures the CIO is as comfortable as possible during the interviews. The level of comfort seems to be reflected in how forthcoming the participant might be with detailed comments about the story being told. Not only do interviews allow the story to be told in the participant's own words, but it is also possible to obtain immediate clarification of comments or elaboration of details. The interviewer should remain neutral and should act as a guide to the relating of the story and as a facilitator for clarification of comments made by the CIO.

Emerging themes were identified by analyzing individual interview transcripts and then by comparing the themes from other interview transcripts. This is a common and accepted practice when conducting qualitative research to support the interpretation of textual data.

Expected Findings

Today, CIOs find themselves drifting between a technically oriented past and a strategic business oriented future. Their past, in general, related to a focus on efficiently employing state of the art hardware and software. The future indicates increasing involvement in strategic business planning at the most senior organizational level to effectively apply information technology to support the attainment of business goals and objectives. To relate a common saying, the CIO role is evolving from "doing things right" as a manager, to "doing the right things" as a leader. Those organizations that can successfully manage the transition of this role will gain competitive advantage. Thus, it is important that both the company and the CIO realize that the CIO role should evolve from an information processing function to a role based upon knowledge management.

In order for information technology to be applied successfully, a team approach is necessary at the most senior level in the organization. It is incumbent upon both the CEO and CIO to accept responsibility to adopt certain roles. For instance, the CIO must accept the responsibility to bridge the gap between information technology and the business. Alternatively, the CEO must understand the IT process just as they understand other traditional areas within the corporation, like accounting or finance. It is the CIO who must ensure that the CEO understands information technology and how it may be applied to accomplish the business objectives.

Comments about what the future holds for CIOs are also interesting. The senior information technology executive is moving away from the "technology" and emphasizing more of the "information." The CIO is becoming more of a "prophet" and less of a "technologist," As a prophet, the CIO must know how technology may be employed to transform the business. Further, the CIO must be capable of leading the more traditional parts of the organization through this transition. While the CIO must educate the rest of the organization about the capabilities of information technology, they can not become too enthusiastic and attempt to push the organization beyond the willingness of the CEO and the rest of the senior management team. A good CIO must develop a thorough understanding of the goals of the organization and how information technology may be strategically applied to advance toward those goals.

While there is a movement toward more of an emphasis for the CIO to understand the business, the CIO must still be the information technology champion within the organization. The CIO needs to know both the business and the information technology. Thus, while the CIOs of the future will be involved in strategy, they must understand information technology and how it can be applied to positively impact the business.

As senior management address the importance of information technology to the functioning of an organization, the formally recognized role performed by a chief information officer (CIO) emerges. The emergence of this role can take on many forms and is contingent upon many factors. Some of the major factors may relate to some of the following items. First, the CIO role may be affected by environmental factors such as size, industry, or organizational structure. A second factor may relate to the level of maturity of the CIO role. Thus, the role in one firm may be contributing more to a firm's competitive advantage. Along with this factor is also the aspect of senior management's interpretation of the value of information technology to the overall operation of the firm. A third factor relates to industry-based government regulations that may exist and perhaps influence the role performed by the CIO in relation to the processes of gathering, retaining, and distributing information.

As the role of the CIO is incorporated into the senior management level, questions arise about how management and leadership of the organization may be affected. That is, are the normal processes of senior managers altered in any way through the interaction with a CIO? For instance, does Mintzberg's managerial roles framework still apply? Can the framework be used to analyze this new environment at the senior management level? Further, are the aspects of leadership affected by the addition of the CIO role to the leadership team? These important questions will be addressed later in this book.

The Rest of the Book

The book is organized into five sections.

The first section of the book provides an historical perspective to the role of the CIO and some background discussion of the project which generated the CIO comments included here. The historical presentation is in Chapter I. This chapter presents a general discussion of the perspective of the role of the CIO and sets the stage for the presentation of the project, which investigated the management experiences of chief information officers. The second chapter presents an overview and introduction to the data gathering part of the development of this book. It describes an overview of the project, including some of the issues that were addressed during the process of gathering the CIO comments.

The second section of the book presents chapters about the CIOs from New Zealand. Five CIOs agreed to participate.

The third section of the book presents chapters about the CIOs from Taiwan. Six CIOs participated.

The fourth section of the book presents chapters about the CIOs from the United States of America. Seven CIOs agreed to participate.

The fifth section consists of three chapters which describe how the results of the interviews were determined and analyzed. There is also a discussion of the content of the themes that were identified. Chapter XXII presents a discussion of the content of the comments offered by each CIO in response to the questions in the interviews. To begin, the chapter provides a discussion of their early life and education, and an overview of the types of positions held before the participant became a CIO. Then, issues are discussed relating to when the CIO first took on the role, what is being addressed currently, and what the CIO foresees having to deal with in the future.

Chapter XXIII presents an analysis of the comments made by the CIOs. To begin, Mintzberg's (1973) managerial roles framework is introduced and the components are described. The themes identified within each of the major categories of the CIO interviews are then mapped onto the roles described in Mintzberg's (1973) framework. This process supports a discussion of the analysis of the CIO management experiences. Further analysis is presented which attempts to determine if there is any variability of issues across the chronological stages of the CIOs' tenure in their position. This section investigates whether the emphasis of the management experiences might change over time as the CIO gains company specific experience. The next section analyzes the comments from a cultural perspective. The seminal work by Hofstede (1980, 1983, 1993, 2001) is introduced and is then employed to compare the comments of the CIOs representing New Zealand, Taiwan, and the United States of America. The last analysis section included in this chapter reviews the concept of leadership and its impact on the role of the CIO. The final section of the chapter presents some concluding remarks.

Finally, Chapter XXIV presents an overview of the final comments made by the CIOs. At the end of each interview the CIO was asked to provide an overall comment from a general perspective about how they interpret their role within the context of their company. The CIO also provided their perspective about their management experiences. These interpretive comments are divided into three main categories. The first category presented here includes comments about the internal operations of the CIO's business unit. The second category relates to the CIO's interpretation of how the information systems business unit should relate to the corporate user community. The third category discusses how the CIOs view their role in relation to senior management. A brief conclusion section ends this chapter.

Conclusion

This book provides valuable insights into the role of the CIO and the necessary interaction with other parts of the organization as well as external relationships. These insights have been gained through in-depth discussions with currently practicing CIOs. Their comments about their management experiences will prove valuable to both currently practicing CIOs and those who aspire to this challenging role.

Chapter II

Historical Perspective

Introduction

The presentation of this chapter starts with a brief discussion of the history of the emergence of the CIO role in organizations. The chapter then discusses some of the current research about the role of the CIO. This section is divided into a discussion of research, which has investigated corporate level factors and research that has investigated unit level factors. Corporate level factors are those aspects in the environment that may serve to facilitate successful performance by the CIO. Unit level factors are those aspects directly involved in the area of responsibility of the CIO within the organization. Finally, conclusions are presented, which outline how the results reported in this book are beneficial to both academics and those practitioners who may be CIOs or who may be considering working toward becoming a CIO.

Emergence of the CIO Role

Some early research identified the emergence of the CIO and the necessary skills for information systems managers.

In 1986, *Business Week* (Bock, Carpenter, & Davis, 1986) reported on the emergence of a new breed of manager, the "chief information officer" and their introduction into the executive suite. The CIO was expected to be able to relate to the company's nontechnical managers and those more technical managers of the then named data processing department. A very interesting point made by the Business Week article was that the emergence of the CIO was similar to the rise of accountants in the 1960s to the position of chief financial officer. Thus, the emergence of the CIO role followed the emergence of the CFO role by 20 years. Further, the role of the CIO included three main functions. They are described as follows:

- Oversee corporate technology
- Report to the highest ranking executive
- Develop long term strategy and planning

Also, in the late 1980s, it was estimated that approximately one-third of major companies in the United States had identified the necessity for a CIO role and had filled the position (O'Riordon, 1987). The emergence of the role suggests that these companies at that time had recognized the strategic importance of information technology and the necessity for a senior manager to hold responsibility for its application in support of business goals.
O'Riordon (1987) suggested the following characteristics of a successful CIO:

- Business-oriented
- Takes a broad perspective of corporate requirements
- Able to work across traditional departmental boundaries
- Understands how technology can support the business operations
- An innovative thinker
- Flexible
- Good communication skills

Job advertisements for information systems positions from 1970 to 1990 were reviewed by Todd, McKeen, and Gallupe (1995). They investigated specific positions related to programmers, systems analysts, and information systems managers. It is the latter position that is of interest here. At the time of their research (Todd et al., 1995), it was considered that successful information systems managers should have a blend of technical knowledge and sound business-related skills. Further, in general, they should possess effective interpersonal skills. Over the 20-year period of their investigation, Todd et al. (1995) determined that there had not been much change in the required skills indicated in job advertisements. This conclusion supported other research conducted at the time (Benbasat, Dexter, & Mantha, 1980; Butt, 1969; Cheney & Lyons, 1980; Cheney & Lipp, 1987; Exton, 1970; Ives & Olson, 1981; Joslin & Bassher, 1976).

Todd et al. (1995, p. 3) conclude with the following: "In summary, most of the findings over the years indicate that IS managers must have good interpersonal/managerial skills and that technical skills while important, are definitely secondary."

Andrews and Carlson (1997) have suggested that the role of the CIO passed through many phases and is in the fourth wave. To begin, the first wave portrayed CIOs simply as glorified data processing managers. The second wave, saw CIOs perform their role as technocrats representing the expertise of the technology and it application. In the third wave, CIOs adopted the business executive perspective. Currently, in the fourth wave, the CIO is working at combining the technocrat and the business perspectives. Arnold (2001) supported this combination, suggesting that while CIOs must still be knowledgeable about technology, they should also be sure to build relationships with other senior members of the organization and to think strategically regarding the application of technology for the overall benefit of the company.

Some time ago, Benjamin, Dickinson, and Rockart (1985) suggested that the emergence of the CIO role represented the recognition of the importance of the role to be played within the organization. More recently, Kaarst-Brown (2005), suggests that it is unfortunate that 20 years later, in 2005, the CIO is still held in lower regard than those senior managers of other more traditional business units. Kaarst-Brown (2005) suggests the reasons for this gap may be attributed to some of the items on the following list:

- Personality conflicts
- Lack of corporate technology vision
- Poorly aligned IT goals
- Lack of business knowledge
- Lack of IT awareness among the business executives
- Incorrect formal structure and reporting relationships

Jones and Arnett (1994) suggested that the CIO role emerged so that one senior executive could be assigned the overall corporate responsibility for an organization's information processing needs. The gap between the organizational and information strategies (Stephens, Ledbetter, Mitra, & Foord, 1992) had to be addressed and resolved (Stephens & Loughman, 1994). It was considered important both for survival and to attain competitive advantage that the business goals are reflected in the actions of the information technology function (Earl & Feeny, 1994).

Kwak (2001) also suggested the CIO role was adopted for one individual member of senior management in 1986. But, it was not a popular addition as the individuals were seen as being more comfortable with computers than with people, especially those people at a senior level in the organization.

In 1998, Korn/Ferry International published the results of an international survey of three hundred and forty CIOs employed by "Times 1000" companies about their changing role within their organization. When the survey results were published in 1998, it was concluded that CIOs found themselves drifting between a technically-oriented past and a strategic business-oriented future. The past related to a focus on efficiently employing state of the art hardware and software. The future indicated increasing involvement in strategic business planning at the most senior organizational level. The report further indicates that those organizations that can successfully manage the transition of this role will gain competitive advantage. Thus, it is important that both the company and the CIO realize that the CIO role should evolve from an information processing function to a role based upon knowledge management.

The Korn/Ferry (1998) report then proceeds to suggest actions for successfully assimilating the CIO role within the organization. These actions include the following:

- Initiate closer involvement of the CIO with other senior officers and include the CIO's perspective before strategic objectives are finalized by the board.
- Address impediments to success, such as lack of planning, skills shortage, and cultural resistance, and review progress regularly.
- Look beyond return on investment and focus on three separate areas: running costs, extraordinary costs, and technology's contribution to business growth.
- Re-examine remuneration incentives, particularly with reference to the need for a broader skill set, including business and financial experience.
- Make sure the CIO's role is challenging and stimulating and the CIO's contribution is acknowledged by senior executives. An understanding of the issues the CIO faces and the achievements accomplished over the year will ensure top performance.

As this role evolves from a technical to a strategic orientation the necessary CIO qualifications will also change. Thus, while the ideal CIO resume will still include technical qualifications, there will be an increasing emphasis on experience in the more traditional functional areas, such as marketing and finance.

In 1999, Armstrong and Sambamurthy (1999) investigated the influence of senior management leadership and information technology infrastructure on corporate assimilation of information technology. One of the major components of their investigation related to IT infrastructure, which forms the basis for any sustained corporate innovation (Allen & Boynton, 1991; Duncan, 1995; Gordon, 1993; Hanseth, Monteiro, & Hatling, 1996). IT infrastructure includes hardware, operating systems, networks and telecommunications, and databases. The findings support the benefits of a sophisticated level of IT infrastructure with the ability to strategically support business innovation.

Another major component of their investigation was the relationship between the CIO and other senior executives. They found that both formal and informal interactions facilitated a mutually beneficial relationship and promoted assimilation of information technology at a strategic level. They also determined that it was the CIOs responsibility to have information technology knowledge and to share it with other senior executives as a formal member of the senior management team. Another interesting finding related to this aspect has to do with the importance for a CIO to have both business and information technology knowledge. It is this aspect that could contribute to a successful relationship between the CIO and senior management.

In order for information technology to be applied successfully, a team approach is necessary at the most senior level in the organization (Maciag, 2002). It is incumbent upon both the CEO and CIO to accept responsibility to adopt certain roles. For instance, the CIO must accept the responsibility to bridge the gap between information technology and the business. Alternatively, the CEO must understand the IT process just as they understand other traditional areas within the corporation. It is the CIO who must ensure that the CEO understands information technology and how it may be applied to the business.

Feld and Stoddard (2004) suggest that successfully implementing information technology must consider factors beyond the technology itself. They state the following:

Making IT work has little to do with technology itself. Just because a builder can acquire a handsome set of hammers, nails, and planks doesn't mean he can erect a quality house at reasonable cost. Making IT work demands the same things that other parts of the business do—inspired leadership, superb execution motivated people, and the thoughtful attention and high expectations of senior management. (Feld & Stoddard, 2004, p. 74)

The role of the CIO is expanding to include more risk assessment, change management, problem solving, and selling at the organizational level (Weiss & Anderson, 2004).

Current Research

This section of the chapter is divided into two major areas. To begin, a discussion is presented about investigations into the corporate level aspects which may facilitate the role of the CIO. These aspects relate to the corporate environment and to such aspects as perceptions, attitudes, and infrastructure. The second part of this section discusses unit level aspects. Unit level is interpreted here as relating to the area of responsibility for the CIO and may include such aspects as CIO skills and characteristics, unit personnel skill sets, and unit infrastructure.

Corporate Level Research

Recently, Kolbasuk (2005) reported that the perception of CIOs within organizations may be evolving. She suggests they may finally be getting the respect they deserve as they become members of the board of directors of large companies. This movement to the board level in the organization indicates that the perception of the CIO role is evolving from a manager primarily focused on regulations, back office operations, and administrative duties to applying information technology at a strategic level to facilitate competitive advantage through an understanding of how business processes function and may be adapted to a changing corporate environment.

Recall that Kaarst-Brown (2005), in contrast with Kolbasuk's (2005) results, found that CIOs are still being held in lower regard than other senior managers of more traditional business units. The contradictory results of these two investigations may be addressed and resolved by the following comments in the remainder of this sub-section. In general, it is incumbent upon the senior management team to adopt an attitude recognizing the important value of information to the corporation. Further, as a consequence of this recognition, the senior management team must also realize that responsibility for the management of this information must reside with one specific senior management individual, and that this individual should be the CIO, who should be an equal member of the senior management team.

In order to apply information technology strategically, corporate information must be considered a valuable resource. Thus, the attitude of senior management must be that managing information strategically should be treated with the same level of interest as managing finances, human resources, operations, and all the other more traditional functions within the organization (Meagher, 2003).

In response to the Feld and Stoddard (2004) research reported above, Dickerson (2004) reported on a self-assessment of his role as a CIO for InfoWorld. He suggested that ongoing challenges exist related to managing partners involved in their outsourcing endeavors, acquiring and maintaining a simplified corporate level technology platform, and ensuring the IT leadership is aligned with corporate leadership and that IT is held accountable for performance. These challenges relate to aspects of the corporate level environment.

Broadbent, Weill, and St. Clair (1999) investigated the ways that information technology infrastructure contributes to the successful implementation on business process redesign. They determined that those firms with a rich set of information technology infrastructure capabilities would have a higher probability of successfully implementing significant changes to their business processes. They defined a rich infrastructure as including those technologies that facilitated boundary crossing and extension of range services.

Another corporate level environmental aspect relates to the existence of a steering committee. Karimi, Battacherjee, Gupta, and Somers (2000) investigated the impacts of steering committees on the management of the information technology function. They defined this committee as a team of senior managers representing major units within the organization and making strategic decisions linking information technology with the business goals. The research results indicated that the existence of a steering committee facilitated a good fit between information technology direction and the business strategy. Further, the function of a steering committee could go a long way in supporting the efforts of the CIO.

An interesting alternative perspective is the information technology competence of business managers. Traditionally, it was the purview of the information technology departments to develop, install, and maintain information systems. It has been determined that increased line manager competence in information technology leads to improved alignment between information technology and business (Reich & Benbasat, 2000). However, few organizations support this idea (Chan & Reich, 1999).

A series of articles reports on the investigations into alignment. Information technology and business alignment refers to coordinating the activities of the information technology unit with the goals and objectives of the business. Luftman & Brier (1999) suggest that senior executives should focus on the relationship between the functional business unit and the information technology area. They should attempt to develop an attitude of mutual cooperation and provide executive support in all aspects of the relationship. Further, Reich and Benbasat (2000) determined that the most important factor for alignment is communication. Information technology professionals must earn the right to play a meaningful role with senior management. This right will be developed through communication and by acquiring shared domain knowledge. Actions that facilitate the acquisition of shared domain knowledge include studying domain knowledge either through reading or attending courses, or through association. Many organizations assign information technology professionals to business units. Alternatively, functional personnel may be assigned to serve in the information technology area. Reich and Benbasat (2000) concluded that line managers with both business and information technology knowledge are catalysts for innovation. Hartung, Reich, and Benbasat (2000) recommend that the business planning process should include consideration for information technology in order to extract the full advantage from current technologies.

Unit Level Research

This subsection presents a discussion of research conducted to investigate aspects of the business unit which is the direct responsibility of the CIO. It is interesting to note that the majority of research relates to investigations of the environment of the CIOs business unit rather than the unit itself. The research that has been conducted at the unit level focuses on identifying core capabilities (Bharadwaj, 2000; Bharadwaj, Sambamurthy, & Zmud, 1999; Clemens, 1991; Feeny & Willcocks, 1998a, 1998b).

Feeny and Willcocks (1998a) investigated the core information systems capabilities for exploiting information technology. Specifically, they attempted to determine which information systems capabilities would be necessary, or should be considered core, in order to facilitate a business's capability to exploit information technology. They identified three general challenges, including alignment, delivery, and architecture. Within the purview of these challenges they identify nine core capabilities which are required to support the exploitation of information technology. They are as follows:

- Leadership
  - Integrating IS/IT effort with business purpose and activity.
- Business Systems Thinking
  - Envisioning the business process that technology makes possible.
- Relationship Building
  - Getting the business constructively engaged in IS/IT issues.
- Architecture Planning
  - Creating the coherent blueprint for a technical platform that responds to current and future business needs.
- Making Technology Work
  - Rapidly achieving technical progress, by one means or another.
- Informed Buying
  - Managing the IS/IT sourcing strategy that meets the interest of the business.
- Contract Facilitation
  - Ensuring the success of existing contracts for IS/IT services.

- Contract Monitoring
    - Protecting the business's contractual position, current and future.
- Vendor Development
    - Identifying the potential added value of IDS/IT service suppliers.

The skill set to support the above capabilities may be described in the context of three broad areas. The first is technical skills. It is suggested that information systems professionals and managers should possess a profound level of knowledge about information technology. This level may be gained through education and extensive experience. The second skill area relates to business aspects such as leadership, business systems thinking, relationship building, informed buying, and vendor development. Again, experience in the business supports the development of this skill. The third area is interpersonal skills. It is important to be able to relate to and work with internal users, senior management, and vendors.

Van der Heijden (2001) expanded upon the Feeny and Willcocks (1998a) framework, developing, among other aspects, guidelines for operationalizing and managing the capabilities of the information technology function. Van der Heijden suggests that "… adopting a capability perspective should allow IT managers to move away from symptom-driven management and tackle the roots of their issues" (Van der Heijden, 2001, p. 20).

Finally, Feeny and Willcocks (1998a) suggest it is very important that the capabilities to be developed within the information systems area must be aligned with the goals and objectives of the organization. Following this line of reasoning, Cash (2005) suggests that the CIO is very well positioned to help the senior management team deal with customer management, especially because of the ability to deal with appropriate information about customers.

Conclusion

This chapter has presented an historical perspective to the role of the CIO. The focus of the chapter has been on the emergence of the role and aspects of the role as identified in current research projects.

Comments about what the future holds for CIOs are also interesting. For instance, the Nolan Norton Institute (2001) suggests that the senior information technology executive is moving away from the "technology" and emphasizing more of the "information." The CIO is becoming more of a "prophet" and less of a "technologist." As a prophet, the CIO must know how technology may be employed to transform the business. Further, the CIO must be capable of leading the more traditional parts of the organization through this transition. Olson (2000) used the term "apostle" in reference to the future role of the CIO. While the CIO must educate the rest of the organization about the capabilities of information technology, they can not become too enthusiastic and attempt to push the organization beyond the willingness of the CEO and the rest of the senior management team. A good CIO must develop a thorough understanding of the goals of the organization and how information technology may be strategically applied to advance toward those goals.

Blair (2005) cautions, however, that while there is a movement toward more of an emphasis for the CIO to understand the business, the CIO must still be the information technology champion within the organization. The CIO needs to know both the business and the information technology. Thus, while the CIOs of the future will be involved in strategy, they must understand information technology and how it can be applied to positively impact the business.

The next chapter presents an overview and introduction to the data gathering part of the project conducted to develop this book.

References

Allen, B.R., & Boynton, A.C. (1991). Information architecture: In search of effective flexibility. *MIS Quarterly, 15*, 435-445.

Andrews, P., & Carlson, T. (1997). The CIO is the CEO of the future. In *Proceedings of the CIO Conference*. Retrieved January 26, 2007, from www.cio.com/conferences/eds/sld018.htm

Armstrong, P.A., & Sambamurthy, V. (1999, December). Information technology assimilation in firms: The influence of senior leadership and IT infrastructures. *Information Systems Research, 10*(4), 304-327.

Arnold, M.A. (2001, June). Secrets to CIO success. *Credit Union Management, 24*(6), 26.

Benbasat, I., Dexter, A.S., & Mantha, R.W. (1980, March). Impact of organizational maturity on information skill needs. *MIS Quarterly, 4*(1), 21-34.

Benjamin, R.I., Dickinson, C., & Rockart, J.F. (1985). Changing role of the corporate information systems officer. *MIS Quarterly, 9*(3), 177.

Bharadwaj, A.S. (2000). A resource-based perspective on information technology capability and firm performance: An empirical investigation. *MIS Quarterly, 24*(1), 169-196.

Bharadwaj, A.S., Sambamurthy, V., & Zmud, R.W. (1999). IT capabilities: Theoretical perspectives and empirical operationalisation. In *paper presented at the International Conference on Information Systems*, Charlotte, NC.

Blair, R. (2005, February). The future of CIOs. *Health Management Technology, 26*(2), 58-59.

Bock, G., Carpenter, K., & Davis, J.E. (1986, October). Management's newest star – Meet the chief information officer. *Business Week, 13*(2968), 160-166.

Broadbent, M., Weill, P., & St. Clair, D. (1999, June). The implications of information technology infrastructure for business process redesign. *MIS Quarterly, 23*(2), 159-182.

Butt, J.M. (1969, September). Third generation management. *Data Management, 7*(9), 38-40.

Cash, J. (2005, September 1). Your new market mandate: Meet the customer. *CIO, 18*(22), 1-3.

Chan, Y.E., & Reich, B.H. (1999). *Current practices to raise information technology competence in business managers*. Burnaby, BC: Simon Fraser University.

Cheney, P.H., Lipp, A. (1987). *Information systems personnel skill requirements: 1978 and 1987*. University of Georgia (Working Paper #28). Athens, GA.

Cheney, P.H., & Lyons, N.R. (1980, March). Information systems skill requirements: A survey. *MIS Quarterly, 4*(1), 35-43.

Clemens, E.K. (1991, September). Sustaining IT advantage: The role of structural differences. *MIS Quarterly*, 275-292.

Dickerson, C. (2004, February 16). Get technology right. *InfoWorld, 26*(7), 26.

Duncan, N.B. (1995). Capturing flexibility in information technology infrastructure: A study of resource characteristics and their measure. *Journal of Management Information Systems, 12*(2), 37-57.

Earl, M.J., & Feeny, D.F. (1994). Is your CIO adding value?. *Sloan Management Review, 35*(3), 11-20.

Exton, W. (1970, July). The information system staff: Major obstacles to its effectiveness, and a solution. *Journal of Systems Management, 21*(7), 32-36.

Feeny, D.F., & Willcocks, L.P. (1998a, Spring). Core IS capabilities for exploiting informaiton technology. *Sloan Management Review, 39*(3), 9-21.

Feeny, D.F., & Willcocks, L.P. (1998b). Redesigning the IS function around core capabilities. *Long Range Planning, 31*(3), 354-367.

Feld, C.S., & Stoddard, D.B. (2004, February). Getting IT right. *Harvard Business Review*, 72-79.

Gordon, S. (1993). Standardization of information systems and technology at multinational companies. *Journal of Global Information Management, 1*(3), 5-14.

Hartung, S., Reich, B.H., & Benbasat, I. (2000, December). Information technology alignment in the Canadian forces. *Canadian Journal of Administrative Sciences, 17*(4), 285-302.

Hanseth, O., E. Monteiro, and M. Hatling. (1996). "Developing Information Infrastructure: The Tension Between Standardization and Flexibility", *Science Technology Human Values*, Vol. *21*, No. 4, pp. 407-426.

Ives, B., & Olson, M.H. (1981, December). Manager or technician? The nature of the information systems manager's job. *MIS Quarterly*, *5*(4), 49-63.

Jones, M.C., & Arnett, K.P. (1994, Winter). Linkages between the CEO and the IS environment. *Information Resources Management Journal*, *7*(1), 20-33.

Joslin, E.O., & Bassher, R.A. (1976, February). System managers speak out on performance directions. *Journal of Systems Management*, *27*(2), 18-21.

Kaarst-Brown, M. (2005, June). Understanding an organization's view of the CIO: The role of assumptions about IT. *MIS Quarterly Executive*, *4*(2), 287-301.

Karimi, J., Battacherjee, A., Gupta, Y.P., & Somers, T.M. (2000, Fall). The effects of MIS steering committees on information technology management sophistication. *Journal of Management Information Systems*, *17*(2), 207-230.

Kolbasuk, M. (2005, September). CIOs get respect. *Insurance and Technology*, *30*(9), 18.

Korn/Ferry International. (1998). *The changing role of the chief information officer*. London.

Kwak, M. (2001, Spring). Technical skills, people skills: It's not either/or. *MIT Sloan Management Review*, *42*(3), 16.

Luftman, J., & Brier, T. (1999, Fall). Achieving and sustaining business-IT alignment. *California Management Review*, *42*(1), 109-122.

Maciag, G.A. (2002, August 19). The CIO challenge: Bridging the gap between IT and CEO. *National Underwriter*, *106*(33), 33-34.

Meagher, R. (2003, January-February). Putting "strategic" into information management. *The Information Management Journal*, 51-57.

Nolan Norton Institute. (2001). Say goodbye to the CIO, welcome to the business prophet. *Information Management and Computer Security*, *9*(2/3), 123-125.

Olson, L.A. (2000, May 8). The strategic CIO – Lessons learned, insights gained. *Information Week*, *785*, 264.

O'Riordon, P.D. (1987, Summer). The CIO: MIS makes its move into the executive suite. *The Journal of Information System Management*, *4*(3), 54-56.

Reich, B.H., & Benbasat, I. (2000, March). Factors that influence the social dimension of alignment between business and information technology objectives. *MIS Quarterly*, *24*(1), 81-113.

Stephens, C.S., Ledbetter, W.N., Mitra, A., & Foord, F.N. (1992). Executive or functional manager? The nature of the CIO's job. *MIS Quarterly*, *16*(4), 440-467.

Stephens, C.S., & Loughman, T. (1994). The CIO's chief concern: Communication. *Information and Management*, *27*(2), 129-137.

Todd, P.A., Mckeen, J.D., & Gallupe, R.B. (1995, March). The evolution of IS job skills: A content analysis of IS job advertisements from 1970 to 1990. *MIS Quarterly*, *19*(1), 1-27.

Van der Heijden, H. (2001). Measuring IT core capabilities for electronic commerce. *Journal of Information Technology*, *16*, 13-22.

Weiss, J.W., & Anderson, D. (2004, June). CIOs and IT professionals as change agents, risk and stakeholder managers: A field study. *Engineering and Management Journal*, *16*(2), 13-18.

Chapter III

Gathering and Organizing CIO Comments

Introduction

This chapter presents a description of the data gathering and organizing activities involved in the development of this book. The objective of this investigation was to document the comments of a CIO within their specific organization about their management experiences. Thus, a narrative inquiry approach was taken to conducting one-on-one interviews.

To begin, some background information is presented which serves to place the investigation within a contextual framework. This background information was employed to facilitate the development of a research question and the consequent adoption of an appropriate research method. Appendix A includes the interview protocol. Appendix B contains the informed consent form. The chapter also introduces the CIOs who participated, along with their organizations. Then a discussion follows about the approach taken to analyzing the comments obtained from the interviews. The process for identifying the themes is described. The chapter concludes with a discussion of some issues that were addressed and resolved during the initial data gathering process and subsequent organization of the CIO's comments to support the identification of themes relative to their management experiences.

Background

The information technology environment in which business is conducted continues to change, creating challenges and opportunities. New hardware and software technologies are influencing business processes, while the pervasive Internet is transforming how business is conducted. The properties of the Internet are changing the competitive landscape and the marketplace is no longer restricted by physical boundaries. Also, enterprise resource planning (ERP) software technologies are providing a cross-functional perspective for managing products, services, and customers. The advent of ERP concepts allows managers to focus on the effectiveness of business processes of the firm within its particular environment.

The challenges and opportunities created by the ever changing information technology environment require a response from senior management to facilitate the effective functioning of an organization. Thus, as senior management address the importance of information technology within the context of the organization, the formally recognized role performed by a "chief information officer" (CIO) emerges (Kishore & McLean, 2002). The emergence of this role can take on many forms and is contingent upon many factors. Some of the major factors may relate to some of the following items. First, the CIO role may be affected by environmental factors such as size, industry, or organizational structure. A second factor may relate to the level of maturity of the CIO role. Thus, the role in one firm may be contributing more to a firm's competitive advantage. Along with this factor is also the aspect of senior management's interpretation of the value of information technology to the overall operation of the firm. A third factor relates to industry-based government regulations that may exist and perhaps influence the role performed by the CIO in relation to the processes of gathering, retaining, and distributing information.

Table 1. CIO-related projects

Reference	Subject
Cannon and Woszczynski (2002)	Lessons learned from Y2K
Grant (2003)	Designing e-business initiatives
Groves (2003)	Internet security threats to organizations' information
Miller (2002)	Characteristics of successful change leaders
Ranganathan and Sethi (2003)	Shared domain knowledge
Reich and Benbasat (2000)	Business and information technology alignment
Sujitparapitaya, Janz, and Gillenson (2003)	Information technology governance related to data warehouse practice
Swartz (2003)	Knowledge management
Xu, Lehaney, Clarke, and Duan (2003)	Executive information systems

There has been some recent research into the role of the CIO. Table 1 presents a sample of projects that investigated a specific topic which allowed comments to be made about the CIO role. However, the main objective of these projects was to investigate a specific subject related to the CIO and not a comprehensive investigation of the overall CIO role.

Further, recent research projects that have directly investigated CIO perspectives include the following. Seddon, Graeser, and Willcocks (2002) surveyed 80 senior IT managers about the benefits for their organizations from various approaches to evaluating IT projects and the IT function. Kishore and McLean (2002) documented the discussion of a CIO panel of nine senior executives and their opinions about the future of virtual organizations.

While the above projects are elucidating, they do not provide an in-depth and comparative perspective to the emerging CIO role. This book describes the management experiences of currently practicing CIOs. In-depth interviews were employed to document and develop a better understanding of the role played by the CIOs within the context of their current organizations.

Research Questions

The interview questions include the following:

- Personal and family history
- Company background
- Why the current position was accepted
- Issues
    - Initial
    - Current
    - Future
- Dealing with users
- Deciding on investments
- General comments about being a CIO

Appendix A includes the complete interview protocol, which served as a discussion guide for the conversations with each CIO. The personal and family history, as well as the background material of the company, provided some context within which to view the CIO comments. The remainder of the interview protocol attempted to document CIO comments about issues the CIO felt were significant. The results of these detailed comments are presented later in the book.

The goal was to document issues identified by the CIO and to explore these issues relative to various corporate and national contexts. In-depth interviews document major issues addressed by the CIO. Issues are identified based upon a chronological discussion of the CIO's career. In general, the role of the CIO is to manage information technology for the benefit of the firm. The activities performed by the CIO will have a direct impact on the firm's bottom line. It is therefore incumbent upon the CIO to ensure that the use of information technology is aligned with the business goals and objectives of the firm.

Method of Investigation

The objective of this investigation was to document the comments of a CIO within their specific organization about the role they play. Thus, a narrative inquiry approach was taken to conducting one-on-one interviews.

Narrative inquiry documents "... a segment of one's life that is of interest to the narrator and researcher" (Girden, 2001, p. 49). It entails "... the symbolic presentation of a sequence of events connected by subject matter and related by time" (Scholes, 1981, p. 205). The narrative inquiry approach facilitates documenting stories that are contextually rich and temporally bounded. The contextually rich concept suggests that those events, which are experienced first hand, are the ones that are most vividly remembered (Tulving, 1972). As Swap, Schields, and Abrams (2001) suggest, employing an approach where research participants relate stories about their personal experiences "... would be more memorable, be given more weight, and be more likely to guide behavior" (Swap et al., 2001, p. 103). The second concept, temporally bounded, suggests that narratives should have a beginning and an ending, along with a chronological description of intervening events. Research suggests that the sequential aspect of relating events contributes to the appropriateness of the narrative (Bruner, 1990; Czarniawska-Joerges, 1995a; Vendelo, 1998).

Narrative inquiry has been employed to investigate behavioral science (Rappaport, 1993), fiction and film (Chatman, 1978), and strategic management (Barry & Elmes, 1997). It has been employed to investigate various aspects of information systems by Boland and Day (1989), and Hirschheim and Newman (1991). Further, Hunter and Tan (2001) employed narrative inquiry to identify the major career path impacts of information systems professionals. They interviewed a number of information systems professionals at various stages of their careers to determine why these individuals changed jobs.

The narrative inquiry approach supports the objective of this project by facilitating an exploratory investigation of the issues involving the role of the CIO. In order to ground the discussion in the research participants' personal experiences, individual resumes were employed as the main instrument to guide the interview and to elicit the narratives. The resume was employed to assist research participants to reflect upon their work experiences and report these experiences in a sequential account of events at they transpired throughout their careers. The resume approach has been used previously in information systems research (Young, 2000). The resume is readily available and an untapped source of data (Dex, 1991), and acts as a milestone reference to assist human memory recall (Baker, 1991). While the resume guided the interview, the next paragraph describes a generic technique upon which the interview was organized.

The long interview technique (McCracken, 1988) may also be used in association with narrative inquiry. During the course of the interview, research participants were asked to reflect upon past work experiences. Initially, "grand tour" (McCracken, 1988) questions were asked. These questions are general in nature and nondirective in manner, allowing the research participant to specify much of the substance or perspective of the interview.

Then, with reference to the interview protocol, questions were posed regarding the research participant's past career and personal management experiences. A chronological process was followed from early life, through formal education, and into the various positions held throughout their career up until the current position. Then, the detailed specific issues of the current position were investigated. Questions were asked about initial, current, and future issues. Throughout this section of the interview, "floating prompt" (McCracken, 1988) questions were asked. The nature of these questions depends upon the content of each interview, and, generally, relate to the researcher's decision to pursue a thread of discussion in more detail. Another concept similar to floating prompts is "laddering" (Stewart & Stewart, 1981). This technique involves a series of "how" questions to facilitate the research participants' elaboration of their comments.

Specific, or "planned prompt" (McCracken, 1988) questions were asked near the end of the interview in order to address issues gleaned from the literature or previous investigations. These planned prompts for this project related to:

- Personal history
- Previous experience
- Activities during a typical week
- Dealing with users
- Deciding on information technology investments

Emerging themes were identified by analyzing individual interview transcripts and then by comparing the themes from other interview transcripts. This is a common and accepted practice when conducting qualitative research (Miles & Huberman, 1994) to support the interpretation of textual data (Thompson, 1997). Based upon the transcripts of these interviews, individual chapters have been developed for each CIO. These chapters also follow a similar format, thus facilitating comparisons. The chapters are written in the first person and each CIO retained the right to make any final changes to the content of their chapter.

Chief Information Officers Interviewed

The identification of potential CIOs to be involved in the book was carried out with the valuable assistance of contacts, both professional colleagues and personal friends. In the first instance, a professional contact, Dr. Kay Nelson, director of the Center for Information Technology Management, at Ohio State University, made the initial introduction to a number of potential participants through the CIO Council of Columbus, Ohio. This contact resulted in the eventual participation of seven CIOs from the Columbus, Ohio, area. The identification of CIOs based in Taiwan involved two major steps. First, funding was provided by the Taiwan Economic Cultural Office (TECO), Canada. The second step involved identification of potential participants in Taiwan. This step was facilitated by Mr. Flandy Su, Chairman of the Bank of Kaohsiung, who is a personal friend. Mr. Su's contacts and assistance with local arrangements was invaluable. Further, Mr. Doug Casement, managing editor and publisher at Computer World and CIO IDG Communications, New Zealand, made valuable contacts with potential participants in New Zealand. Potential participants were also identified by Dr. Paul Cragg in the Accounting Finance and Information Systems Department of the Business School at the University of Canterbury in Christchurch, New Zealand. The interviews in New Zealand were carried out as part of a Visiting Erskine Fellowship provided by the University of Canterbury during the months of July and August, 2005.

The following CIOs agreed to participate in this book and interviews have been conducted with them.

- **New Zealand**
  - Wendy Bussen, director of information technology services, Auckland University of Technology (AUT)
    - Wendy was born and grew up in Huntly, New Zealand. She has a Bachelor of Science in mathematics from Waikato University and a Master of Philosophy in information systems from Auckland University. She joined AUT in 1996.
    - AUT is New Zealand's newest university, although it opened its doors as a postsecondary institution in 1895. The goal of AUT is to produce excellent, capable graduates in relevant fields.
  - George Elder, information and supply chain manager, Tait Electronics Limited
    - George was born in Dunedin, New Zealand, and grew up in Motueka, New Zealand. He has a CPIM certification from the American Production and Inventory Control Society and an MBA from the University of Canterbury. He joined Tait Electronics in 1997.
    - Tait Electronics was established in 1969 with head offices in Christchurch, New Zealand. The company supplies world class radio communications equipment.
  - Rhys Gould, group manager of information systems, Fulton Hogan
    - Rhys was born and grew up in Dunedin, New Zealand. He studied accounting at Otago University in Dunedin. His first job after university was with Fulton Hogan.
    - Fulton Hogan was founded in 1933 as a contracting company specializing in road works, quarrying, and civil construction.
  - Zarina Thesing, general manager, information technology, Pumpkin Patch
    - Zarina was born and grew up in Auckland, New Zealand.
    - Pumpkin Patch was founded in 1990 to provide quality children's fashion.
  - Russell Turner, chief information officer, MetService
    - Russell was born in Gisborn and grew up in Wellington, both in New Zealand.
    - MetService was formed in 1992 to provide weather forecasting service in New Zealand.

- **Taiwan**
  - Lucas Chuang, chief information officer, EVA Airways
    - Mr. Chuang was born and grew up in Madou, Taiwan. He has a Bachelor of Science in mathematical sciences from National Chenghi University. He joined EVA Airways in 1988.
    - EVA was formed in 1988 as part of Evergreen Marine Corporation, the world's largest company for shipping containers and container vessels. EVA is currently the second largest airline in Taiwan providing international passenger and freight service.
  - C. M. Ko, section manager, MIS Department, Compostar Technology Corporation
    - Mr. Ko was born and grew up in Kaohsiung, Taiwan. He studied industrial management at a junior college. He joined Compostar soon after it was formed in 1998.
    - Established in 1998, Compostar is a manufacturer and worldwide exporter of resistors and capacitors.
  - James Lin, vice president in charge of information technology, Taiwan Fixed Network Company (TFN)
    - Mr. Lin was born near Sun Moon Lake in Taiwan. He grew up in Taipei, Taiwan. He has a degree in from Tamsui Oxford University, where he majoring in accounting and statistics with a minor in information systems. He joined TFN in 2003.
    - In 2001, Taiwan Fixed Network Company was granted an integrated network license. Since 1991, the company had operated as part of various organizations within Taiwan. The mission of Taiwan Fixed Network is to provide back end (that part of the network that does not move) connections for all international carriers and mobile phone services.
  - C. K. Tsai, deputy director, Information Technology Division, Chi Mei Optoelectronics (CMO) Corporation
    - Mr. Tsai was born and grew up in Tainan, Taiwan. He has a Bachelor of Science with a major in geology from National Taiwan University in Taipei. He joined CMO in 1998, when the company was formed.
    - CMO, formed in 1998, is headquartered in Tainan Science Park, just south of Kaohsiung, where they are the world leading manufacturer of thin film transistor liquid crystal display products, which are the major components of computer monitors and television screens.

- D. I. Wang, chief information officer, Lite-On Technology Corporation
  - Dr. Wang was born and grew up in Tainan, Taiwan. He has a bachelor's degree in mathematics from a university in Taiwan, and a master's degree in computer science and a PhD in applied mathematics, both from Northern University, Boston, USA. He joined Lite-On in 1998.
  - In 2002, Lite-On Technology Corporation became part of the Lite-On Group. Lite-On Technology has a vision to be a world class producer of light emitting diodes, power supplies, wireless devices, liquid crystal display computer monitors, PDAs, and printers.
- M. P. Wang, general manager, Information Systems Department, China Steel
  - Mr. Wang was born and grew up in Tainan, Taiwan. He has a bachelor's degree in computer science from National Taiwan University in Taipei. He started working for China Steel in 1975.
  - China Steel is an integrated steel mill formed in 1971. With 50% of the Taiwan steel market, the company employs a state of the art computerized continuous casting production process.

- **United States of America**
  - Jonathan Dove, chief information officer, Worthington Industries
    - Jonathan was born in Pasadena, California. When he was eight, his family moved to a farm just outside of Pocahontas, Missouri, where he grew up. He has a bachelor's degree in computer science from Coe College in Cedar Rapids, Iowa. He joined Worthington Industries in 1998.
    - Formed in 1955, Worthington Industries is a diversified custom metal processing company and manufacturer of metal related products.
  - Gary Houk, vice president of corporate information technology and business integration, Online Computer Library Center (OCLC)
    - Gary was born in Akron, Ohio. He lived in a lot of different places growing up. He has a bachelor's degree in computer science and an MBA, both from Ohio State University. He joined OCLC in 1974.
    - OCLC was established in 1970 as a nonprofit member-run organization using computers to improve library productivity by creating and maintaining a shared catalogue database. OCLC also owns and maintains the Dewey Decimal Classification System.

- Marty Luffy, chief information officer, Installed Building Products
  - Marty was born and grew up in Pittsburgh, Pennsylvania. He has a Bachelor of Science in industrial management from Purdue University and an MBA from the University of Dayton. Marty is also a certified public accountant.
  - Formed in 1991, Installed Building Products provides commercial and residential construction services such as insulation, waterproofing, gutters, shower doors, shelving, and mirrors.
- Angelo Mazzocco, vice president and chief information officer, The Dispatch Companies
  - Angelo was born and raised in New Castle, Pennsylvania. He has a Bachelor of Science in mathematics and computer science from Indiana University of Pennsylvania, and an MBA in marketing and information systems from the University of Dayton. He joined the Dispatch Companies in 1998.
  - In 1871, the Columbus Dispatch began printing and selling a daily newspaper. The company currently comprises 14 different entities in television, radio, newspaper, real estate, aviation, magazine, direct marketing, and professional sports.
- Cindy Sheets, senior vice president and chief information officer, Mount Carmel Health System
  - Cindy was born and grew up in Columbus, Ohio. She has a bachelor's degree in medical technology from Ohio State University and an MBA from the University of Dayton. She joined Mount Carmel Health System in 1989.
  - Mount Carmel was formed over 120 years ago by the Sisters of the Holy Cross. Today, it is a leading provider of general health care services in Ohio.
- Kathleen Starkoff, chief technology officer and group vice president, Limited Brands
  - Kathleen was born and grew up in Port Clinton, Ohio. She has a Bachelor of Science in mathematics with minors in chemistry and business from Kent State University, and an MBA from Case Western Reserve with a major in policy. She joined Limited Brands in the late 1990s.
  - Formed in 1963, Limited Brands has over 3,800 retail stores carrying six retail fashion brands, including apparel and fragrance.

- John Zarb, chief information officer, Libbey
  - John was born and grew up in Highland Park near Detroit, Michigan. He has a bachelor's degree from Eastern Michigan University and an MBA from Michigan State University. He joined Libbey in 1996.
  - Libbey is the leading producer of glass tableware in North America. Formed over 185 years ago, the company produces glass tableware, ceramic dinnerware, metal flatware, and various plastic utensils.

Issues Conducting the Interviews

The following paragraphs describe some of the issues which arose when conducting the interviews. Overall, the process went very well. So, these issues mainly relate to making adjustments rather than addressing major problems or concerns.

To begin, it was necessary to convince the individual CIO that his or her participation in the project would be beneficial not only to the project but also to the CIO. Some potential participants were not interested in being involved in the project. These individuals seemed to want to pursue a low profile, either for themselves or for their organization, or both. Other participants seemed very interested in the project but felt they could not participate because of other time commitments. It was surprising how relatively easy it was to convince those who eventually decided to participate in the project. Here it seemed that the participants appreciated the opportunity to tell their story. Agreement to participate was enhanced through the initial contact process. That is, in each of the three countries, initial contact was made with the CIO by someone who knew the CIO. As stated above, the New Zealand CIOs were initially contacted by a research colleague, then a CIO who was not able to participate in the project due to time constraints. The Taiwan CIOs were contacted by a personal friend. Initially, the USA CIOs were contacted by a professional colleague. Then, one of the CIOs who participated in this project initiated further CIO involvement.

One issue that had to be resolved before any data gathering was initiated had to do with confidentiality. Recall that the objective in creating the book was to document the story of specific individuals and their opinions, based upon their management experiences, about performing as a CIO. This objective necessitated the specific identification of both individual and company names. The first step required to address this issue was obtaining approval from the Research Ethics Committee at the University of Lethbridge. This committee provided valuable feedback and suggestions about how to develop and implement an informed consent document. See Appendix B for the approved document. The second step involved convincing the potential participants that they would be satisfied with the result. So, during the initial contact the overall approach was explained. The interviews were audio taped and a transcript was prepared. The transcript was sent to the participant to review and make any changes they thought would be necessary. The participant retained the right to edit the transcript. A chapter was prepared based upon the comments in the revised transcripts. The participant also retained the right to edit the chapter. The right to edit the transcript and the chapter were stated clearly in the informed consent document, which was presented and agreed upon before the interviews were conducted.

During the course of conducting the interviews, meeting times were set and revised based upon the participants' schedules. In all cases, those who completed the process were very accommodating in setting and revising meeting times and responding to requests for further information. Indeed, in many instances information was volunteered by the CIO which eventually proved valuable in the completion of this project.

The interview technique employed in this research project was based upon the McCracken (1988) long interview technique. This technique supports the narrative inquiry approach. Initially, an interview protocol was developed. This protocol was used to ensure consistency of narrative documentation across a number of interviews. When conducting the interviews in Taiwan, the protocol was sent before the interview was conducted. This allowed the participant to prepare some responses in advance of the interview. For each interview the protocol, was used to guide the discussion. This worked very well because each of the participants in Taiwan was of a different culture than the author. Having the protocol in advance contributed to the ease of conducting the actual interview. In some cases, it allowed the participant to organize a translator to help interpret the question or the response during the interview.

When the data gathering process started for the CIOs in the United States, a different approach was initially attempted. Because these individuals were from a more similar culture, the protocol was simply sent to those CIOs who agreed to participate with a request to send back a completed transcript. While this worked for two of the CIOs, it was not successful with the others. The CIOs who expressed an interest in completing this task found that other work-related tasks required a higher priority. Thus, another approach had to be adopted. The protocol was then divided into three major sections. Telephone interviews were scheduled which would be limited to one hour. Three 1-hour interviews were employed to gather the data from the remainder of the CIOs who participated from the United States. This revised approach worked very well. It was much easier to request and arrange this series of 1 hour interviews. This modified approach was then also employed to interview the CIOs in New Zealand. The only complicating factor added for this final series of interviews was the time and day difference between New Zealand and Canada.

In all cases, the protocol was used as an interview guide. At times during the interview the researcher may ask for more detail about a particular comment made by the research participant. This is referred to as either a "floating prompt" (McCracken, 1988) or "laddering" (Stewart & Stewart, 1981). In either case this line of questioning allows the gathering of more detail. It facilitates encouraging the participant to provide further elaboration about the story being related.

Each CIO was involved in the review process for the material about them and their company. For those CIOs who were interviewed each transcript was sent for their review. Any alterations initiated by the CIO were applied to the transcript. The series of transcripts was then assembled along with other supporting data such as the Web site material describing the company. From this assembled material the individual chapters were written. Again, each chapter was reviewed by the respective CIO. Those CIOs who were not interviewed developed their own chapters. A similar review process was conducted with them for their resulting chapters. Any changes suggested by the CIO were adopted into the chapter. As indicated in the informed consent document, the CIO retained the right to edit any material before publication. Every CIO participated in this form of field verification. As participants, it was important that they were comfortable with the process and that they agreed with the contents of the resulting manuscript. Further, this review and verification process contributed to the quality of the information presented in each chapter. In turn, this increased level of participant representation and consistency among the chapters provided support for subsequent analysis and identification of emerging themes.

Organizing the Comments

Qualitative research is an interpretive approach to investigating subjects in their natural surroundings. Thus, qualitative researchers conduct their investigations "in the field."

The main emphasis of qualitative researchers is the personnel involved in organizations.

They spend a great deal of time in organizations and with their representatives documenting situations and gathering organization members' interpretations of situations. So, qualitative researchers attempt to make sense of, or interpret, phenomena in terms of the meanings attributed by those individuals whose opinion is related to and considered important relative to the subject of the research. Qualitative researchers, in order to obtain these interpretations, must work closely with research participants. Thus, those individuals involved with the qualitative researcher are likely considered partners or fellow research participants involved in the investigation of a research question.

Qualitative researchers become closely involved in research situations and with research participants. There arises then a concern about researcher bias. That is, in an interview, questions may be posed in a certain way, or certain aspects of the discussion may be pursued more or less intensively. Some researchers would consider this flexibility to be beneficial, allowing the researcher to obtain relevant data. As Reason and Rowan suggest, "… it is much better to be deeply interesting than accurately boring" (1981, p. xiv). In the end, emphasis should be placed on the research method in order to counteract the potential introduction of bias.

When conducting qualitative research, measuring reliability is difficult. Pervin suggests that reliability in the social sciences research context "… relates to the extent to which our observations are stable, dependable, and can be replicated" (1989, p. 271). That is, can a different person, following the same method, obtain the same results? Here again, the importance of the research method is emphasized. In general, qualitative researchers tend to agree that replication is the best means to validate conclusions determined from qualitative research. A qualitative researcher will investigate a subject area and reach preliminary conclusions about a research question. Subsequent investigations may replicate the research on a broader basis in an attempt to support or refute these initial findings. The most important consideration is that the research method adopted be chosen in light of the research objectives.

As indicated previously, the data gathering method adopted for this project involved a qualitative approach to conducting interviews with CIOs. From the resulting interview transcripts, individual chapters were developed. The content of the chapters may be analyzed within the purview of narrative inquiry and the approach to interpreting textual data.

The approach to conducting qualitative research which employs narrative inquiry has been used extensively in organizational studies (Barry & Elmes, 1997; Boje, 1991;

Table 2. Features of narrative

Feature	Description
Sequence in Time	A narrative should have a beginning, middle, and an end. A chronological sequence of events will add to the richness of the story.
Focal Point	A narrative should be about someone or something, which provides the thread to tie the events together.
Voice	A narrative should be told by someone who presents the story from a specific perspective.
Frame of Reference	A narrative should include a central concept around which the value of actions may be judged.
Context	A narrative should be told within a context for the characters and events. They provide information which may facilitate the interpretation of events.

Boland & Tenkasi, 1995; Christensen, 1995; Czarniawska, 1997; Czarniawska-Joerges, 1994, 1995a, 1995b; Hatch, 1993; O'Connor, 1995; Phillips, 1995; Skoldberg, 1994; Van Maanen, 1988; Vendelo, 1998).

A narrative may be defined as, "... a sequential account of events, usually chronologically, whereby sequentially indicates some kind of causality, and action—accounted for in terms of intentions, deeds and consequences—is commonly given a central place" (Czarniawska-Joerges, 1995a, p. 15). The power of the narrative is in the sequence of relating the events of the story (Bruner, 1990; Rimmon-Kenan, 1983).

Table 2 presents the features of narrative inquiry (Barthes, 1977; Bruner, 1990; Pentland, 1999).

Collecting and analyzing qualitative data requires a significant amount of effort (Luna-Reyes & Andersen, 2003). The analysis of transcripts involves a thorough review of the contents in order to identify common themes (Glaser & Strauss, 1967). The discovery of categories and their revision based upon further review of transcripts entails an iterative process. Thompson (1997) has suggested that interpretation of textual data, or narratives, is iterative, and includes two stages. In the first stage the researcher develops an understanding of each narrative. This requires a thorough reading of the transcript. In some cases multiple readings of the transcript may be necessary. In the second stage the researcher identifies emerging themes from among a number of narratives. Thus, data analysis involves searching for emerging themes, first within an interview and then across a series of interviews. The search for emerging themes is common practice in qualitative research (Miles & Huberman, 1994) and involves the interplay between data from within the transcript and the emerging themes. The process begins with a careful reading of the transcript, where noteworthy phrases or sentences are highlighted. Passages that seem conceptually linked are then considered together and descriptions of the theme or pattern that the groupings share are developed. Grounded Theory (Glaser & Strauss, 1976) facilitates the identification of emerging themes across a number of texts. As the data are reviewed, sets of categories or concepts emerge, which are "grounded" in the data within the texts. Subsequently, the data are reviewed again to identify further evidence that supports or challenges the emerging themes. This second review may lead to the identification of new themes, or a reclassification of existing themes. The role of the researchers throughout this process is, "... to be open to possibilities afforded by the text rather than projecting a predetermined system of meanings onto the textual data" (Thompson, 1997, p. 441).

Interviews may be conducted either face to face or via the telephone. It is important to adopt an approach which ensures the research participant is as comfortable as possible during the interviews. The level of comfort seems to be reflected in how forthcoming the research participant might be with detailed comments about the story being told. Not only do interviews allow the story to be told in the research participant's own words, but it is also possible to obtain immediate clarification of comments or elaboration of details.

The interviewer should remain neutral (McCracken, 1988) and should act as a guide to the relating of the story and as a facilitator for clarification of comments made by the research participant.

Usually, interviews are conducted with participants on the condition that anonymity is ensured. When interviews and specific comments will not be anonymous the result is most often referred to as an oral history. In the case of developing this book, the interview transcriptions have been held in confidence with the participants. However, the resultant chapters specifically mention the name of the CIO and the organization they were employed by during the interview process. The content of the specific chapters has been reviewed and approved by each respective CIO.

Identifying the Themes

This section describes the process followed regarding the identification of emerging themes.

It was necessary before the interviews could be conducted to find individuals who were interested in the project and who would be willing to volunteer to participate. Through various personal contacts individuals were sent information about the project. Those who responded expressing an interest in the project were contacted and provided further information. This information included the informed consent form and the interview protocol, which have been placed at the end of this chapter. It is important to note that those who agreed to participate also agreed to the use of their names and their company name. The participants seemed comfortable with this aspect, especially with the commitment of the author to ensure the participant would retain the right to edit the final version of the chapter.

Individual interviews were scheduled with each CIO who volunteered. Some were conducted face-to-face, while others were carried out via the telephone. In all cases, the interviews were audio taped. Transcripts were prepared from the audio tapes and sent to the respective participant for review. For the most part, any corrections related to spellings of names or towns, or because of inaudible comments made during the interview.

The series of transcripts prepared from the interviews of each participant were used to develop a chapter. Usually, three separate interviews were conducted via the telephone. This allowed efficient scheduling of the participant's time. Each individual telephone interview lasted less than one hour. The face-to-face interviews were usually of just less than two hours. In these cases some material was prepared ahead of time based upon the distribution of the interview protocol. Also, some information was sent after the interview. All of the Taiwan interviews were conducted face-to-face during a 1-week visit to the country. The remaining interviews were carried out over the telephone with the exception of two participants. These two participants wrote their own chapters based upon the interview protocol. While this process of completing their own chapters would have been very efficient for the author, it was found that the other participants had difficulty keeping the task of completing the chapter as a high priority. Thus, the series of telephone interviews were scheduled and carried out. This allowed the participants to commit to a shorter period of time and off load onto the author the more clerical aspects of developing the chapter.

The chapter content was developed based upon the responses to the interview protocol. The major categories of questions were organized relatively close to a chronological sequence. So, to begin the interview, the questions first centered on the participant's early life experiences and education. Then the discussion focused upon the participant's career before joining the current company. Finally, the interview narrowed down to a discussion of aspects related to the management experiences of a CIO at the current company. Within this discussion of the CIO management experiences, a sequential approach was taken. So, issues were discussed relating to those which required the attention of the CIO upon initially accepting the position. Then, current issues were discussed. Finally, the participant was asked to comment upon any issues that were expected to be dealt with in the future. All of these major categories of questions have been employed to structure each interview, then to identify emerging themes, and finally to organize the subsequent chapter regarding the content of the CIO comments about their management experiences.

Conclusion

This chapter has presented an overview of the development of this book regarding the initial phases of gathering and organizing comments about their management experiences from the CIOs who decided to participate. To begin, some background information was presented, which served to place the project within a contextual framework. Appendix A includes the interview protocol. Appendix B contains the informed consent form. The chapter also introduces the specific CIOs who participated, along with their organizations at the time the interviews were conducted. Then, the approach taken to organize the comments is presented along with the process for identifying the themes. The chapter concludes with a brief discussion of some issues that were addressed and resolved during the initial data gathering process.

The results of this investigation will contribute to a more thorough understanding of the management experiences of the CIO and how the role is emerging and evolving in various corporate and national contexts. While the development of an interview protocol was important to provide consistency across a number of interviews, it was also important to allow the participant to pursue aspects of their own story that they considered were central to the aspects of their story about their personal management experiences. This contention between structure and flexibility requires the interviewer to "walk a thin line." The collection of qualitative interview data takes time. It takes a lot of time and effort to read and reread transcripts, and in this case, to then develop a chapter based upon a series of transcripts from interviews with the CIO. This approach adds richness and allows insights of the participant to be gathered. The details of the stories provide a glimpse of insight into the real world of the CIO.

References

Baker, M. (1991). *Research in marketing*. London: MacMillan.

Barry, D., & Elmes, M. (1997). Strategy retold: Toward a narrative view of strategic discourse. *Academy of Management Review*, *22*(2), 429-452.

Barthes, R. (1977). Introduction to the structural analysis of narratives. *Image-Music-Text: 79124* (S. Heath, Trans.). New York: Fontana.

Boje, D. (1991). The story-telling organization: A study of story performance in an office-supply firm. *Administrative Science Quarterly*, *35*(1), 106-126.

Boland, R.J., Jr., & Day, W.F. (1989). The experience of systems design: A hermeneutic of organizational action. *Scandinavian Journal of Mgt*, *5*(2), 87-104.

Boland, R.J., Jr., & Tenkasi, R.V. (1995). Perspective making and perspective taking in communities of knowing. *Organization Science*, *6*(4), 350-372.

Bruner, J. (1990). *Acts of meaning*. Cambridge, MA: Harvard University Press.

Cannon, A.R., & Woszczynski, A.B. (2002). Crises and revolutions in information technology: Lessons learned from Y2K. *Industrial Management and Data Systems*, *102(*6), 318-324.

Chatman, S. (1978). *Story and discourse: Narrative structure in fiction and film*. Ithaca, NY: Cornell University Press.

Christensen, L.T. (1995). Buffering organizational identity in the marketing culture. *Organizational Studies*, *16*(4), 651-672.

Czarniawska, B. (1997). *Narrating the organization – Dramas of institutional identity*. Chicago: University of Chicago Press.

Czarniawska-Joerges, B. (1994). Narrative of individual and organizational identities. In S. Deetz (Ed.), *Communication yearbook* (vol. 17, pp. 193-221). Newbury Park, CA: Sage Publications.

Czarniawska-Joerges, B. (1995a). Narration or science? Collapsing the division in organization studies. *Organization*, *2*(1), 11-33.

Czarniawska-Joerges, B. (1995b). A four times told tale: Combining narrative and scientific knowledge in organization studies. In J.K. Christiansen, J. Mouritsen, P. Neergaard, & B. Jepsen (Eds.), *Proceedings of the Thirteenth Nordic Conference on Business Studies* (pp. 259-273), Copenhagen.

Dex, S. (1991). *Life and work history analyses.* London: Routledge.

Girden, E.R. (2001). *Evaluating research articles* (2nd ed). Thousand Oaks, CA: Sage Publications.

Glaser, B.G., & Strauss, A.L. (1967). *The discovery of grounded theory: Strategies for qualitative research.* New York: Aldine DeGruyter.

Grant, R. (2003). Canadian approaches to e-business implementation. *Canadian Journal of Administrative Sciences*, *20*(1), 3-20.

Groves, S. (2003). The unlikely heroes of cyber security. *Information Management Journal*, *37*(3), 34-40.

Hatch, M.J. (1993). The role of the researcher: An analysis of narrative position in organizational theory. *Journal of Management Enquiry*, *5*(4), 1094-1113.

Hirschheim, R., & Newman, M. (1991, March). Symbolism and information systems development: Myth, metaphor and magic. *Information Systems Research*, *2*(1), 29-62.

Hunter, M.G., & Tan, F. (2001, May 20-22). Information systems professionals in New Zealand: Reflective career biographies. In *Proceedings of the International Conference of the Information Resources Management Association* (pp. 132-133). Toronto, Canada.

Kishore, R., & McLean, E.R. (2002). The next generation enterprise: A CIO perspective on the vision, its impacts, and implementation challenges. *Information Systems Frontiers*, *4*(1), 121-138.

Luna-Reyes, L.F., & Andersen, D.L. (2003, Winter). Collecting and analyzing qualitative data for system dynamics: Methods and models. *System Dynamics Review*, *19*(4), 271-296.

McCracken, G. (1988). *The long interview.* New York: Sage Publications.

Miller, D. (2002). Successful change leaders: What makes them? What do they do that is different?. *Journal of Change Management*, *2*(4), 359-368.

Miles, M.B., & Huberman, A.M. (1994). *Qualitative data analysis: A new sourcebook of methods* (2nd Ed.). Newbury Park, CA: Sage Publications.

O'Connor, E.S. (1995). Paradoxes of participation: Textual analysis and organizational change. *Organization Studies*, *15*(5), 769-803.

Pentland, B.T. (1999, October). Building process theory with narrative: From description to explanation. *The Academy of Management Review, 24*(4), 711-724.

Pervin, L.A. (1989). *Personality: Theory and research* (5th ed.). New York: John Wiley.

Phillips, N. (1995). Telling organizational tales: On the role of narrative fiction in the study of organizations. *Organization Studies, 16*(4), 625-649.

Ranganathan, C., & Sethi, V. (2003). Rationality in strategic information technology decisions: The impact of shared domain knowledge and IT unit structure. *33*(1), 59-86.

Rappaport, J. (1993). Narrative studies, personal stories and identity transformation in the mutual help context. *Journal of Applied Behavioral Science, 29*(2), 239-256.

Reason, P., & Rowan, J. (Eds.). (1981). *Human inquiry – A sourcebook of new paradigm research.* Chichester, UK: John Wiley.

Reich, B.H., & Benbasat, I. (2000). Factors that influence the social dimensions of alignment between business and information technology objectives. *MIS* Quarterly, *24*(1), 81-113.

Rimmon-Kenan, S. (1983). *Narrative fiction: Contemporary poetics*. London: Rutledge.

Scholes, R. (1981). Language, narrative, and anti-narrative. In W. Mitchell (Ed.), *On narrativity* (pp. 200-208). Chicago: University of Chicago Press.

Seddon, P.B., Graeser, V., & Willcocks, L.P. (2002). Measuring organizational IS effectiveness: An overview and update of senior management perspectives. *Database for Advances in Information Systems*, *33*(2), 11-28.

Skoldberg, K. (1994). Tales of change: Public administration reform and narrative mode. *Organization Science*, *5*(2), 219-238.

Stewart, V., & Stewart, A. (1981). *Business applications of repertory grid.* London: McGraw-Hill.

Sujitparapitaya, S., Janz, B.D., & Gillenson, M. (2003). The contribution of IT governance solutions to the implementation of data warehouse practice. *Journal of Database Management, 14*(2), 52-69.

Swap, W., Schields, M., & Abrams, L. (2001, Summer). Using mentoring and storytelling to transfer knowledge in the workplace. *Journal of Management Information Systems, 18*(1), 95-114.

Swartz, N. (2003). The "wonder years" of knowledge management. *Information Management Journal*, *37*(3), 53-57.

Thompson, C.J. (1997, November). Interpreting consumers: A hermeneutical framework for deriving marketing insights from texts on consumers' consumption stories. *Journal of Marketing Research, 34*, 438-455.

Tulving, E. (1972). Episodic and semantic memory. In E. Tulving & W. Donaldson (Eds.), *Organization of memory* (pp. 381-404). New York: Academic Press.

Van Maanen, J. (1988). *Tales of the field.* Chicago: University of Chicago Press.

Vendelo, M.T. (1998, Fall). Narrating corporate reputation: Becoming legitimate through storytelling. *International Studies of Management and Organization, 28*(3), 120-137.

Xu, X.M., Lehaney, B., Clarke, S., & Duan, Y. (2003). Some UK and USA comparisons of executive information systems in practice and theory. *Journal of End User Computing, 15*(1), 1-19.

Young, J. (2000). *The career paths of computer science and information systems major graduates.* Unpublished doctoral thesis, University of Tasmania.

Appendix A. Management Experiences of the CIO: Interview Protocol

Part A

1. Personal History
    a. Where were you born?
    b. Where did you grow up?
    c. Are you married?
    d. Any children?
    e. Please relate a personal interest story.
2. Family History
    a. Parents
    b. Siblings
    c. Where you lived
3. Education
    a. Where and when did you go to elementary school, high school, and university?
4. Previous Work Experience
    a. What companies have you worked for?
    b. What positions have you held at these companies?

c. What were the highlights as far as tasks performed and major accomplishments?

Part B

5. Current Position
   a. Company background
      i. What is the industry?
      ii. When was the company formed?
      iii. What is the company's industry relationship (market share)?
      iv. What is the company Mission?
      v. Are there any unique aspects to the company that you find interesting?
      vi. What is the URL for your Web site?
   b. Why did you accept your current position?
   c. What issues initially required your attention?
      i. Describe the issue.
      ii. Discuss what you did.
      iii. Discuss the final result.
      iv. Repeat the above for another issue.
   d. What issues are you currently addressing?
      i. Describe the issue.
      ii. Discuss the status and anticipated outcome.
      iii. Repeat the above for another issue.
   e. What issues do you foresee addressing or requiring your attention in the future?
      i. Describe.
      ii. How do you plan to address the issue?
      iii. What is the anticipated outcome?
      iv. Repeat the above for another issue.

Part C

6. Pick a week and tell me what you did.

   a. Describe the task.
   b. Indicate the number of hours you spend doing the task.
   c. Was there something that you did not do that week that you normally would?
7. Dealing with Users
   a. How do you determine what your users want/require?
   b. How do you know that you have responded to what your users want/require?
   c. How do you know that you have delivered what your users want/require?
8. How do you decide on investments in:
   a. Hardware?
   b. Software?
   c. People?
   d. Tools?
   e. Techniques and methods?
9. General comments about CIOs and their management experiences

Appendix B. Informed Consent Form

Project Title: Management Experiences of the Chief Information Officer

Investigator: M. Gordon Hunter, Ph.D.

This consent form, a copy of which has been given to you, is only part of the process of informed consent. It should give you the basic idea of what the research is about and what your participation will involve. If you would like more detail about something that is included here, or information not included here, please ask. Please take the time to read this form carefully, and to understand any accompanying information.

You have agreed to participate in a research project that I am conducting. The purpose of this research is to investigate factors involved in the management experiences of Chief Information Officers. Your participation is very important, as it will provide valuable information about this role. There are no right answers to the questions, and the most valuable information for this research is your personal opinions and experiences.

The transcript that you develop is based upon a standard protocol for all research participants. You may choose not to answer any or all of the questions, and your cooperation is completely voluntary. Should you decide to withdraw from the study your transcript will be destroyed.

Subsequent publications will specifically identify you through reflective chronological biographies developed, based upon the data gathered via the standard protocol or background material provided by you. **You retain the right to edit any transcript or resulting manuscript before publication.**

Your signature on this form indicates that you understand to your satisfaction the information regarding your participation in my research project and agree to participate. In no way does this waive your legal rights nor release the investigators, sponsors, or involved institutions from their legal and professional responsibilities. This research is being carried out in accordance with the Tri-Council Policy Statement: Ethical Conduct for Research Involving Humans, and the University of Lethbridge's policies. You are free to withdraw from the study at any time with no consequences. Your continued participation should be as informed as your initial consent, so you should feel free to ask for clarification or new information throughout your participation.

If you have further questions concerning matters related to this research, please contact me, Gordon Hunter, at (403) 329-2672. Questions of a general nature may be addressed to the Office of Research Services, University of Lethbridge at (403) 329-2747.

____

Signature of Participant

____

Date (Day/Month/Year)

A copy of this consent form has been given to you to keep for your records and reference.

Would you like to be sent a copy of the aggregated study results when they are available?

Yes _________ No _________ (please check the appropriate line).

If you responded **YES**, please provide your likely mailing address for six months from now:

____

____

____

Thank you for your participation. Please do not hesitate to contact me if you require further information or have questions:

M. Gordon Hunter, Associate Professor

Faculty of Management

The University of Lethbridge

4401 University Drive, Lethbridge, AB T1K 3M4

CANADA

Telephone: (403) 329-2672

Fax: (403) 329-2038

E-mail: ghunter@uleth.ca

Section II

New Zealand

The chapters in this section are the results of the discussion with CIOs from New Zealand. The New Zealand population on June 30, 2004, was just over 4 million (Economist Intelligence Unit, 2005). About half the population lives in the four main cities of Auckland, Christchurch, Hamilton, and the national capital, Wellington. Because of New Zealand's lack of significant natural resources, recent efforts have focused on the development of a knowledge economy through post secondary education. Through government support, emphasis has been placed in general on value added contributions to the economy.

Information technology plays a small, but growing role, in the New Zealand economy (Ein-Dor, Myers, & Raman, 1997). As Sallis (2001) more recently reported:

New Zealand has a small manufacturing industry and builds very few computer components or peripherals. The nation does, however, have a significant reputation as an IT proving ground and high-volume user of products and services. New Zealand's Internet traffic totals are among the highest in the world. In fact New Zealand has the seventh highest number of Internet hosts per 1,000 inhabitants in the world and the fourth highest number of secure servers per million people.

New Zealand is an early adopter of software development technologies and prolific producer of IT applications. It has a vibrant professional society for individuals ... and an active sales and service industry ... together with several focused professional groups ... Essentially, the IT industry in New Zealand is a value-adding environment, utilizing tools and technologies developed elsewhere. (Sallis, 2001, p. 53)

Sallis (2001) also reported that there is a general problem of hiring capable staff in all aspects of information technology. It seems that this will be an ongoing issue for the foreseeable future.

The individuals who were interviewed represent organizations in Auckland, Christchurch, and Wellington. The following chapters and CIOs are included in this section:

- Wendy Bussen, director of information technology services, Auckland University of Technology (AUT)
  - Wendy was born and grew up in Huntly, New Zealand. She has a Bachelor of Science in mathematics from Waikato University and a Master of Philosophy in information systems from Auckland University. She joined AUT in 1996.
  - AUT is New Zealand's newest university, although it opened its doors as a postsecondary institution in 1895. The goal of AUT is to produce excellent, capable graduates in relevant fields.
- George Elder, information and supply chain manager, Tait Electronics Limited
  - George was born in Dunedin, New Zealand, and grew up in Motueka, New Zealand. He has a CPIM certification from the American Production and Inventory Control Society and an MBA from the University of Canterbury. He joined Tait in 1997.
  - Tait was established in 1969 with head offices in Christchurch, New Zealand. The company supplies world class radio communications equipment.
- Rhys Gould, group manager of information systems, Fulton Hogan
  - Rhys was born and grew up in Dunedin, New Zealand. He studied accounting at Otago University in Dunedin. His first job after university was with Fulton Hogan.
  - Fulton Hogan was founded in 1933 as a contracting company specializing in road works, quarrying, and civil construction.
- Zarina Thesing, general manager, information technology, Pumpkin Patch
  - Zarina was born and grew up in Auckland, New Zealand.
  - Pumpkin Patch was founded in 1990 to provide quality children's fashion.
- Russell Turner, chief information officer, MetService
  - Russell was born in Gisborn and grew up in Wellington, both in New Zealand.
  - MetService was formed in 1992 to provide weather forecasting service in New Zealand.

Table 1.

CIO Name	Company Name	City	Number of Employees	Sector
Wendy Bussen	AUT	Auckland	900	Education
George Elder	TAIT Electronics	Christchurch	1,000	Communications
Rhys Gould	Fulton Hogan	Christchurch	4,653	Construction
Zarina Thesing	Pumpkin Patch	Auckland	2,700	Clothing
Russell Turner	Met Service	Wellington	200	Weather reporting

Table 1 provides some comparative data about the companies involved from New Zealand.

References

Economist Intelligence Unit (EIU) (2005, February 14). New Zealand: Population. *EIU ViewsWire*. New York.

Ein-Dor, P., Myers, M.D., & Raman, K.S. (1997, Spring). Information technology in three small developed countries. *Journal of Management Information Systems, 13*(4), 61-89.

Sallis, P.J. (2001, July). Some thoughts on IT employment in New Zealand. *Communications of the ACM, 44*(7), 53-54.

Chapter IV

Wendy Bussen
Auckland University of Technology

To foster excellence, equity in learning, teaching, research and scholarship and in so doing serve our regional, national and international communities

My name is **Wendy Bussen**. I am the director of information technology services at AUT University in Auckland, New Zealand.

Personal History

I was born in Huntly, New Zealand. It is about a 1½ hours drive south of Auckland. I attended Huntly Primary School and Huntly College, and then went to Waikato University in Hamilton. I lived in residence and graduated with a Bachelor of Science, majoring in mathematics. Ten years ago, I went to Auckland University to study for a Master of Philosophy, majoring in management sciences and information systems.

My first job after university was as an actuarial trainee for National Mutual Australasia in Wellington. I worked there for about 18 months. I could have stayed and studied for a professional actuarial designation, which would have taken 5 or 6 years, but instead I chose to travel. I don't regret that I did. I set a personal goal to go around the world before I turned 30, and I managed to achieve it.

While on my travels, I decided to find employment in England. For 3 years I worked at Unilever Computer Services in London in their operational research division. I was a FORTRAN programmer, writing code for simulation packages. One exciting project I worked on was simulating the addition of a new cutter for the Thames timber mill in northern England.

I was also involved in the establishment of a new division. Unilever wanted to set up a new information centre at their head office. I was seconded to work on the data analysis and graphical representation of data from all the Unilever factories around the world. I had to learn a new programming language called "A Programming Language" (APL). Senior management had never seen the data presented in the graphical format that I developed. This was in the 1980s, when graphical tools were still in there infancy. I was pleased with the results as they showed information about production in a different light. This was greatly appreciated by senior management.

After 4 years living in London, I decided it was time to continue on my travels with the intention of returning to New Zealand. I had some difficulty finding a job when I first returned to New Zealand. My experience was in management sciences and operational research. Most companies in New Zealand were too small to have a department specialized in this type of work. Most computing companies developed business systems. I managed to secure a job with a company called Computer Professionals Limited in Auckland. I coded accounting systems using Visual Basic. After about 2 years, I moved to Quanta Consulting Ltd, as a systems consultant. I wanted to work closer with the client and gain a deeper understanding of business needs and system requirements. Once the client decided to buy the software I would project manage the implementation until the system was up and running. After 2 years working for Quanta, we decided to start a family and I became pregnant with my first child. I had hoped to take on contract work, but when the baby was born everything else took second priority. My focus became the needs of my baby.

Eventually, a friend of mine called and asked if I would consider working part-time at UNITEC Institute of Technology teaching accounting information systems. This was ideal, as the lectures were in the evening and fitted around my family commitments. I enjoyed working with the adult students and spending time during the day preparing my lecture notes. I lectured for about the next 2 years, and then took 6 months maternity leave when our second child was born.

At this time, I started working on my master's degree in management sciences and information systems. I wanted to lecture in the Bachelor of Business program and I needed to have a higher qualification. It was a challenge fitting it in around my commitments; however, it has assisted me with securing the job that I have today.

In 1996, I saw an advertisement for the director of information services at Auckland Institute of Technology (now named AUT University). The position interested me because it offered the chance to use my teaching experience and to move into a senior position. I wanted to apply my understanding of both business and academia. After I had completed my Masters, I was restless and missed the excitement of implementing new technology into organizations. The director position looked ideal. I applied, went for the job interview, and secured the position.

Company History

Our Web site outlines the following history of AUT:

We are New Zealand's newest university, yet we have been educating people in the Auckland region for over a century. AUT first came into being in 1895 as the Auckland Technical School, opening its doors with a roll of 30 students. At that time we were a school for the trades, teaching subjects such as mechanical and architectural drawing, cookery and dressmaking.

In the century since, we have undergone many changes, splitting off a secondary school and helping set up two other technical institutes to accommodate the Auckland region's growth.

In 1989, when we were called the Auckland Institute of Technology, we became the first polytechnic in New Zealand to offer degrees and masters courses. That enabled us to meet the growing demand by industry and the professions to provide higher-level programs that focused on creating work-ready graduates.

One of our greatest moments was at the turn of the new millennium when we became New Zealand's newest university—the Auckland University of Technology. But we are a new kind of university. We take pride in engaging with our communities, undertaking exciting and meaningful research, offering a unique style of teaching and research, and in particular, watching our graduates flourish in their chosen careers.

Although we are a new university, we haven't forgotten our roots. We continue to offer an education that meets the needs of society and is connected to the real world. We still believe that the strongest contribution we can make to New Zealand is to produce excellent, capable graduates in relevant fields.

Our charter outlines the following guiding principles:

The Auckland University of Technology values and is committed to:

a. *International standards of quality in learning, teaching and research,*
b. *Integrating theory and practice with professionally based learning experiences,*
c. *Relevant and contemporary curricula,*
d. *Excellence, innovation and creativity,*
e. *The Treaty of Waitangi and the aims and aspirations of the Maori people,*
f. *Educating for Pasifika peoples' development and success,*
g. *Respect for the dignity of all people and the development of human potential,*
h. *Equity of access, experience and opportunity to succeed,*
i. *Ethical practice in all aspects of the university's activity,*
j. *Kaitiakitanga, sustainable stewardship of resources for future generations,*
k. *Consultative decision-making,*
l. *Environments conducive to work learning and scholarship,*
m. *Effectiveness, efficiency, accountability and service,*
n. *Freedom of inquiry and expression, and*
o. *Its responsibility as critic and conscience of society.*

My Company and Me

I left the software development firm to have my first child. I then had my second child while I was lecturing at UNITEC. I was teaching 10 hours per week and was preparing at home, so the work suited my commitments and the demands of a young family. I was also completing my master's degree at this time. I started to become a little restless and missed the excitement of leading teams and implementing technology into organizations. Accepting the director position at AUT University allowed me to stay working in an academic environment, which I enjoyed, and at the same time have responsibility for commercial decisions. I moved into a more senior management role and was able to work for an organization that is highly regarded in New Zealand.

One of my initial challenges when I started at AUT was building capability in flexible learning. The vice chancellor at the time was keen to ensure flexible learning options in all the programmes taught at the university. I enjoyed seeing how technology could be applied to learning and how it enhances opportunities for students, lecturers, and the organization.

A frustrating experience for me was selling the concept of technology-enhanced learning to the other members of the senior team. While the vice chancellor was very enthusiastic about flexible learning, a good portion of the others were not. The vice chancellor had a clear vision of how he wanted technology to enhance opportunities in learning; others in his team, however, preferred to focus on building capability in other areas. Tension built up within the senior team and at many times I found it difficult to work within this situation and to progress developments in flexible learning.

During this time, I worked on one project, which proved to be one of the most exciting projects of my career. AUT, together with 15 universities from around the world, formed a global alliance. The vision was to work collaboratively and to develop online programmes for students in China. We formed a company, appointed a board, and recruited a CEO. The board met at the partner universities on a regular basis as the strategies were developed.

Another challenge for me was to gain a deeper understanding of network technology. I had always worked as a software developer, and because a good portion of the capital budget was spent on network technology, I learned to ask probing questions and ensure the university made sound investments.

In 2000, I relinquished my responsibilities in flexible learning and had the opportunity to focus on servicing and addressing areas of customer dissatisfaction within the university. I started by implementing a new structure for the IT team. It was a team of 75 staff in total. I created two new departments named IT client services and information services. These were established so that staff could work closer with the customer. They also focused on business process improvement.

An area of dissatisfaction within the university was the overgrown Web site. Technically, the site was fine, but it did not align with marketing strategies. I formed a Web Center and worked with our marketing people to review and redesign the site. I appointed a marketing specialist as the first Web center manager. Dramatic changes were made to the site and how the information was presented. Now, we continually interact with our marketing people to ensure our Web site is providing the service they want.

Another major issue that I dealt with near the start of my time at AUT was putting the right people in the right places. Over time I appointed new managers to support AUT's new direction. On reflection, some of those decisions were quite difficult. Not only was I changing departments, but I was also changing peoples' careers. I now have a team that sees opportunities and responds. They also have a good understanding of what service means.

My Typical Week

My typical week consists of one-on-one meetings with colleagues, direct reports, sometimes meetings with groups of people in working parties, and meetings with vendors.

Dealing with Users

There are different groups of users. I am a member of a senior team called the vice chancellor's advisory board. When he has issues, he will discuss them with this advisory board. I work with the other board members mainly on a one-to-one basis and sometimes with their teams. I keep a close watch on concerns that other senior team members may have or assistance they may need with a new concept.

I like to meet professors when they first arrive at the university. I create a social situation, usually lunch, where I have a chance to get to know them. We discuss what IT can do for them and what their experiences might have been at other universities. This gives me a chance to promote IT and our processes. I have found that this approach works well.

We also have a staff and student service desk, which operates within the ITIL framework. I take every opportunity to reinforce the fact that the service desk is the point of contact for IT problems. We try to capture requests and resolve them straight away (tier one), which is during the initial phone call. About 70% of our calls are resolved at tier one. If that is not possible, the request is escalated to the service desk manager. The manager can remotely take control of the user's computer to attempt to resolve the issue. If this is not possible, a technician is sent to the user's location.

We also have an IT client services department to look after the needs of our clients' information systems needs. The manager of this department sits on various university committees representing IT. We encourage all the major areas in the university to have an IT users group and to have monthly meetings, which we would attend. This is another way we keep in touch with our users.

To determine that we are delivering what the users want, we run customer satisfaction surveys. We analyze the results thoroughly. Recently, we gained some very valuable feedback about mobility from student focus groups.

Deciding on Technology Investments

We now have an IS governance committee. This ensures that investment decisions remain aligned to the strategic direction of the organization and are driven by the business owners. One of our current projects is a customer relationship management system, which is being driven by our communications and marketing area. This is how it should be.

Budgeting for IT investments is part of the planning process. Business users will identify opportunities and include an estimate in their budgets. Because we sit on their user group committees, we can provide input to the development of these estimates. Further, we try to coordinate all of these requests across the units within the university and ensure that they are included on the agenda for the IT governance group.

Current Issues

There are not many current issues that need to be dealt with immediately. Things are actually working quite nicely right now. The team delivers on request and has developed trust among the user community.

We just completed a major project to install voice over Internet protocol (VOIP). The telephone system for the entire university is now based on VOIP.

We are also looking at our current contract with our preferred supplier of desktop computers. Our current contract has expired. So, we have an opportunity to explain our requirements to other potential suppliers. We have centralized our desktop services. This allows us to gain economies of scale both for leasing and for providing services. We try to treat our computers as a commodity. Every 3 years, computers are replaced. Our emphasis is on service to our internal customers.

We are implementing a new time tabling system, which we acquired from Singapore. We have a team of software developers who support our student management system.

Future Issues

The issue of mobility is one we will have to address in the near future. Students are arriving on campus with all sorts of devices, including cell phones. So, we are looking at strategies we need in place to enable this mobility. An independent research firm just completed a student-based focus group project on access to information at

AUT. We obtained some fabulous feedback. Students said they would be interested in owning inexpensive laptops and having access to inexpensive broadband.

Another issue will be the replacement of our core infrastructure. We currently have a 5-year lease on all of our network technology and this expires next year. We see this as an opportunity to upgrade all of our equipment. We will look into the future when we do this replacement at the kind of services we think we will need to supply.

Further, our project office needs to be expanded. We need to look at how we manage our resources across all of our active projects. We also want to pursue opportunities in identifying and responding to situations where we can contribute to business improvement.

Final Comments

The CIO has an interesting role. Some senior managers see your position as having responsibility for only the technical infrastructure. They do not see how IT can contribute to strategic advantage. The CIO must continually persuade and look for opportunities to promote improvement and advancement to senior management. The CIO needs to promote how they can add value to the organizations, more so than other positions. Some management teams are not interested in technology and the challenge for the CIO is to learn how to speak in their terms and look for ways that technology can enhance their business.

References

Auckland University of Technology (n. d.). Retrieved January 30, 2007, from www.aut.ac.nz

Chapter V

George Elder
Tait Electronics Limited

Supplying and servicing world class radio communications equipment

My name is **George Elder**. I am the information and supply chain manager at Tait Electronics Limited.

Personal History

I was born in Dunedin, New Zealand. Soon after my birth, we moved to a small town in the north of the South Island called Motueka. That's where I grew up attending primary and high school. After high school I went to Christchurch and enrolled at the University of Canterbury in the engineering program. After 2 years of study, I decided that university was not for me and went looking for a job to make some money.

I was lucky enough to find employment with Firestone Tyre and Rubber Company. I worked as a tyre builder on shift work. After 6 months I realized that I had to be doing something better. I applied to work in the Technical Services Department. They wanted someone to do quality control and decided I might be suitable. So, I moved into the quality control of the tyre manufacturing process. I was assigned to the Technical Team and we wrote tyre specifications, built experimental tyres, and commissioned new pieces of equipment. I was the quality control officer responsible for ensuring appropriate production tolerances for product from our production machinery. I learned from the ground floor up what makes a manufacturing operation work. I think this experience has helped me in my current position, but more of that later.

I gradually took on more responsibility in the quality control area and became involved in commissioning new pieces of equipment. I would work with the suppliers regarding new products that required major changes in process and I found it was interesting work. I was also working closely with the guys on the factory floor. I always had a good working relationship with these groups.

About 1976, Firestone advertised for people to join their new Computer Department. I had heard about computers and thought computer programming might be interesting. So, I sat the aptitude test that IBM administered in those days. I came through with flying colours and joined the new Computer Department.

Prior to this, Firestone had another local company doing their data processing. But, it was decided to bring the processing in-house with the acquisition of an IBM 370-115. My first task as a computer programmer was to learn COBOL. I was given a "teach yourself" set of material and put in a room for 1 month. I eventually learned to write "Gotoless" programs which were considered important in those days. Over the next 5 to 6 years I progressed through the ranks as senior programmer, analyst programmer, and finally systems analyst, reporting to the data processing manager. I was involved in writing programs for all the company's major business processes, purchasing, inventory, sales, and all the aspects of general ledger. I even developed a set of programming standards.

As I progressed through the various positions in the Computer Department I began to supervise employees. I learned a lot about managing staff then. I think this experience has helped me in my present position.

After about 11 years of working for just this one company, I started thinking about broadening my experience. One day I read an article about a company called Fact International. They produced an integrated information system that dealt with all the systems I had been working on and struggling with since I had joined Firestone's Computer Department. The Fact system was based on interactive screens instead of batch processing. This struck me as the way these systems should function.

I responded to an advertisement for a position at the Timaru Milling Company, a subsidiary of the Goodman Group, which was a large flour milling and food processing company in New Zealand. The Timaru subsidiary manufactured flour and pasta. They had recently installed the Fact system, but they were not getting what they expected from the system. Before I started, the company had hired an independent contractor to develop an add-on system to present the data in a revised format. This was costing Timaru Milling a lot of money. My first role was to resolve this issue. We made major revisions to the Fact system to reclassify the data the way the company operated. The project was a resounding success. The day we printed the new reports we had staff asking for more copies. It was an exciting time. I still have a copy of that year's Board report, which stated that Timaru Milling Company had better computer information than it ever had in the history of the company.

In 1984, I started working for Fact International in Auckland. I quickly discovered that my knowledge of the Fact system and my general experience with manufacturing at Firestone and Timaru Milling were quite valuable. I had not really appreciated that until then. I was doing training on general ledgers for accounting customers and consulting on how to set up the inventory system, how to set up data for manufacturing, and how to establish reporting structures. I mainly focused on understanding the issues that the customers had and how to reflect them in configuring the Fact system they had just acquired. I was responsible for demonstrating the system in their terms. I did this kind of work at a number of companies in the Auckland area.

During that time, Fact decided that they would probably want to open a branch in Christchurch. So, I moved there as branch manager. I was assigned the objective of making a profit from day one, which we achieved! For me the work included the new element of personnel management and a high level of direct sales. From the start of the branch in 1985 until 1988, we added 13 major customers. For a brief period I had the largest customer for Fact. I enjoyed the challenge of building up the branch. It was a lot of work, but very enjoyable. I liked to work with customers and independent consultants, guiding them in how the system could respond to their needs.

Then Fact decided to open an office in Boston in the United States. They invited me to become their business development manager, which I accepted. Part of my job while in Boston was to work with distributors in the UK and Europe. So, we moved to Europe to be closer to the distributors. We lived in Arnhem for about 7 months. My work with customers involved sales and training and ensuring the software was integrated with the requirements of the company. After 7 months we transferred back to New Zealand and I took up my position running the Christchurch Branch.

I was back in Christchurch for about 1 year when a circuitous series of events commenced. First, I left Fact to work for Macpac. They had just purchased a competing system to Fact called The Inventory Management Systems (TIMS). I thought it would be worth my while to get to know all about this other major ERP system being sold here in New Zealand. Not long after I joined Macpac, a company called GEAC purchased both Fact and TIMS and began consolidating the two systems. I took on more of an operations management role at Macpac. I obtained a certification (CPIM) from the American Production and Inventory Control Society and was able to implement many operational changes, including Kanban and pull-type production systems. In 1997, I moved to GEAC to work with the TIMS system. Well, because they had purchased both Fact and TIMS, the organization had changed over the 5 years I had been at Macpac.

When I was approached by someone at Tait I decided to accept the offer. Back in 1987, I had been involved in Tait's acquisition of the Fact system. I had spent time on training and resolving implementation issues. So, I had some background experience with the company and the people. This helped me make the decision to move to Tait.

Company History

Tait Electronics Ltd. was established in 1969 with head offices in Christchurch, New Zealand. Sir Angus Tait had spent the Second World War in the United Kingdom working on airborne radar. He had returned to New Zealand and established a small business building mobile radios. A series of major technical developments by the company saw it progress through the decades from a small 12 employee company to one that today has offices in 10 different countries with almost 1000 employees. Tait also has a network of dealers in over 160 countries which facilitate the export of over 95% of the radios which are still assembled in Christchurch.

The company culture is represented by its responsiveness to customer needs and a focus on the future.

My Company and Me

When I started working at Tait, I was the leader of the BITS team. This stands for Baan implementation and training services. Baan is an ERP system that Tait had purchased to replace the Fact system they had been using for the past 12 years. The team focused on supporting the implementation of Baan, not so much from the users' perspective, but more to do with ensuring that the system was reliable. We concentrated on system reliability, application support, training, and system security.

In the early days, I realized that the BITS team was quite demoralized because they were not recognized for the hard support work they did at all hours of the day and night. To combat this I set up a weekly one page IT news letter that was circulated throughout the company telling everyone what work was being done, who was doing it, and what successes were being attained. Over a period of 12 months, the understanding of what the group did grew and became more appreciated. As a result, the team morale rose considerably over time.

After about 12 months I was offered the opportunity to consolidate the BITS team and the various IT groups into one corporate IT group. The corporate IT group formation was the result of an overall corporate reorganization of the Mobile Radio,

Radio Infrastructure, and Corporate into one operating unit. So, as leader of the consolidated IT group, the role of CIO began to emerge. Remember, though, the title of CIO does not exist at Tait. So, my title was initially, information systems technology manager.

A good example of the emergence of the CIO role is that I sit as a member of the Senior Management Team which reports directly to the CEO. I am also responsible for supply chain management, which is an issue I will discuss later in this chapter.

An issue that I addressed quite early on was standardizing the way things operated in the company. While there had been some stated objectives about standardization, there were a lot of areas where there was not much evidence of standard procedures. We standardized the PC operating procedures. We went from having four different antivirus systems to one. We recognized, for example, that laptops were costing us a lot of time because everyone just bought their own. When they had a problem it took us a lot of time to resolve it. So, we standardized on the laptop, the image, and the operating system. This certainly reduced our maintenance effort. Now we can have an automatic roll out of software to the PCs in the organization through a simple standard menu. I have also established the position of asset and software manager, who is responsible for the licensing and software for all of our PCs. This position has been quite useful for controlling costs and putting the standardization into place.

There was another issue that had to be dealt with along with the standardization process. People at Tait had been able to work quite independently. There was good reason for this. The company employs a lot of very talented engineers who know their jobs and have strong opinions. They are also very computer literate. So, when we started the process of standardization we met some resistance. One of our most visible actions related to laptops. While we were prepared to support a standard PC, we made a strong point that we were not prepared to support any nonstandard PCs. Our approach was to resolve a PC problem by reconfiguring it. Thus, if the PC had any nonstandard systems they would be lost.

Now, we also realized that this standardization process could only go so far. Some engineers in certain areas require unique software applications. Others might require Internet access. We have identified these areas and we respond to their needs. Over time, most groups have come to realize that the standardization approach is best for the overall company. We are pretty much at a point where all IT aspects are managed centrally, including storing all data on a central repository.

Another issue that we had to resolve was the use of open systems. The company wanted to channel most of its resources into product development. While we had to be able to support this effort we had to do it with as lean an operation as possible. We have been able to do that through the wide use of open source systems.

A further issue is more IS related than IT. I use IS to describe the applications and IT to describe the technology. Well, I recognized an opportunity to change the way we operated worldwide. Instead of having each of our branches around the world running with their own database for purchasing, stock control, sales, and finance, we could run everything on a single database from a server in New Zealand. In order to do that, we implemented a virtual private network (VPN) on the Internet. Now we run all of our transaction processing this way. We moved from Baan version 4 to version 5 in order to amalgamate all of our databases and handle the time zone issues. Now the stock control in our branches around the world is mostly automatic with DRP. Whenever the stock goes below a certain pre-established level, it generates a requirement here for manufacturing to build and replenish the stock without anyone needing to intervene. So, we have removed all of the internal purchase orders and sales orders and have simplified the whole business in that respect.

An example of another benefit of this revision is the ability to direct ship. In the past, if Hong Kong placed an order for a customer in China we would have had to ship the product through the Hong Kong office. Now, because all of the data is resident here, we can ship directly to the customer in China. Further, no matter where you are you can track the status of the order.

One little piece of hardware that helped make all this possible for us was Perebit. It is a little box that is put on each end of the Internet-based WAN. It compresses the data by up to 70%. We were concerned about the speed of transmission (latency), especially to places like the UK, which is half a world away. Our people in the UK tell us it seems like the server is just in the next room. So we are pleased with the performance.

My Typical Week

My time at work is usually quite hectic. But the other week I took some time to document what I did over the 5 days. I think the following represents what I normally do. That is, if there is anything "normal" in this job!

Monday

- At work by 8:30 a.m.
- Catching up on status of the system, any issues, and writing up a plan for the week.
- 9 a.m. meeting with a packaging supplier about a new box we are developing.
- 10 a.m. clearing e-mails checking on detail required for the management meeting this afternoon.

- Review of e-sales project progress and checking if there are new customers using it.
- New calendar system for 750 staff went live today, so time to check with the support team about the number and types of calls they are dealing with. Talk to team about progress and some users about the implementation.
- Receive supplier contract from legal people and review with team member.
- 2 p.m. weekly management team meeting, with information on sales and strategic issues that are impacting IT and supply chain.
- Notes to be made from the management team meeting
- Some invoices to be checked off.
- Some positive feedback from the implementation of the new calendar system received by e-mail.
- Check a staff member appraisal record matches my notes and ready for signing.
- Finish about 5:45 p.m.

Tuesday

- At work by 8:30 a.m.
- Check on e-mails and prepare for IS/IT weekly meeting with team leaders.
- 9 a.m. IS/IT weekly meeting with IT services manager and IS development manager. This is to ensure that we are all aligned and working together. Discuss projects for the week, issues that are still outstanding and events we need to be aware of and provide input to. We also look at the weekly company performance metrics.
- Schedule meeting to further Configuration Management Control project where we are trying to change from an environment where every possible product combination is held in a price book, to an environment where customers choose the options they want and configure their own solution.
- Begin writing monthly report for the other senior managers.
- 1 p.m. quarterly meeting on the budget for the next 12 months. At this point we review all IT expenditure and planned expenditure and review the actions we have planned. What capital will be required, what operational areas are not in control and how to keep cost within budget for the next period.
- Meeting to discuss area of reorganization within the business that will result in different resources required in the IS and IT teams in the future.
- Summarize requirements of the Mechanical Engineering team from a meeting last week and remind them of the decisions needed for advancing the implementation of paperless Purchase Requisition processing in their area.

- Finish about 5:30 p.m.
- Tuesday evening spend 2 hours preparing for a staff appraisal meeting.

Wednesday

- At work by 8:15 a.m.
- Clearing e-mails, checking out issues and following up voice e-mail.
- 10 a.m. Product cost reduction steering group meeting.
- 11 a.m. Reduction of Hazardous Substances project steering meeting.
- Staff issue with communication and morale, requires two separate confidential meetings
- 2 p.m. weekly catch up with Group Sourcing Manager
- Meeting with developer over approach to Product Compliance development and if there is a simpler option which will reduce cost and development time.
- 4 p.m. Staff appraisal with team administrator. She is doing an excellent job, is a little under-worked (her view) so we need to ensure she is getting all the tasks she can handle. This role is designed to free team members from administration issues, thus freeing their time to use their unique skills.
- Finish monthly report and forward to other senior managers.
- Finish about 6 p.m.

Thursday

- At work by 8 a.m., e-mails, etc.
- 9:15 meeting about business restructuring in Asia and the impact on both IT systems and Supply chain.
- Find and forward operating instructions of the compliance database to senior developer.
- Discussion with team member about integration of separate databases used for managing component data.
- Discussion with marcomms on how we move forward from version 1 to version 2 of our e-sales project, decision to get a group together and finalize and officially close off version 1 and move all requests to the version 2 project.
- 1pm meeting with cross functional group about the proposed change to a configuration management system in sales with a greater emphasis on modular product. This will require different systems capability to gather the details of

individual components but retain identification of the lot under some suitable identification

- Review proposals for shifting key staff to different employment contract.
- Spreadsheet analysis of Cellular Phone costs and presentation for managers to discuss.
- Discussion with Mechanical Engineering manager on use of purchase requisitions by his team and decision they will need to make prior to implementation.
- Finish about 5:45 p.m.

Friday

- At work by 8:30 a.m.
- Preparation of 1 hour presentation on management of IT Assets, both hardware and software licenses for local CIO group meeting in about 1 week.
- Meeting with IT services manager about use of Skype and how we can be proactive about this tool and its potential savings to the business.
- Discussion with IS Development manager about the IST strategy and the need to have a more formal approach to this, possibly every 6 months. Currently, this is not a regular documented meeting.
- 1 p.m., Sales and Operations planning meeting where the monthly operation plans to meet sales demand are reviewed and adjusted.
- 2 p.m. weekly leadership forum with key team members. We are reviewing our IT operation based on Peter Scholtes book “The Leaders Handbook.” We all discuss and review a section of this each Friday afternoon.
- 3 p.m. meeting to review status and decisions surrounding the new TM8000 packaging which must reduce cost, be acceptable to customers, and protect our product in transit right through the supply chain to the end user.
- Discover that some staff have developed a bad habit of using C drives, investigate and find 5 failed hard drives this week. Send out global message reminder to all staff about company policy in this area for all company data to reside on the network drives.
- Begin spreadsheet to evaluate cost of using 2 different sized boxes in part of supply chain and the financial impact of some smaller lower cost boxes vs. loss of this demand from the purchase price breaks of the larger box.
- Review upgrade and service work planned over the weekend.
- Finish at 5:15 p.m. for the week.

Dealing with Users

Recently, we learned a very valuable lesson about dealing with users. Initially, we talked with a specific group of users and obtained a very clear direction about what they required. When we involved a larger user group, that direction changed. Eventually, when we delivered the system it did not meet the initial requirements and, indeed, all the users were not satisfied. The valuable lesson we learned is that we must take a stronger role in challenging the identification of requirements that have been developed. We must guard against the tendency for "group think." This is especially so when managers tend to dominate the requirements identification process and not listen to their people.

It is also helpful to work with users regarding how their processes might be changed and improved. So, we should not just simply look at how we can apply IT to existing processes. We should consider how IT may be employed to improve their processes. It is also important to work with the users rather than simply insist that IT must be applied in a certain way. There will always be resistance to change. We must be clear that we are on the same side and we want to help the user solve a particular issue.

Along these same lines, we want to move the user from an initial level of concern to a level of opportunity. We want them to focus on the positives. Setting expectations is very important. There is a nice little formula that helps explain what I mean:

CS = P/E

Customer Service = Performance / Expectation

So, it is important to establish an agreement about expectation as early as possible.

It has also been suggested that if you can deliver 90% of what a user wants, you have an opportunity to tidy up the other 10% later. But, you will have the user onside. We have to deliver what the user really wants and not focus on the appealing aspects which may not be necessary.

Deciding on Technology Investments

The corporate budget is derived from the long term company direction and business plans. We review those plans as part of our IT budgeting process. We do not work to many hard and fast rules with investments. We will do a return on investment analysis. But, with IT projects it can be difficult to determine, for instance, the value of a new server. So, we mainly concentrate on insuring we respond to all the issues. We must, however, run within a fairly tight budget. We prepare corporate budgets on a 3 monthly basis and extend them out for 15 months. During our budgeting process, we review the projects we know are coming and what improvements we know we are going to have to make. We might have a new application in the wings and we have an expectation of what that is going to require in the way of software, hardware, and support. We may have to renew a software maintenance contract or implement some new IT tool. So, we establish some guidelines as to what we think we are going to need to spend.

We can respond to new opportunities. If we decide that something else, outside of our plan, is more important and the company agrees with us, then we can switch to the new opportunity. We have a steering group that meets about every 6 weeks. We can present revisions there and obtain approval.

Current Issues

Right now, we are installing an online sales system. Internally, we are having some interesting debates. We are talking about whether it becomes part of our existing distribution channel or whether it should operate independently. We are also trying to decide if it should be initially employed to reduce the cost of doing business or to expand the business. For the past 20 days, we have had a small prototype system in place for some selected customers. They realize that this is a test system and there might be some wrinkles. But, they realize along with us that this system will be a benefit to us all.

We are also in the process of rolling out a new corporate calendar system. We have again taken a low cost approach to this project. We will go live on August 1 with an overlap to allow people to re-enter their meetings and tasks from the old calendar. We decided that it would be easier to ask everyone to re-enter their own data rather than rely on a migration tool. This process will also re-enforce the training sessions.

We also have a project in the area of improved sales price book generation. We are giving tools to the sale people to help them configure solutions and develop pricing alternatives based on the different radio components that we sell. This will allow the sales people to make detailed presentations on unique products. It will give them the ability to do more quotes in the same time more accurately and more professionally, and they will then be able to flow the information back through the ERP system for configuration, manufacture, and eventual delivery of the product.

We have a number of supply chain issues. That is why part of my title includes supply chain management. We are at the start of a project to improve how we manage our inventory. We are rationalizing our product packaging. We are also working on compliance requirement to Reduction of Hazardous Substances (ROHS). This is a European Union regulation restricting the use of hazardous materials in electronic components and we have to comply by June 2006. We have to change materials right across the company. It involves changes in our data, changes in our procedures, certifications from suppliers, and testing to make sure replacement components produce the same performance as original components.

We have a number of projects in other areas of the company. We are negotiating with our laptop supplier for new laptops that respond better to our performance requirements. We are in the process of removing the manual purchase requisition and implementing part of the Baan ERP system to handle this process automatically.

Future Issues

One issue that stands out more than the others regarding the future is security. A few years ago, we hardly ever thought about security. Now it is a major topic. We have one and a half positions fully dedicated to dealing with things like spam and antivirus requirements. We have an online sales platform and our sales people want to be able to access the system and their files from wherever they are.

The company overall is becoming more dependent on IT. There was a time even since I started working here that if the network was down for an hour people were not happy but they could carry on with other tasks. Now if it is down for 2 minutes, everything comes to a grinding halt. We have customers around the world who cannot be given answers on stock availability if the system is down. We are moving to a paperless organization and now most of our business data is automated. We must provide constant access to this data. We are building in redundancy through the duplication of servers. We also respond further to security concerns by placing the servers in different locations around Christchurch.

We are looking to pursue the idea of vendor managed inventory (VMI). So, our supplier will hold the inventory until we need it here for our production process.

Final Comments

I see a CIO as having to have a very good understanding of the business. I am sure this is nothing new. But it is important. The CIO needs to look at the issues and requirements very broadly and understand the systemic picture. The CIO must understand that a change in one area may manifest itself in another area sometime in the future.

You may have noticed the frequent use of the term "we." This is a good reminder that a CIO is dependent on the team. I have a very strong and capable team of 23 people in IS and IT at Tait, and a reasonable proportion of my work is planning for, supporting, resourcing, and representing this team. Without their work, effort, and skills, the results would not come.

I think the CIO should have stronger business knowledge than IT knowledge. The IT knowledge may be needed to be able to deal with specialists. I depend very much on the skills and capability of the IT specialists within my department. There are areas that, because of the rapid development in the IT world, I am not as up to date on some of the technical aspects. But the CIO needs to be able to speak the language of both the specialists and the business people.

The CIO role gets you involved in the detail of almost all aspects of the business. In order to reinforce this and confirm my competency, I returned to university in 1999, and completed an MBA over 2½ years, while still working full time, finishing with an excellent mark in 2001.

Chapter VI

Rhys Gould
Fulton Hogan

A market leader in the road building & civil engineering industries.

My name is **Rhys Gould**. I am the group manager of information systems at Fulton Hogan.

Personal History

I was born in Dunedin, New Zealand. I grew up there and took all my schooling in Dunedin. I studied accounting at Otago University in Dunedin. While I majored in accounting I also took courses in management, economics, and as they called it then, information science. I wanted to have as many options as possible regarding my future career.

I very nearly did not go to university. I had all the information to go to Australia to learn to be a race car driver. The only trouble was I did not have any money. It was kind of a cross road in my life now that I look back on it. I will always wonder what could have been.

My first job after graduating from university was with Fulton Hogan, where I currently work. I started 3 days after my last exam.

Company History

Fulton Hogan is a diversified company with operations in New Zealand, Australia, and the Pacific Basin. Our Web site includes the following description:

Company Profile

Fulton Hogan is a roading and infrastructure construction company founded in Dunedin in 1933 by Jules Fulton and Bob Hogan. Since that time we have grown to employ over 4,000 staff ... constituent divisions represent a broad range of products and services in the roading, quarrying and civil construction sector, and hold strong positions in their respective markets.

The things we do:

With over 70 years of experience, Fulton Hogan is a market leader in the road building industry, and has pioneered new engineering and construction techniques at the same time as gaining a reputation for completing projects on time, regardless of the contract's size. In conjunction with this, we are a major supplier of roading materials and other quarry products, including concrete aggregates, sand, sealing chips, asphalt aggregates and railway ballast.

Fulton Hogan is also a market leader in civil engineering projects, with expertise in everything from bridge and dam building through to tunneling, pipelaying, earthworks and airport construction.

As well, the company has made a substantial investment in facilities for the manufacture of bitumous materials, so whether you need to surface a driveway, a road or an airport runway, Fulton Hogan can produce the materials required and lay it as well.

In addition, we are the specialists in road marking, highway maintenance, drainage, earth moving, road transport, heavy haulage, ready-mix concrete, pre-cast and pre-stressed concrete production, facilities and project management, sporting surfaces and laboratory and technical services.

How we do it:

The Fulton Hogan Group is equally committed to four separate policies, and these are:

- *Quality: Fulton Hogan is committed to providing its customers with the standard of service and product that meets their expectations every time. Most of the company operations are certified to comply with ISO 9001 standards, and process improvement is part of every employee's job.*
- *Safety: As well as maintaining ongoing training in health and safety issues, Fulton Hogan monitors employees' fitness and health, minimizes all risks and hazards and works with staff to provide a sage workplace. Our safety standards are a demanding as our quality standards.*
- *Environment: It is our goal to minimize the impact of business operations on the environment. To achieve this, we consider the environmental issues at the planning and decision making stage, consult with authorities, communities and other interest groups, monitor all discharges to the environment and carry out regular audits of management plans with the environment in mind.*
- *Training: An ongoing training programme is in place to further develop the technical, managerial and operational skills of the staff.*

My Company and Me

My father had met a person through work who was employed at Fulton Hogan. I provided my personal information to this contact person and an interview was arranged. I really did not know what job I was applying for. But, I started as an assistant accountant in an unofficial graduate training program. We now run this program more formally. But back when I started it was very informal. I was very fortunate to have a mentor who was very helpful in a number of ways. His name is Jim Miller. He has since retired. When he was my mentor he was the director of finance and the unofficial CIO. He was very strong in leading the business forward in terms of growth. This was not just the case in financial aspects but also the actual management of the business.

So, I reported to Jim. I made up my own program. He left me to my own devices and would review what I was doing. Jim would give me some high level suggestions about what I should do. But for the most part, I was given the responsibility to establish my career with Fulton Hogan. On my first day of work, I met with Jim and we discussed what I would be doing. Well, that afternoon I went straight to a sealing crew working on roads around Dunedin. I was quite excited about this assignment because I was tired of spending time inside studying.

I spent just over a year in the field. I worked on different facets of the business from the grassroots level. From a process point of view, I got to understand the business from a very low level. I think this experience was quite important. I had to earn my keep. I was working as a laborer, driving trucks, driving rollers, quarrying rock, making bitumen and paint and all the activities that Fulton Hogan does. I really enjoyed this work.

Now, because I also had this mentor, Jim, who I was reporting to occasionally, I would write a report about my activities. The process of writing the report and discussing my activities with Jim would get me thinking about the overall business. Jim wanted me to think about who the customer was and how I should respond to the customer. I would consider such things as internal relationships, the payments trail, and where opportunities were for improvements.

I always talked with the foreman or the department manager to explain that I was not a spy from head office. I had a few challenges because people thought I was a spy and that I might be useless at my assigned tasks. I remember having to sort one guy out. Subsequently, he came to rely on me in other situations and on other projects. We developed a mutual respect for each other and our contribution to the company.

Jim Miller, my mentor, went on to be managing director. He was a very valuable person in my early experiences at Fulton Hogan. He taught me a lot about customer service. There was one episode where he taught me to look upon him as a customer. It was a simple task. But, it proved to be a very valuable lesson. Jim asked me to photocopy something for him one day. Instead of taking the document out of the file, I simply copied the pages. I saved myself a couple of minutes. Jim was not impressed because the copies had a black line down each side. I challenged him in that I thought he wanted a copy right away and that the information he wanted was more important than the form in which it was presented to him. Jim reminded me that it was important to check with the customer about quality and timelines of the presentation. He also pointed out that there are both internal and external customers. In this case, the internal customer was my boss. This was a good lesson for me about checking to see that I was meeting my customer's requirements. It is a lesson that I will always remember.

After my initial experience working in the field, I spent some time doing basic administrative functions in our head office. One assignment was in the computer room, where we processed transactions related to accounts payable, banking, and the sales revenue side of the company operations. This assignment helped me to learn about the various business processes and how they all fit together.

My next assignment was to spend time on a construction site involving a project to stabilize a landslide. During the day, I was responsible for all the administration to do with the project. At night I would occasionally drive a dump truck with a subcontractor who was a friend of mine. Again, both experiences were enjoyable and proved beneficial later in my career. I learned a lot about the necessity to ensure that all of the data was processed through our job costing system. I also identified ways to efficiently enter the data to ensure we had the most current and accurate information coming from our general ledger system. Later, I developed what I call my "project pack" which includes the tools necessary to keep track financially of our construction projects. I shared these packs with other parts of the organization. I do not like to have to reinvent the wheel and I was keen for other people to learn from my experience.

I was then asked to move to Gisborne on New Zealand's North Island as an administration manager for that region. We had established an office there about 18 months prior to my assignment. We had a couple of road maintenance projects that were not making any money. In consultation with the regional manager we decided that we should attempt to acquire contracts for other types of services beyond road maintenance. We thought this would not only help to grow our operation in the region but would help make us profitable. While the regional manager would focus on operations, I was to be responsible for all of the office procedures. So, I set about establishing new systems for revenue recognition, stock management, and truck allocation. Our plan was successful. We doubled our staff, bought a whole new plant, established new departments, and won new contracts.

It was also at this time that I started getting experience supervising people and working with groups. As the company grew, more people were reporting to me. We were also developing new information systems. At this time, we were developing and modifying our existing enterprise resource planning (ERP) systems. I was involved with the job costing and project management, fleet management and fixed asset modules. I worked closely with an individual in our Auckland office. I eventually moved to Auckland to work for this person as a management accountant.

Auckland was a relatively big office. I was able to see that some of the processes I had developed in the smaller offices could be applied equally well in this larger office. So, I set about establishing common procedures around work flows and job descriptions. I also conducted training sessions about the functioning of the processes and how information technology would help make the processes more efficient. After about 3 months, I took over the Auckland office as administrative manager. This gave me some added responsibility because our Auckland office was large enough to have two branches. We processed a lot of data for month end cheques and payrolls.

After about 2 years, we had a reorganization at Fulton Hogan, mainly because of our growth. I became a business manager, which has since been renamed as commercial manager. I was responsible for the financial aspects for a larger area and I was also involved in mergers and acquisitions. I participated in developing market plans and planning for growth. I used to collect the city council planning for growth documents. This was an exciting time. I was involved in projects to set up new asphalt plants and new building sites. For mergers and acquisitions I participated in our due diligence and evaluations, and then the transition management teams after we finalized the purchase. All of these activities required me to take responsibility for the coordination of the introduction of Fulton Hogan Administration and information systems. I was responsible for bringing the acquired financial systems into our systems and ensuring the appropriate level of training for our new staff.

I had all sorts of steep learning curves for all the above assignments. I mean this in a positive way. I enjoy a challenge. I like working with people and I was lucky to be able to form a very good team. I was also very lucky to have the support of my boss.

We started to realize that with all of our growth we would soon out grow our existing ERP system. A large project was formed and I was assigned the project manager role. I worked very closely with our chief financial officer at the time. We assessed, acquired, and implemented a JD Edwards ERP system. This project went very well. Just after its implementation, I was offered, and accepted, the position of Group Manager of Information Systems. This position was created as a result of another reorganization precipitated by our growth and the implementation of our new ERP system. The position is in effect our CIO at Fulton Hogan. I accepted the position because it was a new role and it was going to be another challenge. I would be a leader in establishing a new way of doing business at Fulton Hogan.

Initially, I had to define what my role was going to be. I did not come from an information technology background. I came more from the business side with a customer emphasis. So, I talked with a lot of people within our company and even from other companies. I wanted to have a business focus for me and my team. That is why we are information systems and not information technology. I wanted to emphasize the application side.

The information systems function is situated at the group level. We have three main operating companies each with their own CFO who reports to a CEO. Each of the CEOs reports to the managing director. I report to the group CFO, who in turn reports to the managing director. Those of us at the group level work within the context of the big picture for the company. We also play a coordinating role. This is especially important for the development and implementation of information systems. We must have consistency across our three operating companies.

Not only did I initially have to define my role, but I also had to decide how my part of the organization would function. This required the development of job descriptions and the building of a team. Perhaps rather than building a team it was more about changing the direction of an existing team. The existing team had been heavily involved in the JD Edwards ERP implementation. Now we had to change our focus to support all the aspects of information technology and telecommunications. But, I still wanted the focus to be on information systems. So I planned that the team would provide the conduit between the information technology world and our business.

I also decided that while we needed a lot of resources within the information systems area, I did not want to create a large business unit. So, I maintained a small core team and we developed relationships with partners. We work with various partners and will accomplish some of our work through outsourcing.

Another issue I dealt with initially was our help desk. I thought we were doing a good job of managing the infrastructure. But we needed to gain the confidence of our customers. We had to show them that we could listen to them and that we could be relied upon to help deliver solutions. So, I had to establish roles, assign people to these roles, and ensure they understood what they should be doing. As they say in baseball, "start putting some runs on the board."

To support this initiative, I established a group level information systems steering committee. We also set up steering committees for each of the three businesses. These four committees represent our approach to governance. The membership of these committees is made up of business people as opposed to information technology people. Initially, the committees did focus on managing information technology. But, I think we are moving away from that focus. This movement is represented by two aspects. First, the business-oriented members had to learn something about the potential uses of information technology. Second, we all had to gain an understanding of what were the needs of the business and how we should align information technology to support those needs.

There are some similarities among the three operating companies. So, we could have projects that run across the group rather than just one individual company. Human resources and customer relationship management are examples. We use the group steering committee to ensure consistency for these types of systems.

I see my role as educating "upstairs" as well as "downstairs." Everyone should be aware of the impact information systems and technology can have on the business. In the past it seems that the company viewed information technology as a necessary evil as opposed to an enabler. So, I gathered some data about how people within the company viewed us. This data provided input to the steering committees I discussed above. I also gathered some data about where people wanted to be in the future regarding the use of information technology. This future orientation gave us some good ideas about how to proceed to design a strategy to become recognized more as an enabler.

Part of my strategy around developing a team for information systems was to have people involved who were customer focused. We have a very diverse group on the team. Some work with the stability of our core systems and others work at the innovative leading edge.

Our customer focus and development of reliable systems has had an impact on how our company deals with clients. For instance, not only have we won jobs but, in some cases, we have been invited to tender for jobs because of our ability to provide information to clients. Two people from my team work directly with our engineering staff together with councils or regional authorities. We are very proactive about providing information on the contracts we have. In some cases, the client may not even re-tender because they are so satisfied with our involvement. Internally, our engineers will now invite someone from my team to accompany them to help them win a job.

My Typical Week

In this section, I present my activities organized by what I do each week and what I do on a monthly basis.

Weekly

Communication:

- Discussions/planning with staff on "business as usual" and projects – 1 day.
- Discussions/meetings with vendors – ½ day.
- Discussions/meetings with stakeholders (internal customers) – ½–1 day.

Financial:

- Reviewing and signing off on expenditures – 2–3 hours.

Management: Normally 1 day

- Develop/establish key performance indicators (KPI)
- Develop/establish job descriptions
- Planning for team training and development
- Budgeting
- Preparing agenda or minutes
- Planning my own work – developing operational plans in relation to our strategy

Other:

- Involvement with reviewing the setup of new projects/jobs for my team – 1 hour
- Reading articles/research material – 2–4 hours
- Traveling (sometimes on the phone with staff, vendors, or customers) – 3-4 hours
- Review of Intranet Communication Tool – 1 hour

In general, I would normally be in my office for ½ of the week. For the other ½ I would be out and about.

Monthly

- Financial
    - Capital expenditures (Capex)
    - Monthly profit and loss statements
    - Cost to complete on IT/IS projects
    - Job review
- Preparation of Monthly IS Management Report
    - Circulated to senior management of operations within the business units so they know what is going on in the overall company
- IS Team Meeting
- Review of two page initiative/ideas
- Video conference with our IT staff in Australia
- Visit to Australia and our other main office centre (like Auckland)
    - Meet with CEO, CFO, and IT representatives of each of our operating companies
- Meetings about specific issues or challenges

Dealing with Users

We have developed an overall information systems strategy based upon discussions with our internal users. The various business units may make a request within this strategy to respond to an opportunity or address an issue. A two page description of the situation is developed and that is where we become officially involved. We certainly offer to discuss the situation in the development of the two page request. The steering committee for the particular business will make a decision about whether or not to proceed. If the decision is that the project will not proceed, it is parked for future reference. If the project is going to proceed, a business case is developed. This is where we become heavily involved in the investigation of options. The business case will include a calculation of ROI, but we do not concentrate solely on that aspect of project evaluation. It is perhaps more important to ensure the result of the project fits with our current strategy. The steering committee again evaluates the business case. Given approval here the project is initiated.

After the project is completed, we conduct a debriefing session. There is always a hand-over process between the project manager and the functional manager. Then we try to have the functional area focus on business as usual.

Deciding on Technology

We will develop a business case for all of our investments in technology. We may rely upon vendors, customers, or other outsourcing partners as reference points. We try to avoid the "bleeding edge" of technology and stay reasonably boring with our use of technology. Again, our strategy dictates our overall approach to investments. If we are looking at a technology that will help our internal clients, we will certainly involve them. If, for example, we think that personal digital assistants (PDA) might be helpful, we most certainly will obtain input from our clients. But, we would not involve them in our infrastructure decisions about, say, a new server.

Current Issues

I am part of a senior management team involved with acquiring new businesses. Currently, we are looking at an acquisition in Australia. From an overall company perspective, we have a strategy of acquiring businesses with similar operations throughout the Pacific basin. My involvement in this process is to ensure we also have a strategy and operational plans around due diligence for information technology and information systems. I am responsible for the assimilation of the acquired business into our existing business. But my role is not just to address the challenges of resoling information technology issues around acquisitions. I also represent the New Zealand head office in this Australian acquisition. We have two members from our Australian operations and two members from the Australian company we are acquiring. So, this involvement requires me to participate beyond the narrow focus of information technology. This certainly contributes to a higher profile for me and the CIO role.

Another issue we are addressing right now is business continuity planning. This is a difficult issue because it is not necessarily seen as a tangible activity and it is not easily understood. Our group steering committee is working on this issue. Soon we will appoint a business partner to help us work through this project. I like to remind everyone involved that business continuity planning is about the basics. You know the boat needs to be afloat before it will win the race!

When we complete our business continuity planning, I expect to have a strategy around making sure that the information systems are going to be stable. I want to be sure that our information systems are going to work every day. They are going to be robust and stable. If for some reason the technology is not available we have to have a plan in place to continue to achieve our business goals. It is very important that the rest of our company is on side with this plan. They need to understand it is important to have a contingency plan. They must be willing to pay for it. It is a matter of ensuring they recognize the benefits of such an investment.

Another issue relates to the development of a long term strategy for our infrastructure. In the past, we would simply buy another server. We are in the process of moving to a virtualized server environment. What we need to develop, going forward is a plan for when and why we would acquire more infrastructure capacity. The plan would also address how we might acquire this excess capacity.

We also need to have more of a focus around costing. In the information systems area we used to take the "big bucket" approach, where if we wanted a server, as I discussed above, we would just buy it. Now we have different operating departments representing different operations within information systems. These areas are; infrastructure, applications, and user support. We also have a number of different projects. So, it is necessary to have a higher visibility for costs. We need to have the discipline early on to identify what the estimated costs will be and then for reviewing the actual costs at the end of a project. They way we are increasing this visibility is through our budgeting system. So, each business unit is responsible for the costs of their information systems. We will help them make the decisions about information system development or maintenance. But, they will be responsible for the cost and the management of the information system.

An aspect of the costing issue relates to differentiating the cost of applications from infrastructure. We can specifically identify the cost of an application and charge it to an operating unit. Even when more than one operating unit is involved with the same application we can establish an allocation process. The cost of infrastructure is more difficult. So, for now this cost is part of my budget.

Future Issues

An issue that we will have to deal with in the future has to do with the company's ability to change. Here is an example of what I mean. There seems to be a hold up in terms of data flowing through the system. Now I do not simply mean the computer system. I include all the manual processes within the system as well. Indeed, there is a blurred line between what is automated and what remains manual. So, a foreman in the field fills out bits of paper regarding such things as project status or labor usage. These bits of paper come to the office, get input, and then come out on a report somewhere. My team and I know that more of this process can be automated. But, we must convince management that we can improve the process by applying information technology. The resolution of this issue will take time. I think we have the framework in place to support these types of initiatives. What remains is for us to demonstrate and convince management that we can apply the appropriate technology to improve our processes.

Because of our strategy of acquisition, we must be able to efficiently integrate the acquired businesses into our operations. We need an enterprise architecture that can support this integration process. The key aspect is to have the hardware and the methods in order to carry out this process. Our plan is to integrate the acquired businesses with the way we do things. We recognize that because we are taking over an existing business that they may not have made investments in information technology in the recent past. So we will have to do a lot of work to assimilate their operations with ours. While we want to have them adopt our processes, we do not want to significantly affect their existing culture. This is a fine line that must be dealt with appropriately. We have to appreciate what is different and what is the same between our company and the one we are acquiring. It takes a lot of communication to decide what to change and what would be beneficial to retain. We want to take the best of both worlds and bring the two entities together.

I see the information technology world and the administration world converging. It is not just about how the technology operates. It is becoming more about how the technology supports what the business wants to do. The functional business units are becoming more knowledgeable about applying information technology to their operations. So, as a CIO representing information technology we have to get involved in and be sure we understand the overall process.

An interesting future issue has to do with the use of robotics technology in the field to help us do our work. We employ global positioning systems (GPS) to view the terrain and existing infrastructure at a construction site. In the future, I foresee us employing this technology so the machines could perform tasks based upon various inputs. For instance, we could take as input data about the terrain and infrastructure (such as gas mains or live wires) and the desired final result. An on-board computer could then calculate the most efficient approach to completing the task and then guide the machine to perform the necessary activities. The machine driver would be there just to respond to any anomaly that might be identified. So, the skills of the driver might be different in the future. Perhaps we will need people who have grown up playing computer games!

Final Comments

I am more interested in methods than in tools. For instance, the generic approach to project management will help us implement technology that will be beneficial to the overall company. In our case it seems that project management is about being involved in multiple projects. We have to analyze the activities and ensure the results are appropriate for our business needs.

I also think it is important to develop some key performance indicators (KPI). It is important to establish these measures and then determine how we are doing in providing service to our company. We know what initiatives we should pursue that will support our company strategy. We need to know how well we are doing.

References

Fulton Hogan (n. d.). Retrieved January 30, 2007, from www.fh.co.nz

Chapter VII

Zarina Thesing
Pumpkin Patch

Australasia's Leading Children's Fashion Brand

My name is **Zarina Thesing**. I am the general manager, information technology at Pumpkin Patch.

Personal History

I was born in Auckland, New Zealand. Until I was 10 we lived in Waitakere in west Auckland, where there is a lot of bush and it is slightly rural. We then moved to Lynfield, Blockhouse Bay, another area of Auckland which was known for its harbour and more "out of town" position. I lived there until I got married at 26.

I started primary school in Waitakere. I finished primary and intermediate schools in Lynfield. Then, I attended a public high school. I attended the University of Auckland and earned a Bachelor of Commerce in information systems.

My university degree included a work experience project paper. I was assigned to a company called Peace Computers. They specialize in computer systems for utilities, specifically energy billing systems. I worked in a team of three people on the development of a general ledger system for a client company called Wyatt Machine Tools. It was an interesting process and great experience.

After graduating university, I started working at Peace full time. I was involved initially in designing and writing common modules for the energy billing system. We were developing function-oriented services, rather than everyone just coding a process themselves. I worked on a generic rate calculator and an address finding function. I coded in Informix, a 4GL language. For another energy company, I was involved in the development of an equipment management system. This system kept track of the maintenance and replacement of power poles.

While I was at Peace, I progressed from developer to a systems designer role. I cannot stand chaos, and like to be organized. I like those around me and working with me to be organized. So, I moved more into a systems design role that enabled me to identify areas of work that required development, and assisted in developing, designing, and also co-coordinating the developments for my designs.

After three years at Peace, I moved to Software Consultants Limited, and was assigned to work with BellSouth, a telecommunications company in start up mode in New Zealand. I was head hunted by the consulting company through a girl friend who worked for them. I was not really looking for a new job. They were interested in my skills as an Informix developer for Bellsouth and I decided to take on the new challenge, as I was keen to experience development for another company and the establishment of the company in the New Zealand market.

I was involved with BellSouth on and off for about 5 years. As New Zealand operations were smaller than around the world, we were a trial site for a new cellular billing system from the USA. We had a lot of issues getting the system running and there was no reporting module. I was brought on initially to assist in developing reports that were required for the business, especially the finance team who needed more information on call volumes and flows to set products in the system, which enabled revenue to be gathered. I was also involved in the development of a commission system so that they could have information about how to increase sales of GSM cellular phones to ensure BellSouth could take on their competitors.

For another assignment at Software Consultants, I worked for the New Zealand Navy. A facilities maintenance management systems (FMMS) was acquired to help maintain two new frigates which had recently been purchased. The information system did not have any documentation and the original contract did not include any training. I was asked to provide a systems manual, and developed the necessary training program. I also advised them on system interfaces and other change management systems. While I was on this project, I also did a lot of project coordination. When I think back on this assignment I recall that we really worked hard, but we had a lot of fun as well.

For my next assignment at Software Consultants, I was appointed project manager for the health authority product range. This predominately consisted of a contract management system. We modified it for the Southern Regional Health Authority. This was my first role as project manager, and it involved leading a team of developers to rewrite the CMS system for the Southern Retail Health Authority. I had to manage this project in such detail that every week I could tell if we were on schedule and budget (or note). As this was my first project management role and I was very sure the project was going to be kept on track, I was probably a bit intense for the team. I was a new manager and I demanded a lot. But we did it and it was a great achievement. I think this assignment is where I developed my reputation as a good project manager. Certainly, the experience was very valuable. I learned to always use peoples' strengths and to divide the work out to the right strengths. This meant the whole team could succeed and get the work done. The next system development was to change the system for another customer, which only required a few small changes. It was not the challenge I was looking for. I felt I had reached the end of the road for this experience and it was time to move on.

I decided to try the contract market. For all the time I had been working for the consulting companies, I had seen the bills coming through and so I knew how much they were charging for my services. I also knew that the clients always wanted me and my skills and never wanted me to leave. I was young and confident. Despite feeling confident, I did not expect to get a contract straight away, and I was just looking. In my first interview, I was successful! I won a contract with Wilson and Horton. This company at the time owned and operated one of the largest papers in New Zealand, the New Zealand Herald. I worked at installing a billing distribution system. The contract was initially for 3 months. They were anxious to have the project completed before Y2K. So, my project management skills served me well. Eventually, as each contract was extended, I worked at Wilson and Horton for about 18 months. Over that period, I replaced about 12 information systems.

Two items were very important to me as I looked back on that experience. The first item had to do with requirements identification. In my initial interview, I had asked if they had specified the detailed requirements for the system they had purchased. They had not. This, during my interview for my next contract, was a key question. I only wanted to be involved in projects that had taken this crucial step. I did, however, choose to take the Wilson & Horton project. The fact that we did not have requirements up front created a lot of needless work. We had to get the system over the years of implementation to work the way the company wanted, rather than knowing this up front. To be fair, there were a significant amount of changes, such as different owners and CEO's, that also changed the requirements during the project. The other item important to me was my reporting relationship in the role. I was not working within the information technology department. I was working in the functional unit that required my services. This was probably viewed as an oddity, especially by the folks in the information technology department. As the project was critical to the success of invoicing customers for their newspaper, I was also able to raise issues to the CEO when necessary. This was a very good line of communication for me as project manager. I could easily talk to him about various project issues. It was a rather unique situation. I was young, a contractor, and outside the normal information technology department structure. I was able to get things that were necessary to ensure the success of the project. The new system consolidated all the decentralized databases around the country into one main database to enable the call centre to work with the information. It was a huge initiative, which had a direct impact on the company's bottom line.

It was at this time that I started to realize that career was not everything in life. I had worked very hard in each role since leaving university and had gained many skills in systems development and implementation. I started thinking about what I wanted to do next. I set my goal of being an information technology manager at a smaller company thinking this may give me more breath of experience and general management skills in a company, so, I went looking. I saw an advertisement for Pumpkin Patch and went for the interview. It was a difficult decision to leave Wilson & Horton. I felt like I had to "start again," but believed there was more opportunity longer term for me at Pumpkin Patch. I started at Pumpkin Patch on contract as a contract project manager.

Company History

Pumpkin Patch was founded in 1990. The best description of the company may be found on the company Web site, where it states the following:

Pumpkin Patch is Australasia's leading children's fashion company, and is increasingly recognized as an international brand representing innovative design and quality product.

Our product range encompasses all stages of a child's growth—from baby to toddler, primary school kid to pre-teen—including clothing, nightwear, accessories, rainwear, footwear, teddy collection and bed linen coordinates. Pumpkin Patch also caters for Mums-to-be with a stylish maternity collection. There is also our fashion mini-brand for discerning pre and early teen girls—Urban Angel.

The entire Pumpkin Patch collection is designed by our in-house team who ensure each garment is fresh and stylish with a distinctive design signature.

Pumpkin Patch employs over 3,000 people, produces 2,000 styles per season, and our fashion forward children's wear is sold through over 190 company stores worldwide. The collections are currently available in numerous countries and regions including New Zealand, Australia, the United Kingdom, Ireland, the United States, Asia, and the Middle East.

Pumpkin Patch predominantly sells through its own store network in New Zealand, Australia, the United Kingdom, and the United States. We have also developed a number of other successful approaches to selling our products internationally including forming partnerships with successful international retailers such as David Jones in Australia, Nordstrom in the United States, and Jawad in the Middle East..

Pumpkin Patch has a strong history of revenue and earnings growth, with analysts forecasting approximately $375 million in sales in the 2007 financial year.

Pumpkin Patch is at an exciting stage in its development with a strong and growing core business in New Zealand, Australia, United Kingdom and international sales offering future growth opportunities opening stores in the United States.

My Company and Me

When I joined Pumpkin Patch, we had a technology team of about eight people. Our support area was running very well, and technology was mainly being deployed and supported in the retail store and distribution divisions. Any projects that were carried out took an ad hoc approach based on what the users required. This was effective, as IT was "close to the business" but prioritization and project process was an area I set out to improve.

In the beginning, and to address the issue of how we were going to approach projects, I started talking with everyone in the company. My primary objective was to get to know everyone and to understand the business. I spent about 3 months doing this and documenting my understanding. I made a presentation about the issues as I saw them, and what I thought we should do about them. Some technical issues had to be addressed, such as data fragmentation. We were also going to concentrate on solving the business needs specifically around the "Design and Buy" area, rather than the mainstream distribution and retail.

Along the way, a major business issue related to our recently initiated expansion plans into the United Kingdom. We had slowly grown from the New Zealand and Australian market. The UK market was new and we were under a lot of pressure to make it operational and efficient. This expansion was made all the more difficult by the distance and time zone difference. We were learning as we went along. Another problem related to customs clearances. We spent a lot of time just trying to clear stock through the customs process, including knowing what products could go to the UK and what their related Customs tariff codes & import documents were. To solve this, we first developed a "Design & Buy" system, which stored all product information as it was designed in a system. This was then able to have custom related information stored in it to ensure we could efficiently clear stock into the UK. We did a good job, and it was really good to see the challenge that had been set in 2000 become automated 3 years later, which gave us the ability to take on the next challenge!

Initially, for me, I had to get used to a different way of managing. In my past work experiences I was used to a very formal and vertical structure with a CEO and a board. At Pumpkin Patch, the managing director would talk to different managers abut their operations and about the overall business in general. It is a very flat structure. As a consequence, people who had been at Pumpkin Patch for some time thought you could just turn information technology on at will. They did not realize there had to be a process to follow to successfully complete a project. You know in a small business you can build a little database, get it up and running and look really good. But longer term solutions cannot be constructed successfully that way. A process has to exist, be understood, and be consistently applied. I do think that the managing director understood and agreed with me about this, and for the most part so did everyone else.

The flat organization structure was for the most part very positive for me. I was able to very easily gain access to the managing director, and his priorities and views on how things needed to be tackled. This access facilitated quick decisions and the availability of funds to make changes and implement systems. Also, the culture was very nurturing to try new things. We could develop a concept or idea into an information system and pilot test it in a part of the company. If it worked it would be expanded throughout the company. If it did not work we would move on to the next project. The culture was very forgiving.

Another initial issue had to do with staffing. At the start of my tenure, we had a number of contract developers. Their skills were good. But we made a decision that we wanted to have our own permanent employees. We wanted people to be with us for the long term. We wanted them to care about our own coding standards and be dedicated to the challenges thrown at us, and we were especially interested in people who wanted to work at Pumpkin Patch. This approach not only reflects what we wanted to do in the information technology area, but this is part of the overall culture of the company. So, we grew slowly and continuously, always ensuring continuity through acquiring the necessary skills and retaining those skills within the company.

My Typical Week

I meet with my managers individually every 2 weeks. At the moment I have five managers. So, these meetings take at least one day. We call this their "progress meeting." I have a busy schedule seeing managers, reviewing where they are with various activities, and discussing progress or issues. These discussions often cover the following topics:

- Project and progress
- Team issues and their resolution
- Larger team issues
- Suggestions for continuing work
- Encouragement from me to support progress
- Business requirements and opportunities

I also have a "Heads of IT" meeting every week, where all my managers meet together. This enables us to work more closely together and share ideas going forward. We like everyone to agree on our way forward rather than working as individuals. When we get full consensus, things happen!

The managers who report to the "Heads of IT" meet fortnightly. It is good to see this level of management taking ownership of team issues and assists in the communication across the team. This consists of project managers, help desk managers, and so forth.

We like to communicate to the entire team as managers. We have recently devised a newsletter that is sent out via e-mail monthly, Pumpkin Techs. This serves the purpose to keep everyone in the team informed of recent achievements, latest team movements, and Pumpkin Patch business issues. We meet with the entire team monthly and have a guest speaker from the business come along to address how their area runs and the current challenges.

Then, more often than not I attend a breakfast or luncheon seminar. I am especially interested in retail information technology issues. I try to maintain contact with my peers from other companies. I find updates on technology to be very helpful, as long as they are targeted. I do not have time to read everything. So, I have to focus on the topics that apply to Pumpkin Patch.

I meet formally and informally with my peers at Pumpkin Patch. These are the general managers of our other departments. In some cases, I have to book specific times with these managers. Others prefer an informal drop in approach. We generally discuss issues related to things our team might need to do for the departments.

I try to visit my team of people to say "hi" daily and see how they are doing. This is difficult. But, I think it is essential to keep people motivated. As managers, we are trying to find more time for the individual weekly, say, just for a coffee, to keep in touch with their issues and ensure we can identify with their challenges.

I work from home on Mondays. This is my time and it is wonderful. I am able to set what I need to achieve and it actually all gets done. Most of this time is spent reading. I review contracts and business cases that my managers have produced. I read all the project documents that I have to approve. Our approach to system development includes the production of documents at the end of each stage, which requires my approval. We want to monitor progress and control any changes from our original plans. I encourage my managers to have "time out" from the team weekly and ensure they are organized and on top of things. As the company is constantly moving on to the next challenge, we can at times be "on the run" and it is important in leading the team that we stay focused on the things that matter.

Every Friday, I meet with our change advisory forum (CAF) group. We review all the changes submitted by the various information technology team members. We want to ensure each project stays on track and that there is no duplication across projects. We also aim to keep the risk of change to the existing business operations to a minimum by ensuring all team managers are aware of the changes and how they affect their areas of responsibility. This process has been in place for the past 6 months. We are all very pleased with the process. The process is based on the ITIL concept of a change advisory board. We prefer the term "Forum."

Also, I try to meet regularly with our managing director to discuss current issues or those that I foresee in the near future.

Dealing with Users

At Pumpkin Patch, we have two categories of internal clients. First "sponsors" are the managers of the business units that request our services and from whose budgets will flow the funds for the development and implementation of a new or revised information system. Next, the "users" are those individuals who work within the business unit and who will interact directly with the information system.

My managers will interact with the sponsors on a fortnightly or monthly basis. We talk with them all the time about what they need, what the next request might be. When a project starts, we want to be clear about the specific objectives. We then carry out standard technology project steps such as requirements, design, and so forth. We are encouraging more user involvement, especially at the end, to ensure acceptance of the system. This includes a step called user acceptance testing (UAT).

After the project is complete, we conduct a project review to ensure the outcomes have been achieved and ensure key learning's are feedback into the next project.

Users have access to our help desk. Based upon user contact we will write change requests. We will investigate in more detail the specific requirements. We may respond directly or initiate the project process explained above.

If we start to receive a myriad of calls to our help desk, we will investigate the situation. Right now, it is more of an informal process where I will talk to the sponsors or the users. Based upon this feedback, we may decide to take some action either at the project level or with more appropriate training for the users.

Deciding on Technology Investments

I will work with the sponsors before the start of a project to determine the costs of any technology-related aspects. Together we have to justify any expenditure to support the business objectives of the project. We will both sign off on the plan and proceed with the project. It is quite a fluid approach.

There is an overview process to these detailed project decisions. Our managing director and I will review the project and expenditure plans. Within our budgeting process, I have responsibility for both technology capital and operating expenditures. Once these budget items are agreed upon, it is my responsibility to operated with the budgeted amounts. Of course, if I find out that I might have an over expenditure I, along with the appropriate sponsor, will meet again with our managing director to revise our plans.

Most of our ongoing expenditures are included in the technology operational budget. Once we establish this budget, it is my responsibility to ensure the rest of the business continues to receive the agreed upon level of technical service, such as computer response time. Again, I regularly discuss any issues that may arise here with our managing director.

Current Issues

An issue we are currently dealing with now I will call scalability. As the company expands we have to stretch our systems. Some systems were not written with the knowledge of the kind of expansion we are experiencing now. So, we have a constant challenge to ensure our systems can respond to the company expansion. We try to respond by making continuous small changes. This is a low risk approach which allows us to invest where it is most needed, and then move on to ensure continuous operations.

As we grow, another issue arises about managing our people. Remember, when I first started we had eight people in the information systems area. Now we have 45, and that number is still growing. We got a lot of our decisions made informally, and now we follow, out of necessity, a formal process for decision making. Our teams are very business focused. That means my managers need to be business people first. That is hard to intertwine with their technical skills.

We want to retain our people for the long term. When we hire people we try to ensure that they will be comfortable in our culture. I tell them it is flat, fluid, and things will move fast. We want people who are dynamic and flexible. We have good incentives for people to stay. But, if it is not working out, as in most employment, it will be hard for them to continue and I encourage them to make the choice.

We have spent a lot of time making our project process clear. We have adopted a methodology that we follow as closely as possible. We also need strong project sponsors who can set priorities and make decisions about their projects.

We also must ensure that our information technology strategy is aligned with the business. We all meet regularly. I think my managers have a good feel for the business. But it is a formal feel. I want them to develop a real feel for the business. I challenge them to get out to a store and get to know the store manager at a personal level. I think in the long run this will make our information technology services better and we will more easily be aligned with the people on the front line.

Right now, our key limitation is access to skills. For instance, for the last 6 months we have been short four people on our help desk. We look for qualifications and the right fit. We will not hire just based on skills set, and we take a great deal of time finding a person for one role, as it is imperative for the entire team's success.

Future Issues

The first issue, and there may be many parts to this issue, is my team. The team is now large compared to our size just a few years ago. So, now we need a more formal organization and reporting structure. This may impact our culture. Another aspect to the team issue is ensuring we have the appropriate skills. Now we have a telecommunications network that stretches around the world. We need skills for establishing and monitoring this network. We could outsource all of our infrastructure skills needs. But, as I said earlier, that is not the overall company approach. As the company grows we want to develop a team. We want an expert team that is tight, highly efficient, and that does things that are quite special for Pumpkin Patch. In order to do this, in the future we have to make decisions every day about how we can continuously improve.

Another issue relates to the growth of the company. Pumpkin Patch started out in New Zealand and Australia. The first expansion was into the UK. Now we are moving into the United States. We are also developing a wholesale division. These expansions have been slow and cautious. This is the company philosophy. So, the question is, with all these expansion plans, what does it mean for our use of information technology? The answer, in a word, is scalability. We have to have information systems that can handle the anticipated expansion. We have to have the skills that will facilitate our growth. In all the comments I am making here, I feel confident that we are currently addressing this issue and that we will be able to respond adequately in the future.

As we have grown in the number of people, we have not added any more space. So, we have people sitting on top of each other. Well, we are a tight group, but not that tight! We are looking at new office space to resolve this issue. This might seem like a small issue, but I do not think it is. Because I want to continue to have a highly regarded team spirit, the new space is very important.

As we grow our infrastructure will have to keep pace, and as we add more remote users latency becomes an issue. Our technology must be able to respond to users who need to interact with our information systems. Thus, we need to decide if we will proceed with a centralized or decentralized model for our future expansions plans for our infrastructure. Whatever we do, it has to service our business needs.

As we expand more into a global environment, we are encountering new issues. For instance, one of our employees in the UK visited our wholesale site in Saudi Arabia. The Internet service was not acceptable. So, we are investigating mobile access broadband and not land lines. This is certainly an issue we will have to resolve as we start dealing more with global suppliers.

Final Comments

My main observation is the CIO is a business manager. The CIO must know the business. You must be in touch with the business and where it is going. From my technology degree I know enough about that. I understand the process approach. But, as a CIO I have to be able to work with people and I most certainly have to be able to lead those people.

Everything we do is justified through a business system. We have to prepare a business case. We have to understand what the business needs and how information technology can bridge the gap and provide what is needed.

So, I see my role as keeping in touch with the business, managing my team, and knowing the industry and everyone involved. The CIO must maintain those relationships that can influence and obtain commitment from the business to apply technology for the overall benefit of the company.

I believe that in the future information technology will continue to develop and rapidly change. In 20 years time, the information technology environment will be very different. All the business users will be capable of dealing directly with the technology. This is like today where we all can deal with the telephone, even though not too long ago, it was a novel technology that required someone else to dial the number for the user. So, in the future, information technology may become more responsible for the inner workings of the technology platform, but the users will be responsible for their own application systems. This will make things move even faster. They will be able to use the technology the way they want to.

References

Pumpkin Patch (n. d.). Retrieved January 30, 2007, from www.pumpkinpatch.co.nz

Chapter VIII

Russell Turner
MetService

A global leader in valuable weather and presentation services

My name is **Russell Turner**. I am the chief information officer at MetService in Wellington, New Zealand.

Personal History

I was born in Gisborn, a little town on the east coast of the North Island of New Zealand. We moved to Wellington when I was two. I attended a public elementary school and then a catholic secondary school where my mother was teaching. I obtained an A bursary and went to Victoria University where I focused on physics. I have completed my third year, taking such courses as digital electronics and quantum physics. But, I have not finished my degree. I took what at the time was a very high paying job as a computer programmer. I had planned to return and finish my degree after I had some experience under my belt. But, I have not yet done it.

This high paying job was with Praxis Software. I was a junior programmer using Pascal and COBOL languages. The systems were real estate tracking using point of sale, and warehouse management. The clients for these systems were local wholesalers who were importing products from India. The mark-ups on equipment and clothing were significant, sometimes in the tens of thousand percent. This created an issue for me as a COBOL programmer. I had to determine how to handle such large percentage figures.

At the beginning of 1986, I took a job with Colonial Mutual in Melbourne, Australia. They are quite a large superannuation and insurance company. This was my first experience with a large company with a lot of programmers. I mainly worked on a system that computed calculations for superannuation and payments.

Next, I moved to a supplier of Colonial Mutual. I was involved with package delivery to customers. These were superannuation systems. Also, while I was here I worked on payroll systems. At the time Australia was building a new parliament house in Canberra. We developed a payroll system for the commission responsible for the construction.

I then moved to Prismac, still in Melbourne. This company focused on check processing and image processing systems for banks. This was quite interesting as the use of this technology was just emerging. We would take standard UNISYS machinery and program them for individual banks depending on their specific needs. They were high volume check processing machines, which were quite large. They could be as long as 10 meters. At the time, imaging technology was just emerging, which would eliminate the physical encoding of the check amounts.

But, in 1989 my wife had a baby and we decided to move back to New Zealand to be close to our parents.

I took a job with Phillips, New Zealand. They are a Dutch company which had developed an optical laser disc technology. The intention was to convince large government departments to scan and archive their documents onto laser disc. My experience in imaging technology helped me get this job. We were able to sell the system to various government departments. My role at Phillips was a technical product manager. I worked with organizations to determine what was possible and how our system could be implemented. So, that was when my programming career ended. I moved more into a consultative or product management role. After only 1 year, Phillips decided to close their Wellington office.

I then moved to KPMG Peat Marwick. They were looking for consultants who had experience with document imaging systems. I joined them as a consultant to develop a strategy for providing document imaging consulting services. I did seminars on document imaging and the benefits that could be obtained. We attracted a lot of work from clients for projects around their perceived need for the technology.

One of our major clients for this service had a significant need for document imaging with respect to the national grid. They were still documenting the grid by hand using India ink. These were lovely works of art going back to the 1940s. This was a significant project to convert these diagrams to electronic images. So, with everyone's agreement, I moved to a specially established subsidiary to complete this project. I spent the next 2 years working on this project.

My next move was to Tel-Itel as a consultant, where I worked on some interesting projects, including a document imaging system for one of New Zealand larger government departments. We did quite well, bringing in the project on time and on budget. At the time, the government was under pressure for having too many projects which were over budget and taking more time than they should have. So, they publicized our project as an example of a successful project. On another project, we developed a network management operation support system. This is where I learned more about taking a structured approach to project management. Now my experience was taking me further away from development and more into the management side.

While there have been a number of different jobs at different companies, there seems to be a pattern of moving through the technical experience and on to management related positions. This trend becomes more evident with my next job.

In the late 1990s, I went to work for Saturn Communications, a cable TV company that was going to set up its own telephone network. It was going to install a new telephone network on top of its existing cable TV network. They were successful in Wellington, and later in Christchurch. This was the first time that a company was going to build a network with wire in the ground that was not owned by New Zealand's monopoly telecommunications company. So, it was a very interesting time to be involved in a company that was going to build the entire infrastructure of a telecommunications organization from scratch.

My role was to install the operational support systems, such as customer billing. It was quite a challenge. I learned a valuable lesson over this period of time. I learned what not to do. You can learn what to do from books. Making a judgment about what you are not going to do can be more valuable. The ability to make these kinds of decisions comes mainly from experience.

Over the next few years, there were a number of mergers. I had started off at Saturn as a project manager responsible for specific system implementations. Then Saturn merged with Telstra. Then Telstra-Saturn merged with Clear. Again there were some major system integration projects.

This period of time and experience showed me the leading role that information systems have on the development of products and processes for the entire company. It is the processes and methods used within information technology that can be quite powerful when used elsewhere in the company. It was this realization that led me to look for another opportunity. I was responsible for application development and project management. I wanted to be more involved in the business operations side and, for instance, change management. So, when the opportunity came to move to MetService, even though it was somewhat smaller as far as staff and budgets, the role interested me. I got to look after the whole pie rather than just part of the pie.

Company History

Our Web site provides the following historical information:

The observation and studies of New Zealand's weather started as early as the 1840s. The weather forecasting service began in 1861, when a spate of shipwrecks prompted the Government to start a storm warning service as part of the then Marine Department.

Forecasting remained a marine service until 1926, when it became part of the newly-formed Department of Scientific and Industrial Research. At the outbreak of World War Two in 1939, forecasting became part of the Royal New Zealand Air Force. The focus on aviation continued with a move in 1964 to the then Department of Civil Aviation, which in 1968 became part of the new "super ministry", the Ministry of Transport.

During the 1980s there was increasing pressure on government funding for meteorology in New Zealand, together with a government-wide move to "user-pays" for specialized services, and to more autonomy and accountability for government departments. A combination of commercial competition in the deregulated market for meteorological services, and reform of publicly funded science, led to the establishment of two government owned companies in July 1992.

- ***MetService**, a state-owned enterprise. Our business is operational meteorology, and we provide weather forecasting services to three main customer groups:*
    - *The Minister of Transport (for the people of New Zealand)*
    - *Civil and Military aviation*
    - *Media and Industry*
- ***National Institute for Water and Atmospheric Research** (NIWA). As one of nine New Zealand Crown Research Institutes (CRIs), NIWA's mission is to provide a scientific basis for the sustainable management of New Zealand's atmospheric, marine and freshwater systems and associated resources.*

Vision

- *A global leader in valuable weather and presentation services*

- *Growing through customer appreciation of our innovative solutions, operational excellence, and outstanding service*
- *Profitable and well organized by highly skilled enthusiastic and alert people passionate about the success of our company*

In our annual report for 2004-2005, we state the following:

The social and economic impact of weather is something that can't be ignored. Controlling the weather is impossible but forecasting it has an impact on businesses and lives around the world. MetService and its subsidiary Metra work with customers from New Zealand and the Pacific Islands to the Middle East and Europe. They rely on us to understand their needs and deliver the right information, in the right format, at the right time, to wherever they may be.

Metra is a subsidiary of MetService, which was formed to conduct international media, aviation, and energy information dissemination business.

My Company and Me

When I joined MetService, the first thing I did was conduct a SWOT (strengths, weaknesses, opportunities, and threats) analysis. I wanted to find out where we were doing well and where we were not.

The first issue that I identified was our approach to project management. There was no specific approach to the projects we were working on. There was no architecture plan. Everything seemed to be ad hoc. We were just reacting to projects as they came in. We were not seen as proactive and leading the company in leveraging the benefits of information technology.

We also had many legacy systems because there was no long-range plan. There was no active plan to retire and replace systems.

Dealing with Users

The steering committee that I established when I first arrived has been very helpful. I get a "heads up" on all the business plans and how information technology will be involved. I know what they want now and what they are intending to do over an extended period of time.

We have also devised a procedure of engagement. Initially, our business analysts will sit with the users and try to understand the idea. They will document the size and shape of the project along with the priority and maybe even some comments about possible solutions. There is no charge, or budget allocation for this initial process. This means that we are more likely to be engaged by the user community to talk about what they need.

We really have to manage change during our projects. We want our users to know that they can make changes but we also want them to know the affects of those changes. What they ask for initially is not necessarily what they end up with. It is important that they get what they want. So, there must be very good reasons to make a change during the project.

At the end of the project, we conduct a survey which asks all the usual questions. We ask if they got what they wanted. We want to know if they were kept informed throughout the entire process. We ask about their involvement in testing the system. It is a brief survey, but I think it is important to do and it provides very valuable information.

Deciding on Technology Investments

Our investment decisions in technology are all based upon our architecture plan. We know, based upon the plan, where we want to be in 6 years. So, it is just a matter of conducting the necessary projects and acquiring the technology as we proceed. There may be projects that require us to diverge from our plan. We have to be able to make a very good business case to do so. We might install some obscure database in some part of the company for an immediate tactical reason. Then we must plan to bring it back into the fold and align it again with our overall architecture plan.

Current Issues

As I stated above, I determined that we needed a standard approach to conducting projects. We needed something that emphasized the front end of a project. More work needed to be done at the analysis stage. Now we have a steering group with representation from all business units. All project proposals must pass through this group. It is this group that will approve a project and decide on its priority. Now the rest of the company does not feel that we are doing the prioritization. They feel they are more in control of the process.

I have also restructured my unit to put more emphasis on project management. I have hired a new project manager. We are working at creating a customer-oriented approach to projects.

We are also taking the opportunity to review some of our vendors. With my telecommunications background, one of the things I naturally paid a little bit of attention to was our telecommunications infrastructure. MetService makes a fairly extensive use of a very geographically diverse network. We have stations scattered around the country in quite remote areas. So, for this network we do not necessarily need high speed, high capacity. But, it is very diverse geographically. Also, we looked at the band width for our international operations. A lot of our data comes from overseas, such as Washington and the United Kingdom. We receive about 600 gigabytes per month, which is reasonably significant. So, we have documented all of our telecommunications requirements and issued an RFP. We are just completing the evaluation of the responses and will be making a decision soon.

Another area where we are quite active right now is with the implementation of ITIL. Our operations group is running fairly well. However, the processes are based on ISO manufacturing standards, which emphasizes more on procedure manuals. We do not think that is what should be used to direct the quality of the daily operations of an information systems unit. So, everyone has taken the initial foundation training course. We are now looking at aspects related to incident management and problem management.

We are also addressing business continuity. This is especially important because of our issue of legacy systems. We also have to consider that Wellington is in an earthquake prone area. Therefore, we rolled these requirements into our telecommunications RFP, which I described above. Because of our legacy systems issue, the architecture of the systems is not amenable to splitting across multiple locations. We certainly do not want to have a mothballed system somewhere remote, which may or may not run when you need it. We would rather have the production process and capacity split across multiple sites. Then we would be capable of running independently and, in case of an emergency, at a lower capacity. But we need to decide on how we arrive at the situation where we can have a diverse operation. First, we have to strengthen the existing architecture. So we are moving to a new location that is more resilient to earthquakes. It will also have improved fire detection and suppression. Second, we will pursue the architecture plan regarding the establishment of two separate sites.

Many of our staff members have been here quite a long time. They know our systems very well. They also know the business very well. Therefore, the quality of the work being done is actually quite high. There are relatively few bugs. As we move into our architecture plan, we will have to look at acquiring new skills. I expect to do this through training and hiring.

Future Issues

I think the most difficult aspect about the future for us will be maintaining the momentum set out in our architecture plan. We have identified about 25 subprojects which will be necessary to complete the plan. But, there are always business pressures to drop the long term initiatives in favor of addressing a more immediate sort term goal. So, we have had to fit our long term projects around everything else that is going on. We have to be aware of the other business unit's resource forecasts and what they are projecting to do. Thus, it is very important over the next while to map out our resource demands reasonably accurately. Recall that I have experience with large migration projects dealing with customers and moving them from legacy systems. These projects almost always clash with more immediate business imperatives. We have to be a bit more like a nimble mammal ducking and diving among the feet of the dinosaurs!

Final Comments

Does information technology give a company a true advantage? Is it a true differentiator? I think for the most part the answer is "no." I could not say that e-mail is a differentiator in our company. But, how it is used might provide some differentiation. I think what differentiates one company from another is the processes around the use of technology. So, the role of the CIO is not so much about telling everyone about a new technology. The role should be more about determining the processes for the effective use of the technology. Most business functions can be enhanced by the proper application of information technology. The way it is adopted is more important than what is adopted.

References

MetService (n. d.). Retrieved January 30, 2007, from www.metservice.com

Section III

Taiwan

This section includes the results of discussions with CIOs from Taiwan. At the end of 2003, the Taiwan population was 22.6 million (Economist Intelligence Unit, 2004). The main two cities are Kaohsuing in the south and the capital, Taipei, in the north. Taiwan is the leading global manufacturer of computer hardware (Chuang, 2004; Tsan & Chang, 2005). It produces most of the world's computer notebooks, digital cameras, and cell phones (Chen, 2005; Dean, 2003). Overall, Taiwan has a reputation for global competitiveness and rapid growth (Wang & Chang, 2005). Taiwan companies focus on innovative approaches to low cost operations and forming mutually beneficial supply chain partnerships.

The individuals who were interviewed represent companies in Kaohsiung in southern Taiwan and Taipei in northern Taiwan. The following CIOs agreed to participate:

- Lucas Chuang, chief information officer, EVA Airways
  - Mr. Chuang was born and grew up in Madou, Taiwan. He has a Bachelor of Science in mathematical sciences from National Chenghi University. He joined EVA Airways in 1988.
  - EVA was formed in 1988 as part of Evergreen Marine Corporation, the world's largest company for shipping containers and container vessels. EVA is currently the second largest airline in Taiwan, providing international passenger and freight service.
- C. M. Ko, section manager, MIS Department, Compostar Technology Corporation
  - Mr. Ko was born and grew up in Kaohsiung, Taiwan. He studied industrial management at a junior college. He joined Compostar soon after it was formed in 1998.

  - Established in 1998, Compostar is a manufacturer and worldwide exporter of resistors and capacitors
- James Lin, vice president in charge of information technology, Taiwan Fixed Network Company (TFN)
  - Mr. Lin was born near Sun Moon Lake in Taiwan. He grew up in Taipei, Taiwan. He has a degree in from Tamsui Oxford University, where he majored in accounting and statistics with a minor in information systems. He joined TFN in 2003.
  - In 2001, Taiwan Fixed Network Company was granted an integrated network license. Since 1991, the company had operated as part of various organizations within Taiwan. The mission of Taiwan Fixed Network is to provide back end (that part of the network that does not move) connections for all international carriers and mobile phone services.
- C. K. Tsai, deputy director, Information Technology Division, Chi Mei Optoelectronics (CMO) Corporation
  - Mr. Tsai was born and grew up in Tainan, Taiwan. He has a Bachelor of Science with a major in geology from National Taiwan University in Taipei. He joined CMO in 1998, when the company was formed.
  - CMO, formed in 1998, is headquartered in Tainan Science Park, just south of Kaohsiung, where they are the world-leading manufacturer of thin film transistor liquid crystal display products, which are the major components of computer monitors and television screens.
- D. I. Wang, chief information officer, Lite-On Technology Corporation
  - Dr. Wang was born and grew up in Tainan, Taiwan. He has a Bachelors in mathematics from a university in Taiwan, and Masters in computer science and a Ph.D. in applied mathematics, both from Northern University in Boston, USA. He joined Lite-On in 1998.
  - In 2002, Lite-On Technology Corporation became part of the Lite-On Group. Lite-On Technology has a vision to be a world class producer of light emitting diodes, power supplies, wireless devices, liquid crystal display computer monitors, PDAs, and printers.
- M. P. Wang, general manager, Information Systems Department, China Steel
  - Mr. Wang was born and grew up in Tainan, Taiwan. He has a Bachelors in computer science from National Taiwan University in Taipei. He started working for China Steel in 1975.
  - China Steel is an integrated steel mill formed in 1971. With 50% of the Taiwan steel market, the company employs a state of the art computerized continuous casting production process.

Table 1.

CIO Name	Company Name	City	Number of Employees	Sector
Lucas Chuang	EVA Air	Taipei	5,000	Airline
C. M. Ko	Compostar	Kaohsiung	4,200	Electronics
James Lin	Taiwan Fixed Networks	Taipei	1,200	Telecommunications
C. K. Tsai	Chi Mei Optoelectronics	Tainan	10,000	Electronics
D. I. Wang	Lite-On	Taipei	3,800	Electronics
M. P. Wang	China Steel	Kaohsiung	8,727	Manufacturing

Table 1 provides some comparative data about the companies involved from Taiwan.

References

Chen, T. S. (2005, Summer). Joining the global village: Taiwan's participation in the international community. *Harvard International Review*, *27*(2), 24-27.

Chuang, S. (2004, April 12). Taiwan gains IT edge with speed and skill. *Asia Computer Weekly*, 1-2.

Dean, J. (2003, August 8). Taiwan, a tech bellwether, brightens. *Wall Street Journal*, p. B4.

Economist Intelligence Unit (EIU) (2004). Taiwan: Population. *EIU ViewsWire*. New York, March 8.

Tsan, W. N., & Chang, C. C. (2005). Intellectual capital system interaction in Taiwan. *Journal of Intellectual Capital*, *6*(2), 285-298.

Wang, W. Y., & Chang, C. C. (2005). Intellectual capital and performance in causal models: Evidence from the information technology industry in Taiwan. *Journal of Intellectual Capital*, *6*(2), 222-236.

Chapter IX

Lucas Chuang
Eva Airways

Just relax, your home in the air.

My name is **Lucas Chuang**. I am currently the chief information officer at EVA Airways.

Personal History

I was born in Madou, a town with a population of around 50,000 located in the southern part of Taiwan. I attended elementary and middle high school in Madou where I was born. For senior high school, I went to Tainan. Then, for university I went to Taipei. I received a Bachelor of Science from National Chenghi University in 1979, with a major in mathematical sciences. Immediately following university, I did my military service. I served as a second lieutenant in the Marine Corp. As a radio operator on board a destroyer, I was responsible for coordinating fire support for landing operations.

I joined Evergreen Marine in 1981 as a programmer, and was transferred to Evergreen's New York office in 1983, where I was in charge of a team of about

10 software development personnel. In 1988, I returned to Taipei as a manager for software development. Soon after my return I was lucky enough to be assigned to a team of about 20 people responsible for all information technology development for the formation of an airline company as part of Evergreen Marine. I was the project manager in charge of a team which built a new generation air cargo system. I believe it was the first client/server based air cargo system installed in the airline industry.

Company History

The idea of starting a new airline in Taiwan was pioneered by Evergreen Marine Corporation in mid-1988. I was one of 20 team members assigned to organize the formation of EVA Airways. At that time Evergreen was the world's number one in shipping containers and container vessels. The timing seemed right to extend the company further into other forms of transportation. Also, while there were a number of domestic airlines in Taiwan, there was only one international carrier. So, a market was identified. Our experience shows that this was a good decision, as we have done well financially.

Formal government approval was obtained in 1989 and the inaugural flight was July 1, 1991. The mission of EVA Airways is to become the best service airline. We focus on safety and service. Our freight ton kilometer (FTK) rating for 2003 placed us seventh in the world.

Currently, we are the second largest airline in Taiwan. We fly to more the 40 destinations in Asia, Australia, New Zealand, Europe, and North America. Our fleet in 2005 includes Airbus A330-200s and Boeing B777s for long haul flights. The backbone for our future will be the Boeing B777s

My Company and Me

I took the position of chief information officer (CIO) at EVA Airways 2 years ago.

The first major issue that I had to deal with is the lack of staff. Because of a downturn in the economy, we had not hired staff for some time. Our entire IT operations and systems development involved only 145 people. We could have used around 190. So, we were understaffed, and our people were under a lot of pressure. They were working a lot of overtime. I worked with our Human Resources Department to try to increase our staff compliment. I received a lot of help from our users. They were always willing to express their need for more services from my department. This was very helpful, especially when they stated their needs in front of senior management. Now we have about 189. While the numbers are now sufficient, we also have an issue with our staff being under skilled. But, I will discuss this topic a little later here.

Because we were so understaffed, we were under a lot of pressure and the environment was not very good. Therefore, I tried to create a more positive environment to make my staff feel more comfortable and hopefully happy to continue to work for EVA Airways. I was very concerned about losing any people. I could not pay more money to keep them. The salary levels are fixed and senior management was not prepared to make any adjustments. Anyway, the pay would be about the same at other companies. I felt that a happy environment would help people decide to stay with us. Fortunately, not many left. I tried to make the work environment friendly. I showed everyone I cared about them individually. I asked about their work, their home, and their kids.

Another issue had to deal with my experience. Before I became CIO, I was responsible for application development. I did not have any experience with the technical side of the IT department. So, I have to rely quite heavily on our technical staff. But, perhaps that is a good thing because this allows me to focus on the business aspects of employing the technology. I can concentrate more on the public relations aspects of the information technology department.

The former CIO was promoted to the chief executive officer (CEO), my boss. He is very knowledgeable about my area, and very helpful. It is also very good to have a CEO who understands the potential benefits of employing information technology. He was recently promoted again, this time to Chairman of EVA Airways.

My Typical Week

The time I spend at work involves the three following specific activities: responding to e-mail, administrative duties, and attending meetings. I spend approximately 1½ hours per day responding to both internal and external e-mail. I usually take about ½ hour each day to deal with administrative tasks such as leave requests or expenditure approvals.

Normally, I spend most of my time in meetings. Twice per week, I have an information technology review meeting. In this meeting we review our information technology services and operations. Also, in this meeting we may look further into the future to ensure that our information technology strategy is still in alignment with our business needs and expectations. Also, on a weekly basis I may be involved in four or five project status review meetings. On a monthly basis, I attend meetings related to company department heads and the CEO and Chairman, an information technology coordination meeting with other companies in the Evergreen Group, and something we find is becoming more important these days is a meeting regarding information security. I also have quarterly one-on-one meetings with our CEO and Chairman regarding overall information technology project status reviews.

I spend the rest of my time doing something I wish I had more time to do. I try to comfort our business users. I believe it is my duty to try to ensure a high level of user satisfaction within the company regarding the information technology that we provide. I think this is a very important part of my job as CIO.

Dealing with Users

We have a saying in English; "... toss the requirement over the wall." This seems to apply to our users. We have difficulty trying to get them to describe what they want from the IT department. So, there is a gap between the user and the IT department. We have established a business unit to bridge between the two groups. This bridging unit, called systems support, can state the business requirements very clearly. The unit provides the first line of support. In many cases, it is a matter of understanding how the system works and what it is capable of providing for the user. Another important function of the systems support unit is the consolidation of requests. The staff of the unit knows both IT and the business requirements. They are able to match them. Also, they are able to identify priorities of requests. I think this unit has provided a good benefit to both the users and the IT department.

Deciding on Technology Investments

We have an annual budgeting process where all of our business units document their plans for next year. The plan will include a discussion of any new system development that may be necessary. When we come to the start of a specific project, the user department must prepare a business case. If it is necessary to acquire some new technology, it is the business case that is employed to justify funding. The final decision is made by our CEO.

During the year, we may make a budget adjustment. If we can identify where a change should be made we will do so. We may be over budget on some projects and under on others. So, this will give us an opportunity to revise our project priorities.

Current Issues

While I am pleased we have been able to increase our staffing levels, it has created an issue. We have about 50 new staff members now. They are mainly new university graduates. They have to become knowledgeable about the company and the technology we employ here. Therefore, training is important. It is not only the technical skill sets that are important but also the management skills. The most difficult aspect for IT people is the gap between business and IT. I think this applies to all types of businesses. But, it is an important issue for us at EVA Airways. These new people are the most junior people on a project team. They need to know how to manage, how to work as a team member, and take responsibility in performing their duties in the team. We either use classroom training or we send them to work with our users for a short period of time.

The technical skills we teach in training are unique to the airline industry. We use a very large mainframe. We run around 6000 programs, which mainly use Assembler and COBOL with CICS. When EVA Airways was first formed, we purchased the software systems from British Airways. I realize these are relatively old programming languages, but these are the languages of our legacy systems. So, we are mainframe based and we use second and third generation languages.

We do our own in-house training for project management. For some time now we have used the Project Management Institute's material. We use their book, which outlines the project management body of knowledge. We have been able to tailor it specifically to our approach to projects here at EVA Airways.

Another issue we are working on now relates to outsourcing. When we were understaffed, we found it necessary to outsource some of our projects. The problem is that the outside vendors are not familiar with our business. So, for each project with an outside vendor we are spending a lot of time and effort to teach them about our system. For these outsourcing projects, we are over budget on 70% of them. This is caused by either the vendor not knowing our business, and thus spending more time on the project, or because they underestimate the scope of the project. I think it would be better to find a long-term partner who understands our business. The companies that we are dealing with are local Taiwan companies. They mainly do the coding in Assembler for modifications to our existing systems. They may do some Web programming for our new online systems, but in either case it remains important that they understand our business. We tried to outsource some of our work to India, but that was not a successful venture. There was a gap between the requirements we would specify and the resulting code. I think it relates to a language issue. In both countries English is not the mother tongue, but, all the communication was in English. This was especially the case for documenting the system specifications. Anyway, we always had to further develop the code after it was returned to us.

Another current issue relates to integration. In the past, we acquired many systems from different vendors or other airlines. Each system is unique. So, we seem to have a bunch of information system islands. They do not have many links and those that do exist are quite complicated. We are developing a data warehouse to facilitate this integration. We have completed the first phase for our passenger systems. Phase two will be for the cargo systems. There is a lot of work to do on this issue and we currently have quite a long backlog of projects.

Future Issues

There are many interesting issues associated with the use of technology and the airline industry. Indeed, we have identified and are working with IATA on four major initiatives.

One of these issues relates to e-tickets, which, have been in existence for some time now, but only as an option. IATA is pushing for complete e-tickets by 2007. This will save a lot of money compared to the use of a paper ticket. An extension of the e-ticket relates to interline e-tickets. Right now, we can issue an e-ticket for our portion of a passenger's flight. However, if another airline is involved we have to issue a paper ticket. In the near future, the interline e-ticket approach will allow us to issue an e-ticket for the entire flight, even on other carriers. We expect to be capable of issuing interline e-tickets by April 2005. Its subsequent use will depend upon the capability of other airlines to accept and issue an interline e-ticket. But, the schedule is very much dependent upon the other airlines and their priority for the development of this service.

The second issue or IATA initiative relates to radio frequency identification (RFID). While no industry related decisions have been made regarding RFID, we are currently investigating this technology. We expect that when a decision is made we will need to implement a solution very quickly. We expect RFID to be applied to baggage handling. Instead of the bar code, which is currently used on baggage tags, a RFID chip will be used. The current bar codes do not attain 100% accuracy, and some bags are lost. This can be very expensive, especially when the bags miss a connecting flight. But, RFID will increase the accuracy of the baggage handling system.

So, RFID has a potential to benefit the baggage handling process. It may also be used to replace the bar code on boarding passes as well. However, one of the issues to be dealt with here relates to passenger privacy. For security reasons, if a passenger does not board an airplane, we must remove their baggage. This is a complicated procedure, but we must do it. Another concern related to this situation is determining where the passenger is. We could, with RFID, track the person within the airport. Being able to track the person's movement within the airport could be a good service if we can ensure they do in fact board their flight. However, there is also concern about the invasion of the passenger's privacy. This issue has yet to be resolved. It is interesting to note, though, that the technology is available. It is just up to society to decide if its use will be an overall benefit and acceptable.

Here is another subissue that has to do with RFID. Companies like FED EX, and UPS currently use RFID to track each individual item. But, they are what I would call an integrated shipper. They are the forwarder, the carrier, and they provide the ground transportation. In our case, we only provide the carrier service. In order for us to deal with other corporate entities in this chain, we will have to become a sort of virtual integrator. It will be necessary to develop a standard interface among a number of trading partners in order to use RFID to track shipments that involve a number of different companies providing different services.

The third issue relates to the automated ticket boarding pass (ATBP). These machines are used to record who has boarded the plane by reading the magnetic strip on the back of the passenger's boarding pass. There is a machine stationed at each boarding gate. It is only used during the boarding process. This is expensive and inefficient. The machines are very expensive to maintain. If the boarding pass had a bar code or an RFID chip, then we could use portable readers. With a handheld boarding pass reader, we would need fewer machines. This would result in a more efficient use of the readers and consequently less cost. Until the RFID privacy issue, discussed above, is resolved, the bar code approach would also produce a good benefit.

Finally, the fourth issue relates to the common use self service (CUSS) kiosk. This unit is a self-service check-in and seat selection. This process is very efficient for domestic flights. But, it becomes more complicated for international flights. Once a flight is going to cross a boarder we need to ensure that the passenger has a valid passport and, in some cases, visa. The CUSS kiosk cannot check these kinds of details. Further, for some international flights we have to provide a complete passenger and crew manifest list to the destination country before the flight may depart. Again, the CUSS kiosk cannot provide the necessary information. We are not sure how this issue will be resolved.

Final Comments

I find I have to split my time between external and internal duties. I refer to my external activities as public relations and my internal duties as human relations.

Internally, I try to create an environment where my staff can have fun. I always try to be friendly to my staff. As I said earlier, I ask about their family, and how their children are doing. I want my staff to feel respected. I think this is very important.

Also, internally, I focus on training. I think it is one of my responsibilities to build our people's knowledge. Every year we have a program of courses, not only for skill sets but also for management issues. I invite my colleagues from other companies to give us some lecture. I think it is good to have some information from companies other than the airline industry.

In all of this approach to human relations, it is important to be able to retain my staff. It can be very costly when someone leaves the company. When you lose a person you have to find a suitable replacement. While you are looking there will be pressure on the people who have remained because there will be fewer people to work on the project. Then the new person will take some time to become familiar with the project. Overall, the project tends to fall behind schedule and the project team members feel pressure.

Externally, I work with our business users and also our business partners. When I became CIO, I assigned my managers to become account managers. I asked them to visit our business users frequently. I wanted my managers to understand what the business users wanted. I also wanted my managers to inform the business users of what we had done for them and what we could do for them. I wanted my managers to treat the business users as customers. It is important that there be good communication between these two groups.

We enjoy good long standing relationships with or business partners. We use IBM's mainframe for our Passenger Systems, Revenue Accounting Systems, and Maintenance and Engineering Systems. The languages of these systems include IBM's Assembler, COBOL, IMS/DB, and IMS/DC. We have installed many Dell Desktop computers and servers in Taiwan and also in our overseas stations. Our Air Cargo System resides on an HP server. Most of our open systems run under a Microsoft platform. Finally, NCR is our outsource developer for our EDW (Enterprise Data Warehouse) system and it runs on an NCR computer.

Finally, if you want to facilitate change within an organization, it is important to focus on three aspects. First is mindset. People feel more comfortable when they can identify a goal. But, the personal goal and the company goal must be the same. So, we have to ensure we have the same mindset and that we are going in the same direction. Second, people must be competent. You must have employees who are capable of doing the job. I use the term "organizational capability" for these first two aspects. For each project or change initiative, it is important to review and understand your organizational capability regarding mindset and capability of each person. The third aspect is rewards. If people perform well, it would be good to give them a wage increase. This would provide an incentive for everyone if he or she knew a wage increase was possible. Unfortunately, we have very little flexibility in this matter.

Chapter X

C. M. Ko
Compostar Technology Corporation

The best supplier of electronic components

My name is **Chin Ming Ko**. I am currently the section manager, MIS Department at Compostar Technology Corporation.

Personal History

I was born in Kaohsiung and I grew up there. I attended Chen Hsien Elementary School and Shin Jen Junior High School. It was a new school and I entered it in the second year of the school. Then, I studied in Chi Shan. This is a senior high school. I studied automotive repair. This school is very far from Kaohsiung, so I had to live by myself near the school. After senior high school, it was difficult to find a job, so I returned to school. I studied industrial management at a junior college. This school is located in the north of Taiwan, so I had to move again.

My first position was with HJC, a company which actually owns Compostar. When Compostar was formed, I worked partially for HJC and partially for Compostar. I was very interested in working for Compostar only because of their use of ERP systems. While my boss at HJC originally did not want me to go, I eventually was able to join Compostar full time.

But, between working for HJC and Compostar, I worked at Chan Ming for about 6 months. The company manufactures stainless products. I worked in the operations management area doing quality assurance.

I was able to return to Compostar when they were hiring in the management information systems area.

Company History

Compostar, established in 1998, is a manufacturer and worldwide exporter of resistors and capacitors. Our products include thick film chip resistors and multilayer ceramic chip capacitors. We have ISO9001, ISO9002, and ISO 14001 certification. We have fully automated manufacturing lines for our chips.

As stated on our Web site, our vision includes the following:

- Become a leading manufacturer of chip component
- Develop the latest technology to become the leader of the industry
- Recruit proficient staff and create the exceptional corporate culture
- Develop the global market and establish offices in every well-known city

In the multilayer ceramic chip capacitor market, Compostar is currently ranked third in Taiwan and tenth worldwide. Among the top three companies in this market in Taiwan, we are the youngest. So, we are very proud of what we have been able to accomplish in such a short period of time. We believe it is our products' quality that is the most important reason for our present success in this market.

My Company and Me

As I said above, I really wanted to work for Compostar because of their ERP system. These kinds of systems are new and I thought I could learn a lot. So, I started working here in November 2001. I remember my first day of work. There was a typhoon. When I arrived at the Compostar offices everyone had already gone home. This was a surprise. At HJC everyone would continue to work even during a typhoon day.

When I first started at Compostar, I worked in the operations management area. Because of the focus of my earlier studies was in industrial management, I felt I could do a good job. In fact, if anybody had a question about the system they would come to me. I always tried to help others with their questions about the system. I was also assigned to work on systems in purchasing, sales, and the warehouse. I also worked on our human resources information system.

A major issue at the beginning of my tenure with Compostar had to do with our users. There was very little communication with the users. I spent a lot of time visiting the factory. I talked with the users about why they spent so much time on information management. I think this communication helped us to understand the requirements of our users.

Another issue that I had to deal with initially was our system to help us respond to our customers. As our sales revenue grew, the number of customers also grew. All of these customers would make inquiries about the status of their purchases. We needed a system to help us respond to these inquiries. We were able to develop a system that met these requirements.

My Typical Week

I work from Monday to Friday.

On the weekends I spend time with my family. We usually go to a mall or have some outdoor activity. I seldom have enough leisure time.

Dealing with Users

We have a system for documenting user requirements. Smaller issues may be dealt with face-to-face. However, larger issues may require a meeting between us and the user department. At these meetings, it is important for all of us to ensure we understand the requirement.

Based on our understanding of the requirements we may either develop a new system or modify an existing one. Sometimes, we simply suggest a change to a manual process. We think it is very important to consider other areas of the company when we are making these kinds of changes. So, we will attempt to see if there is another area of the company that could also benefit from this change. If we can see that there may be an application which could be applied in another area, we will approach that area to consider making the change. We would do this after responding to the initial request.

After the requirement has been met, we attempt to obtain feedback from the users about their satisfaction. We contact the user to ask them to comment upon our service.

Deciding on Technology Investments

At Compostar, we make these kinds of investment decisions based mainly upon service requests from the users. We develop an annual corporate plan from which a corporate budget is prepared and presented to our vice president. The budget for each department will include a component for information technology. This component taken together from all the departments will show us what we need to invest in regarding hardware, software, people, and tools.

It is interesting to note that these types of decisions are made differently at HJC. Because of the lack of resources at HJC, we focus on solving problems related to our current key issues. If the issue is not so important, we may develop a solution later. For example, we are currently focusing on our assembly system. So, the major investment in technology is related to this system. Consequently, there is not much money spent in the other areas of the company on technology investments.

Current Issues

Currently at Compostar, we are very pleased with our ERP system. But, we want to improve on our systems that help us deal with customers and suppliers. Over the next 2 years, we will focus on this area.

We have to be able to respond to different shipping requirements for different customers. It seems that each customer has their own requirements for the packing of components we produce. We must be able to package our products in response to the customer's requirements. This is how we provide good service to our customers. Along with being able to provide custom packing, we must be able to correctly label the contents of the package. So, we must also be able to generate a label in response to the customer's requirements.

When dealing with our suppliers, our purchasing department issues a purchase order either by FAX or by e-mail. We would like to create an electronic system to issue purchase orders to our suppliers. We currently share our production plans with our suppliers via e-mail or FAX. With an electronic system, the production information will be shared automatically.

Here is an interesting point. Remember, I came to Compostar to work on an ERP system. Now HJC, where I used to work, has asked me to help them install an ERP system. What is even more interesting is that HJC will soon have an ERP system that is more advanced than the one at Compostar. The system at HJC will be able to provide some of the electronic services that I mentioned above. The system at Compostar will not be capable of the same level of service.

Future Issues

In the near future, I will continue to work on the installation of the ERP system at HJC. However, once that has happened, I expect my attention will turn to Internet security and antivirus systems. As we continue to expand our use of the Internet we remain concerned about security and viruses. For the past few years HJC has not been profitable. But I must be able to spend money in order to acquire and install our ERP system and our antivirus system. So, now it is important for me to be able to work with limited resources and within restricted budgets in order to obtain the greatest effect.

Final Comments

I really enjoy this job. I work 24 hours a day for my information systems department. My mobile phone is always switched on. I feel a great sense of responsibility for my information systems department.

Good communication between my department and the users is very important. With good communication we may be able to develop information systems that will run smoothly. We have to learn to be patient with our users. Some users may not be able to express their requirements as specifically as we would like. We have to be patient and ensure that we continue to communicate.

References

Compostar Technology Corporation (n. d.). Retrieved January 30, 2007, from www.compostar.com.tw

Chapter XI

James Lin
Taiwan Fixed Network Company

Dominating the new theatre of telecommunications

My name is **James Lin (Yutang)**. I am currently the vice president at Taiwan Fixed Network Company in charge of information technology.

Personal History

I was born on January 26, 1964, in the Sun Moon lake area in the middle of Taiwan, where you can find much beautiful scenery of our country. This is a very beautiful part of our country. I do not remember much about this because we moved to Taipei when I was two years old.

I took all of my education in Taipei. I started elementary school in 1970, junior high in 1976, senior high in 1979, and university in 1982. For my university studies I attended an Oxford version of a Taiwan university, named Tamsui Oxford University. My major was accounting and statistics with a minor in information systems. I think this major has helped to deal with financial matters in my position. After university I served my compulsory military service for 1 year and 10 months in the army.

My first position was with American Express. I was an authorizer involved in making approval decisions about transactions with very high purchase amounts. In the late 1980s, the process was very complicated. There was not much credit card use in Taiwan. Most of our authorization calls were related to foreigners wanting to make a purchase with a foreign currency American Express card.

During my time at American Express we made a lot of changes. We were the first company to implement the use of an American Express card using local Taiwan dollars. We attempted to install and use an early version of automated teller machines (ATM). However, we could not convince the government to change regulations regarding electronic transactions. Sometimes technology moves faster than government regulators.

I was also involved in setting up the very first online transaction between the bank and a department store through an X.25 Packet Switch Network. Here is a bit of history surrounding this project. At the beginning of Taiwan Credit Card market, we simply installed terminals at merchant sites, called point of sale terminals. Because there were not many transactions at that stage the merchants used dial up telephone lines. When the card was read by the terminal it automatically dialed our data centre and the phone call would be charged to the merchant. At that time, normally the approval process would take between 15 and 20 seconds. With a single merchant, this process was acceptable at that time. However, for larger stores with many sales counters, there was a problem. Not only were all the approval calls very expensive, but they created too much traffic for the telephone lines. So we set up a dedicated network with leased line connections to these large stores. With this infrastructure in place we were able to authorize a transaction within 2 seconds. This is called X.25 Packet Switch Network, which has now been implemented in all the Acquiring Banks in Taiwan.

With the front end process resolved it was time to automate the back end support. We initiated a regional project called, "Merchant Process Reengineering." There were 12 countries involved and I represented Taiwan. I flew to Singapore, Australia, and Hong Kong to acquire the new technologies and implement the new electronic terminals, called electronic data capture (EDC) terminals. Before the acquisition of these terminals, all merchants used to reconcile the batches of records of receipt (ROR) and send to the acquiring bank for settlement. This was very time consuming and required a large number of internal staff. With the new EDC terminals, all the approval transactions would be batched automatically and the bank would settle with the merchant online with payment made by the next day. Both the bank and the merchants were much more satisfied with the process. All the back end support personnel were eliminated.

Later on, I was assigned another task of setting up an American Express Data Centre for Taiwan. The company was good enough to send me to IBM for 6 months of training. Then I established the necessary infrastructure for IT and the Data Centre, including all the networking, intranet, internet, and AS/400 infrastructure. When I left American Express 6 years later we had grown from 60 people to around 600 staff.

I joined Citibank in 1995. I had made a presentation about how the AMEX (American Express) system worked and they became very interested in having a similar system infrastructure. Though the process was similar, the volume of transactions was significantly higher than AMEX. This provided a challenge to the newly designed infrastructure to support and handle the huge volume of transactions. I was pleased that Citibank was willing to provide strong support for this venture. They now have a mature world wide system to support the Credit Card acquiring business. After the merger of Banking and Credit Card businesses in 1996, I was reassigned as project manager in charge of the Banking system. This assignment included the Teller, Sabre Platform, Systematics, and other Consumer Banking systems.

I was recruited by Standard Charter bank in 1999. They were having problems with their technology and the system was failing regularly every day. The package they offered to me was very attractive! So, I decided to take the challenge. Within 3 months the system was stable and was providing the necessary service. This again proved my capability to perform as an IT professional and a problem solver. I was quickly promoted to senior manager.

In 2002, I was asked to join Far Eastern Bank, a small local bank in Taiwan. The transaction volume of the Balance Transfer in Credit Card business is strong, about 30 Billion NT (New Taiwan) dollars. The major assignment for this position was to establish the overall IT infrastructure to support the challenge of introducing new technologies and to replace the Core Banking System. After 1 year of service, I moved to my current position at Taiwan Fixed Networks. Of course, the offer was better and there were more challenges ahead.

Company History

In 1991, the Pacific Electric Wire and Cable Group of companies ventured into the wireless communications field, establishing markets throughout South East Asia. In conjunction with Motorola, the Group developed the world's first mobile telephone communications system in 1993. A member of the Group, Taiwan Cellular Corporation (TCC), founded in 1996, began providing mobile telephone services and quickly became the world's fourth largest mobile telephone company and the fastest growing telecommunications company in the World. By late 2000, TCC surpassed five million subscribers, firmly establishing itself as Taiwan's largest mobile telephone enterprise.

In early 2001, Taiwan Fixed Network was granted an integrated network license. The mission of Taiwan Fixed Network is to provide the back end connections for all international carriers and mobile phone services. So, Taiwan Fixed Network focuses on that part of the network that does not move. We provide all the back end connections for all the internet service providers.

My Company and Me

The biggest challenge we are currently facing relates to the "last mile." This term represents that part of the fixed network which connects the home phone to a telecommunications service. We have a large market share in trunk lines and leased lines. But our market share of the last mile is very small. Our vision is to be a market leader in last mile services. Recently, we had an internal strategic planning session to see what we could do. We know the telecommunications industry, fixed network, and cabling. We plan to be the first company in the private sector to provide last mile services. Luckily, of all the private sector firms, we are the best. But the government continues to regulate this part of the industry and we have a difficult time establishing our market. We must lobby the government to change the regulations so that private sector companies can become involved in the last mile market.

As vice president of information technology, I am in the position now to handle all of our IT related services. There are three separate departments that report to me. They are Billing System Support, OA & Data Centre Support, and Project Management Support. There are a number of challenges that we are addressing. Each is discussed below.

Challenge: Outsource or In-Source

While I think outsourcing is possible, it is important to be sure that you "own your *Core Competence*." By this I mean you have to have your own forces who have the capabilities to build your own core systems. Otherwise, you may ask an outsourcing company to perform a task for you and you will have to rely upon them for priority of effort and cost.

The outsourcing company may have their own set of priorities which does not relate to yours or to providing you with an appropriate level of service according to the signed service level agreement (SLA). Also, they might quote a price which may be very much higher than it should be. They may consider the request beyond the initial scope and will require you to pay extra. So, because of these issues we decided that we wanted to own our core competence. I was assigned the mission to in-source rather than outsource.

Challenge: Unstructured Systems

Our systems are not modularized or functional. If we try to change something there is a good chance that everything will not link together. Let me give you an example. If you look at the top of the residential buildings in Taiwan, you will see an additional one or two stories added on after the construction. This is "illegal construction." It is very difficult to change these structures because any kind of modification may cause the added floors to fall down. This is the same for our systems.

In the past years, users have asked for changes and they have been accommodated. So, now we have to be careful that when making changes we don't bring down the entire system. We have to restructure the systems to legalize them. I have set up some teams to address this challenge. One team is for service requests. Another team is focused on restructuring our billing system. We will try to modularize all of these functions.

Challenge: System Integration

To address the integration issue, we have implemented an ERP system, specifically ORACLE Solution. This system is very expensive, but it is necessary because our systems are very complex. We have a number of systems which should be integrated. We have a GIS system to keep track of our buildings and all of our cables. The system has all the maps of our facilities. We also have a materials management system (IMS) and an order management system (OMS), which send commands to all the PBX to activate hand phone calls.

Challenge: Storage Bank

We are also concerned about resource management. Because technology changes so fast we must be sure that we are not left with some outdated technology. For example, our Engineering Department wanted to have their own PCs, servers, and storage. But, in order to have a more efficient approach to storage, I implemented a "storage bank" concept across all departments activating fiber connections. So, everyone has all the storage they need and our overall costs have been significantly reduced.

Challenge: Project Management

Currently, we are at a very critical point with our IT support. We have just implemented a project management standard operating procedure (PM-SOP). We have been developing SOPs for a lot of our processes so that we will have a standard approach. We are doing the same for our approach to project management. We have established a project management office, which will employ SOPs for all of our projects. The project office will manage the requests from user departments and the conduct of feasibility studies.

I expect our finance guru to be not only a budget watchdog, but also a partner who whips the department into line with the CEO's business objectives and speaks the CFO's language. Return on investment (ROI) will be the key for the management decision as to whether or not to proceed with the project, either budgeted or not budgeted. Thus, the potential investment must be justified. The project manager will take the lead of the project and conduct review meetings with related user departments and associated vendors. At every project stage, the user department project manager must sign off before proceeding further. Project members and others up to the vice president level must sign off. In this way, the projects will be managed easily and we will be able to more easily control change during the project.

All the projects should be the responsibility of project managers, who have to ensure the quality and accuracy of the service delivered.

My Typical Week

On Mondays, I review my weekly schedule and identify the major tasks for the week. We have a regular executive meeting on Tuesday afternoons where we review our weekly achievements with the chairman, the general managers and all the vice presidents. Also, IT Department meetings are conducted on a bi-weekly basis and an IT Cross-Department meeting is held once a month to resolve any outstanding IT issues.

On a monthly basis, we review our financial situation. All the major and critical issues are brought into this meeting for discussion and decision.

Dealing with Users

We have a specific roadmap for each individual service unit, which we review with all user departments on a quarterly basis. This helps us coordinate our service delivery to the user departments. All the service issues and requests are turned into action items, called projects. All the IT projects will be conducted and led by our project management office, which employs our project management standard operations procedure (PM-SOP).

The PM-SOP ensures the following:

- Information technology provides the service that the users want
- Users are fully involved in the project
- Information technology provides the product that the users want

Regular project review meetings are conducted with the related user departments according to the stage of the project. The project manager in the user department must sign off at each stage of the project to ensure the delivery of the service matches with what was originally agreed by the user and IT.

Deciding on Technology Investments

The telecommunications industry is relatively competitive. We need to apply new technologies to support our business growth and to further increase our market share. Most of our systems, including the billing support system (BSS), operation support system (OSS), and ERP, have been built on the Sun platform. In terms of systems' performance at this stage, while we have a small customer base, the systems operate well. With future anticipated expansion of our business and our customer base, we will need to investigate new technologies and identify next generation platforms for support.

Basically, we will visit the major carriers in the United States, Europe, and Asia. We will visit their physical operations and ask for their consultation on the technologies they have already implemented and those they plan to implement. We will also benchmark local carriers regarding their proposed technical solutions. Any new technology will have to accommodate our existing approach to operations. We do not want to implement a technology simply because it is new. It should be the right fit for our company.

We also want to convert our existing proprietary system to an Open platform. This will enable us to be more flexible when implementing new technologies and also to gain an advantage in hardware and software price bidding. In conjunction with these acquisitions, we will need well-designed training courses for the technical skills necessary to drive the new technologies. Legacy systems, their platform, and tools (Pro-C, Delphi, and PHP) will be replaced with new technologies (J2EE). The overall system architecture will be reviewed and revised in order to cope with the new business needs.

The system development lab is where we apply and test the new technologies to see if they will be beneficial to our company. We have developed standard SOP coding approaches with appropriate check-in and check-out procedures to ensure we can control the quality of our software developed before it is allowed to operate in our production environment. The most critical point is the stability and flexibility of our systems.

Current Issues

The major issues we now have are restructuring the billing support system, building a sales support system, and integrating cable TV billing and the billing support system.

The existing billing support system originated from a mobile billing system which was not initially designed for the fixed network operations. After running for 4 years, the system has become a "monster" which is very difficult to maintain. The system is not modularized or functionalized. So, one single function may link with up to 100 other programs. We have established a separate project team dedicated for infrastructure redesign to rebuild the entire system. We anticipate that this project will take 1½ years to complete all the necessary tasks.

The sales support system does not exist. Currently, all the required functions and reports are carried out manually. The sales team has six temporary staff to determine the necessary data and manually produce daily reports every morning. We have determined that the Sales Support System will consist of eight major subsystems, including: Sales Incentive System, Campaign Management System, Customer Support System, Sales Tracking System, Contract Management System, Telemarketing Management System, Dealer Management System, and Prospect Management System. All of these projects are currently underway, and we anticipate their completion by the end of this year.

After the acquisition of Pacific Cable TV in March of this year, we have an added mission to support and integrate this business function into our existing billing support system. The cable TV business is outside the scope of our original fixed network business. However, we anticipate completing this integration by the end of this year. The challenges never seem to stop!

Future Issues

Our overall investment in information technology has been over 10 Billion NT dollars. During this year we plan to initiate three major projects, including Server Consolidation, Back-up Integration, and Disaster Recovery.

The Server Consolidation project will help us to streamline the processes and consolidate related services. Thus, specific server boxes will be easy to manage and the associated maintenance costs will be reduced dramatically. The Back-up Integration project will consolidate our back-up mechanism and centralize all back-up in to one central storage and back-up library. This will reduce the back-up license fee, speed up the back-up process, and simplify the back-up procedure. For the Disaster Recovery project, we plan to establish business continuity and the ability to replicate all of our necessary data at a remote site in order to respond to any potential disastrous event.

Final Comments

What is a CIO? Someone once told me the “CIO” stands for “Career is over!” I would rather say that CIO stands for “Cooking in the Office.”

I am cooking every day in the office with new ideas, new technologies, and new challenges. As long as you adopt the right technology and methodology and deliver the right recipe, you will perform your role well. Management support is a key to your success. Be sure to serve the right meal.

Before we partake of the meal, “God bless us all.”

Chapter XII

C. K. Tsai
Chi Mei Optoelectronics (CMO) Corporation

Business as a way to persue fulfillment

My name is **Chun-Kuei Tsai**. I am the deputy director in the Information Technology Division for Chi Mei Optoelectronics (CMO) Corporation. Our head office is in the Tainan Science-Based Industrial Park just north of Kaohsiung, Taiwan.

Personal History

I was born in Tainan city and I grew up there. My elementary school, junior high school, and high school education was all in Tainan. I pursued my Bachelor of Science (geology) at National Taiwan University in Taipei. I served my obligatory military service as an artillery lieutenant. After my two years of military service, I attended graduate school at National Taiwan University, again majoring in geology.

My first job was with the TAIYO YUDEN Company, Taipei. This is a Japanese company manufacturing capacitors in Taiwan. I started working in the computer room. Soon, I was promoted to computer room supervisor, then MIS computer section unit leader and eventually, I became deputy manager of the MIS computer section. During my four years, I took part in developing systems for sales & human resources.

From 1988 to 1997 I worked in Chi Mei Corporation (CMC). Initially, I was a computer room supervisor. I was involved in establishing a fiber optics network for each of our factories. In 1993 I was promoted to deputy section manager. During the 10 years that I worked at CMC, the company grew quickly. In the beginning, most of the customers had offices in Taiwan. As the business grew, many overseas customers approached CMC to purchase our chemical products. At this time, our company became export oriented. I was then responsible for developing an order management system. This process was made difficult because as the revenue grew by a factor of 10, we did not recruit in many areas of the company, including the Dept. of Information Systems. Starting in 1995 I played a major role in a large project at CMC. We decided to replace our old ERP system.

In 1998, I transferred to Chi Mei Optoelectronics (CMO) when it was formed. Initially I was MIS deputy manager, then MIS manager. Currently, as stated above, I am the deputy director of the Information Technology Division.

Company History

Both Chi Mei Corporation (CMC) and Chi Mei Optoelectronics (CMO) are part of the Chi Mei Group. The Group is a conglomerate of many companies mainly in the manufacture of digital application products. While we work towards producing many different high quality products our business philosophy is best represented by a quote from our founder, W. L. Shi. It goes as follows:

There will probably be no Chi Mei business enterprises after 500 years, but the Chi Mei Hospital and Chi Mei Museum will remain forever.

As you can tell, we are a philanthropically oriented organization. We are famous for our unique management style and corporate culture.

CMO is headquartered at the Tainan Science-based Industrial Park about a one hour drive south of Kaohsiung, Taiwan. We are the world leader in our field. We produce thin film transistor liquid crystal display (TFT-LCD) products which are major components for computer notebook panels, desktop monitors, and large screen televisions.

As we state on our Web page:

The evolution of digital technology has given birth to new digital application products that have made life more convenient and more enjoyable for people all over the world. All digital products require a display interface of some kind in order to show their content; as a result, display interface technology has become a major focus of attention within the IT and electronics sector, with several different technologies vying for dominance. Companies have allocated substantial resources to develop new technologies and applications, working to give humanity as a whole a higher level of visual enjoyment.

We have many very large manufacturing complexes in the Tainan science park. In the near future we will invest a significant amount of money to build next generation plants to meet customer demand. We also want to play a leading role in the further expansion of the science park by establishing and supporting a number of TFT-LCD related companies. We feel that the promotion of local sourcing plants will greatly improve the overall supply chain efficiency.

My Company and Me

When CMO was formed I was working for CMC. I was assigned to work for CMO as the head of the MIS Department. You have to recognize that CMC is an established and traditional company. Everyone at CMC knows the business rules and business processes very well. So, at CMC when a request is made for a service from the MIS department or information technology the users know very well how to describe their requirements. However, CMO is a relatively new business having been formed in 1998. Many of the employees came from other companies, some from different kinds of companies. So, the challenge was to be able to have the users describe their requirements. This was difficult because of the variety of backgrounds of the users. Also, because we were a new company we did not have established procedures.

Also, early on we decided to install an ERP system. This was the first major system installed at CMO. We chose Oracle and we follow the Oracle operation standards as much as possible. Our decision to adopt Oracle was mainly based upon our understanding that it was more flexible than the other alternatives. We had to persuade our users to follow the vendor procedures outlined by Oracle. Following these procedures has made it easier for the users to describe their requirements and then for us to respond with the appropriate customization and modification. One of the areas that required our attention related to a unique aspect of our situation here in Taiwan. Our tax regulations are different than other countries. This required us to do some customization of our Oracle system. This modification works well for us.

My Typical Week

All IT department managers have to attend a weekly meeting every Tuesday. In this meeting department heads will report what they have done and what issues they have encountered. Other IT department heads will try to offer suggestions about dealing with various issues. For those issues which can not be resolved during this IT meeting, a separate special meeting will be held with the appropriate users in order to deal with the issue. For some special projects, a weekly project review meeting will be held to discuss the project status.

Dealing with Users

We employ two approaches to determine and collect user requirements. One approach is through interviews. The major purpose of these interviews is to collect information about each department's plan for the next year. Right now we are interviewing our finance people and our production people about what they want to do next year. We are especially interested in identifying any plans that will affect my IT department. This approach is used mainly for long range planning.

For smaller requests we have an established requirement management system. These requirements are documented and submitted to my department. We respond by assigning someone from my department to resolve the request. This is like a computerized help desk. Another aspect of our requirement management system is the ability of our users to document their satisfaction with our service. So using this system our users can make a request and then provide us with feedback about how we responded to that request. I am very pleased that our users are very satisfied with our response and service.

Deciding on Technology Investments

All of our technology investment decisions follow the same path. First, we will sit with the users to discuss their requirements. We try to ensure that the users can describe their requirements and that we understand what they want. From there we forward the information to our IT committee. This formal committee will review the technology requirements across the entire organization and set priorities. The final priority and budget is set by this IT committee. Members of this committee come from our user community as well as some of our IT managers.

Current Issues

Now, we are addressing two major issues related to integration and communication.

The integration issue involves our fabrication processes. Remember we manufacture thin film transistor liquid crystal displays. Based upon our customers' needs and the state of the technology, these products may be manufactured differently. Thus, we refer to these different fabrication processes as different generations. So, for example fabrication one is generation 3.5, while fabrication two is generation 4. This just means we are manufacturing different products. But, we must be able to keep track of the differences in the fabrication cycle. We have a number of on-going projects regarding the integration of information from these different processes. The integration will result in providing information at a corporate level for orders, sales, and other financial information.

The second major issue relates to communication. This issue is related to our integration efforts described above. Every manager involved in each of our fabrication processes will have their own view of how to manage their own area. From a management of information perspective we need to convince each manager that a similar reporting process is good not only for them but the overall company. The process of developing a common reporting process is underway. I am confident that we will be successful with this project.

Future Issues

One of the major issues we have to deal with in the future is to ensure that our IT service can respond to our specific business trends. In our business the crystal cycle is about two years. So, every two years a new generation of our product will be produced. We need to be able to support this trend by providing appropriate information to our fabrication managers.

Another related issue we are investigating is the development of a data warehouse. Because of our short crystal cycle we need to provide management with information very quickly. We especially need to provide information to top management within a very short time frame in order for them to react as quickly as possible to any changes in our operating environment. By the end of this year we expect to have a system in place.

There is a final issue that we are not sure what we will have to do. But, we know we will have to respond in some way again to help senior management. We at CMO want to be the world's largest supplier of our product. Right now we are fourth in the world. This objective will require us to significantly increase our sales and consequently our production. Thus, we are looking at expanding into mainland China. We know IT will be involved in this expansion. We are just not sure how.

Final Comments

Currently at CMO we do not have a CIO position. The role of CIO, however, is performed by the IT committee I mentioned above in the technology section of this chapter. Not only does the committee make technology investment decisions, it also discusses and sets the future direction for the use of information technology within the company. Perhaps in the future this process will be delegated to one position. Then we will have a CIO.

When we do implement the CIO position, I do not think it is necessary that we fill the position with an IT person. In fact, I think it is more important that the CIO be more close to the business. We are a very young company and there are a lot of changes taking place. It is very important that all of our company leaders know and understand our business.

Chapter XIII

D. I. Wang
Lite-On Technology Corporation

A world-class excellent company

My name is **D. I. Wang**. I am currently the chief information officer at Lite-On Technology Corporation.

Personal History

I was born and grew up in Tainan, Taiwan. I graduated from a university in Taiwan in 1975 with a bachelor's degree in mathematics. After the 2-year military service, I went to the United States of America for my graduate studies. I attended Northeastern University in Boston and obtained a master's degree in computer science. For my PhD studies, I switched back to applied mathematics. I finished my PhD in 1985 with a concentration on optimization. During my studies at Northeastern, I was a teaching assistant. I did this for 8 years. I realized that I did not want to teach for the rest of my life. So, I returned to Taiwan and found a job in the electronics industry.

In 1986, I joined a defense contracting firm here in Taiwan. I was an associate scientist. My major work was in the area of computer application development, specifically the weapon system development, which was part of a very large scale project. I was able to gain a lot of experience with the project management. Every morning we would have a review meeting at 8 a.m. to discuss the issues that had arisen the day before. We would discuss how we should respond to these issues and what activities were required. This experience eventually helped me when I joined Lite-On Electronics.

I was very interested in changing my career and getting into business. So I left the institute and joined an electronics company as the special assistant to the chairman and the VP of the sales and engineering. The company produced power supply equipment. It was a good company. I worked there for 20 months. In July 1998, I joined Lite-On Electronics as the chief information officer. My first challenge was to implement the ERP system. We were attempting to implement SAP in over 11 sites in five countries, including Taiwan, USA, Hong Kong, Thailand, and China, at the same time. I am very glad that we had a very good partner, Price Waterhouse Coopers, on this project. We had 100 people working full time for 15 months. The implementation went very well and the ERP finally went live successfully. The system has been running very smoothly since then. The experience I had gained in project management really paid off. This project was the largest in scale in Asia Pacific at the time.

Company History

In November 2002, four companies in Lite-On Group merged together to form the new Lite-On Technology Corporation which has product lines of light emitting diodes (LED), power supplies, wireless devices, liquid crystal display (LCD) computer monitor, PDA, and printer. In addition, Lite-On Tech. has a sister company, called Lite-On IT, which produces DVDs.

Lite-On Technology Corporation has a vision to become a world-class excellent company. We will accomplish this goal through our commitment to research and development. We employ excellent manufacturing technologies to produce quality and distinctive integrated digital products. As outlined on our Web site, we have made a commitment to quality, integrity, and innovation.

Quality

Our commitment to quality is strongly supported by our "Golden Triangle of Operational Excellence" strategy: the ability to generate revenue growth, healthy profit margins, and strong cash-liquidity. High quality standards are always at the core of every one of these activities, and our unrelenting dedication to these ideals leads to customer loyalty and satisfaction.

Integrity

Integrity fosters trust. We place great value on creating technologies that incorporate the human touch. Every day, we earn respect of shareholders, customers, and employees as we strive to expand and enhance the value of our company while following best-business practices.

Innovation

We honor and nurture the spirit of innovation while striving to be creative and responsive to customer needs. This in turn helps strengthen our competitive advantage in the global marketplace.

Dealing with Users

We approach "dealing with users" from the perspective that we are the leader and the driver. We are the ones who must facilitate the change. We work with the users if we want to implement a new system for them. We show the users how the new system will help them.

We try to ensure that they understand the functions of the software. We also try to understand their processes and how they manage their internal operations. Together, we will develop a business case which thoroughly documents their requirements. This process also includes conducting a gap analysis, identifying what we have and what we would like to have. Before we formally kick off the project, we know exactly what we want and what we can give to the users. We have a thorough understanding of the complete business processes. This will help us to manage their expectations. This process allows us to fully communicate among all layers of the user community, including the CEO, the business unit heads, and the users.

Additionally, we have developed a formal feedback system. We compare the initial business case with the final result of the project. If there is a negative variance, we will take corrective actions until the original target is reached. If there is a positive variance everyone is happy and committed to the continuous improvement process.

Deciding on Technology Investments

There always seems to be a shortage of internal resources. So, we work with hardware and software vendors and also system consultants. We have to leverage these external resources. We treat them as partners and work with them when making our investment decisions. I think the key aspect is creating value. We try to create value for our organization and for our partners.

Current Issues

The current challenge that I am dealing with now is the gap between IT and the users. IT is usually ahead of the users in terms of using the systems and knowing what the system can bring to the operations in the form of benefit. IT has to lead, teach, and coach users on the use of the systems. This engagement period is quite long because users are normally slow to change. It is time consuming for IT to ensure that users realize the benefits. I do think, however, that this is a normal process for any new system to be implemented. We have to determine the requirements of management. Then we have to manage the expectations of the managers. This is very important. We have developed formal processes to help us understand the requirements.

So, IT is the driver in this company. It is IT that is driving the change. The users are reluctant to change. IT must encourage, facilitate, and lead them to change.

Another challenge we are facing is getting the users to set priorities for IT initiatives. Too often they focus on their numbers for revenue and profit. The users do not put the IT projects (actually in most cases the business projects) as a high priority. It is a challenge to convince the users that we need to work together. IT often has to demonstrate the potential benefits in order to solicit users' involvement and dedication. The only way I know to overcome these difficulties is working hard and spending time with the users.

As I said above, Lite-On Technology is the result of the merger of four companies in Lite-On Group. These four companies used different ERP systems—SAP, Oracle, JDE, and TipTop (a local software product). After the merger, SAP was chosen as the platform for the ERP solution. So, the other three ERP systems had to be converted. This challenge was not difficult technically. It was difficult on the business and user side. Because the users had already invested substantial amounts of time and money to implement ERP system, it was difficult to convince them to convert the system into SAP. The users had difficulty seeing the benefits of standardizing the ERP platform. They could not see the difference. We have spent a great effort and finally convinced them that one ERP system can provide a significant benefit at the corporate or group level. This project has been underway for 2 years since the merger. It will continue to be our major focus over the next budget year.

Another major initiative at this time relates to the concept of a "War Room." We have to provide our senior management with the worldwide and most up-to-date information for effective decision making. We have built our business intelligence (BI) system in addition to the decision support systems (on top of the four ERP systems). It is quite unique as no one has done it before in Taiwan. This BI system resides in the war room and is used for our senior management meetings.

Future Issues

Normally, we spend 3 months planning our annual budget. We would like to acquire a package that will help us with our budget planning and subsequent consolidation. We will work with a planning consultant to help us with this system.

We would also like to introduce a supplier relationship management system (SRM). We spend about 80% of our revenue on the purchase of materials. With revenues of about US$6 billion, we would be spending US$4.8 billion on procurement. Therefore, it is extremely important to be able to manage our purchases. We hope the SRM can provide a platform for most procurement processes.

Final Comments

I think the CIO role must be a strategic one. I am required to attend the company profit and loss meetings. I have to understand the business as well as the technology. But, more importantly, the CIO is looked upon by senior management as the driver for business transformation. If there is going to be a change through the use of technology, it is the CIO who must be able to know how this technology can be applied to the business in a beneficial way. So, I must have expertise in both business and IT.

Of course, as the CIO I must lead our department. It is important for us to maintain good communications with the user community.

Finally, I think we should view the CIO role as a strategic partnership with the CEO.

References

Lite-On Technology Corporation (n. d.). Retrieved January 30, 2007, from www.liteon.com

Chapter XIV

M. P. Wang
China Steel

My name is **M. P. Wang**. I am currently the general manager of the Information Systems Department at China Steel.

Personal History

I was born and grew up in Tainan City. Except for my university studies, I have lived in Tainan City all my life. I attended elementary, junior, and high schools in Tainan City. In 1969, I went to Taipei City to attend National Taiwan University. My major was computer science.

When I graduated from university, I served 2 years military service. Then, in 1975, I started working for China Steel and I have worked here all of my working life. Initially, I was an electrical engineer. I was promoted to section manager of our iron making electrical section in the electrical and instrumentation department. Then, I was the assistant general manager of the electrical and instrumentation department. My most recent previous position was as the general manager of our public affairs department.

At China Steel, I have been involved in four expansion projects. In all cases, the projects have been completed on time and within budget.

As the assistant general manager of Y6, the electrical and instrumentation department, I was also responsible for process control computers. I led the department to obtain ISO9001 certification. We were able to accomplish this task very quickly, completing it in just 1 year.

I was then appointed general manager of our Public Affairs Department. In discussing this appointment with the president, I expressed my reservations because of my background and experience. I did tell him, however, that I was very enthusiastic about the appointment. He told me that was good enough for him to appoint me to the position. We have an old saying, "the event broke all the glasses of the experts." What was even more exciting was that in 2000 the ruling party in Taiwan changed. At that time I assisted the newly assigned Chairman of the Board to communicate with the media. I helped him to speak with the media and to conduct TV interviews.

Between July 2000 and May 2004, I was assigned as assistant vice president at Kaohsiung Rapid Transit Corporation (KRTC), a subsidiary company of China Steel responsible for the Kaohsiung subway project. My duties were to supervise the contracting of all the electrical and mechanical systems for the KRTC project. During this time, I supervised the completion of the basic design for all systems. More importantly, I was able to work with the qualified suppliers and generate a 15% savings from budget.

Company History

China Steel is a large integrated steel mill. The company was formed about 30 years ago, on December 3, 1971. At that time, the company adopted the state of the art 100% continuous casting production process which was subsequently computerized. This approach allowed China Steel to gain international competitiveness. We have a 50% market share in the Taiwan steel industry.

Our company Web page outlines our manufacturing processes as follows:

- ***Raw material preparation:*** *Coal, iron ore, and limestone are unloaded to the storage yard first. Coal is then transferred to the coke oven plants to be produced into coke; iron ore and limestone are transferred to the sinter plants to be produced into sinter.*
- ***Iron making:*** *Iron ore, sinter, coke, together with flux are fed into the blast furnaces and they are ignited to produce molten hot metal and slag. Hot metal is then transferred to the basic oxygen furnaces by railway torpedo car.*
- ***Steelmaking:*** *Hot metal and steel scrap are charged into the basic oxygen furnaces to be produced into liquid steel which is mostly transported to the*

refining stations for treatment, and then it is sent to the continuous casters to be produced into slabs or blooms which are semi-finished products.

- ***Rolling:*** *Blooms are fed into the billet mill to be shaped into billets and further processed into bars or wire rod products in the bar or rod mills. Slabs are fed into the plate mill to be shaped into plates or further processed into hot rolled products in the hot strip mills. Hot rolled products can be further processed to produce cold rolled products in the cold roll mills.*

The mission of China Steel is to establish value of our existence as an asset to society and the nation. We want to strengthen the basis of heavy industry and contribute to the development of society and local communities.

China Steel employees also provide another comparative advantage. The employees are competent and innovative. They have participated in the development and diversification of the business. We have many excellent training and development programs.

We are proud of the values we have adopted. Our company Web page provides some valuable comments as follows:

Mr. C. C. Ma, the first chairman of China Steel Corporation, defined the CSC values as teamwork, entrepreneurial approach, innovation, and practicality in the inaugural issue of the "CSC Bimonthly" published on January 28, 1976. While doing so, he laid the cornerstones of CSC's corporate culture. Mr. Ma hoped that CSC employees would apply what these values represent to their day-to-day work and living, so he elaborated them in an article published on January 1, 1981 in the "CSC Bimonthly." Mr. Ma felt that although these values enabled CSC to become a good corporate role model at home and to reap fame abroad, both intrinsic and extrinsic changes in the business environment call for new connotations to these values. Such changes prompted Mr. Ma to exhort CSC employees again with an article in the special edition of the "CSC Bimonthly" to commemorate CSC's twentieth anniversary.

Teamwork means replacing internal rivalries with coordination and cooperation, with a common goal in mind, the corporate objectives. CSC is a mammoth company with complex work processes and sophisticated equipment. What contributed to CSC's success was teamwork, not individual efforts. Mr. Ma strongly felt that CSC had to be an organic whole. So there was special significance when he placed teamwork at the top of the four values. CSC emphasizes the importance of the entrepreneurial approach because the fundamental reason why a company exists is to deliver returns and sustain growth. It does so by observing the basics of entrepreneurship; namely the mobilization of resources to take advantage of opportunities to provide customers with new or continuously improving products and services. In 1977, prior to becoming state-owned, CSC succeeded in its vigorous efforts to secure from the government the relaxation of a number of the restrictions that hamstring state-owned companies. As a result, CSC became a unique state-owned company in that it was able to operate like an ordinary business during its 18 years (1977-1995) under state ownership, years that covered the most crucial period of its development. In other words, in spite of state ownership, its decision-making process and day-to-day operations largely followed the practices of entrepreneurial approach instead of counterproductive, and sometimes even detrimental, bureaucratic practices. The shedding of its status as a state-owned business in 1995 has given it greater room for independent decisions. More than ever, it is aware of its responsibility to provide superior products and services to its customers, and to make contributions to both the neighboring communities and society. To its employees it provides an environment to grow professionally and intellectually, and to its shareholders satisfying returns on their investments.

Being innovative keeps a company abreast of the latest development of an industry. A company should never be contented with its past laurels. Instead, it should have the courage to innovate. The courage to try something new should be valued, and mistakes should be forgiven so long as they are not deliberate or illegally motivated. CSC has always placed extra focus on research and development. Only by offering innovative products and services to customers can a company survive the competition in the marketplace.

Practicality means the state of being sensible and realistic. It is also the characteristic that CSC employees proudly possess. They live in a world of real situations and events rather than theories. They make sensible decisions to deal effectively with the problems at hand.

One aspect which I really like about China Steel is the corporate culture. All of our employees follow the cornerstone of our corporate culture as outlined above by former Chairman Ma. China Steel is a very good company for its employees. The average age of our employees is over 47 years. Our employees stay with the company for a very long time. Their effort in working toward a common goal is incredible.

My Company and Me

I accepted the position of general manager, Information Systems Department because it represented another interesting challenge for me. We do not have a specific position with the title of chief information officer (CIO). But, we have decided for the purposes of this chapter, I perform the role of CIO for China Steel. My scope is mainly to deal with ERP.

When I first started working in this current position, there was one major issue that required my attention. I had heard from a number of sources that users were not satisfied with the service provided by my department. It was my impression that this was our attitude of communication rather than a reflection of the performance of my department. My people had been working very hard. So, I visited all of our major user departments. I visited 15 departments overall. I sat with the department manager and the engineer in charge and had a detailed conversation. Based upon my experience in the public affairs department, I think that face-to-face communication can be very helpful. I asked them about their complaints, their requirements, and their plans. I think they felt better just because I was showing an interest in their problems. Then, we developed a short term and a long term strategy for each individual department. I also implemented a help desk so that my department could respond to their problems immediately. We are now in the process of documenting calls to the help desk so that we can analyze the data to identify the types of problems we have to deal with. We realize we have to provide a good service. But we also have to find out what that service should be. The help desk data will help us plan for our services. So, in order to have the spirit of good service, we must develop a plan which hopefully will satisfy all users.

So, I think the attitude of the users has changed regarding my department. Every time an issue arises I go there first. It is important that I show interest in the user's issues and that my department can react quickly to show immediate improvement in the situation. Thus, the users have become more positive about my department because we are more proactive in dealing with their issues.

My Typical Week

I spend a lot of my time attending meetings. At my weekly managers meeting, we share information, review work progress, and discuss any issues my managers think are important. This meeting usually takes about 1½ hours. Those in attendance include me as the chair, my assistant general manager, the three section managers, and two department staff.

I also attend different monthly, bimonthly, quarterly, half-yearly or yearly meetings. There is a long list of subjects that we discuss at these meetings, including the following:

- Software quality
- Internal communications
- Half year planning

- Procedure review
- Department target review
- Human resources development
- Customer relationship innovation
- Knowledge management
- ISO 9001 review
- ISO 14001 review
- OHSAS 18000 review

As you can see, I have many meetings to attend. Some of them are related to the management of our department and some are related to that of the company. Individual review or group discussion on certain jobs are also major activities.

I also try to find time to keep up to date with what is happening in the field of information technology. I read IT-related reports and papers, and try to gather industry information. Sometimes, I attend some training programs or seminars related to either IT or management issues.

Dealing with Users

In the past, we would develop an IT budget for the entire company and share that with the user departments. I have changed this process. Now we ask the users to develop their own IT budgets. Of course, we help them to develop their own budgets. This way the user knows the costs of IT and they become very aware that changes will also cost money. I think now the planning process is much more thorough than it was in the past.

Every half year, we ask our users to develop a plan for their requirements for the use of ERP. These plans provide us with information about what support will be necessary for that following half year. We just finished developing the requirement summaries for the first half of 2005. We have six teams involved in developing our application software requirements. With these plans the engineer in charge, along with the user, will finalize the scope, how big the each project will be, and how to resolve the project to the satisfaction of the user.

At the beginning of each project, we work with the user employing a fixed format to document each request. We also have a set of procedures that we follow. Each project requires the user's signature agreeing to the above process. We realize there will be change. But, we would like to work with the users to minimize any changes. We try to point out that each change will cost money.

For scheduling to work on the identified plans I have asked my staff to allocate only 80% percent of their available time. Then, if some urgent requests arise we may have available time to respond. For example, this month the company wants to pay an extra bonus to every employee. So, we have to adjust the payroll system. We are able to do this because of the unscheduled available time.

If the users ask for more services than we can provide, we have a process to deal with that. Through our department they may arrange to contract outside services. We will help them to negotiate prices and sign the contract.

We mainly develop our application software by ourselves. However, we sometimes will outsource some development. We may outsource noncritical systems. For example, we hold an annual shareholders' meeting. We have a system to manage the meeting process. The system helps us to register attendees upon their arrival and to count the votes for the election of board members. We also have systems to manage employee medical records and another one for our company library. We consider these systems to be noncritical and we outsource their development and maintenance. Also, we may outsource a project because we do not have the required domain knowledge. So, we will hire a consultant who knows more about the project than we do.

We have two approaches to ensure we have responded appropriately to our users. First, we focus on communication throughout the entire process. Our engineers work very closely with the designated user. We try to ensure we are working with the right person. We want to work with only one person and in one department. In the past, when we work with more than one department the process becomes difficult because each user may have a different opinion about the system. We actually have a joke about this. When two departments have a war about a system the battleground is our department!

The other approach to determining our user satisfaction is through a survey that we ask the users to complete after the system has been installed. We are receiving some valuable comments from our users about our approach to projects.

I would like to see an independent unit established within the company to evaluate the request for services. In some cases, we should not be responding to a user's request because it will not be a benefit to the company. So, we need a unit to show the user that their request should not be processed. For the time being, I am performing this task.

Deciding on Technology Investments

We have an established procedure for making decisions about investments in technology. First, we ask several suppliers about a suitable solution. Then, we finalize the required specifications for the proposed system. These specifications are then sent to our purchasing department, who will contact potential suppliers. The purchasing department will forward the supplier responses to us. We will compare the responses using evaluation criteria developed with the users. Once we make the decision we will forward the information to our purchasing department for them to proceed with the appropriate supplier.

Current Issues

I am currently working at addressing three major issues. They are promoting business intelligence, establishing a wireless network, and analyzing the potential use of radio frequency identification (RFID).

The first issue, promoting the use of business intelligence, will allow managers to analyze vast amounts of data in a simple and easy way. Because business intelligence may mean different things to different managers, we are encouraging the department managers to identify their needs. We are also looking a various data mining techniques which could support the business intelligence effort. I am working very closely with the managers on this issue. Now, we have 10 departments which have volunteered for training and to set up example cases. As we get fruitful results from these participating departments, we hope to inspire all of management to become involved with the business intelligence initiative.

The second issue relates to establishing a wireless network. Some of the work we do in the plant requires the ability to be mobile. We also want wireless capabilities in our press room. But, these are the only two areas where we need wireless capability. The rest of our facilities can use wire connections because there is no need for the computers to move around. With the wireless network we are looking at how we establish and maintain security.

The third issue I am currently working on is RFID. Our plant is now producing beyond the original design capacity. The plant was design to produce 8 million tons per year. But, we are now producing 11 million tons. We have many trucks coming and going. Our facility is very congested. So, with RFID we will be able to keep track of the distribution of products. We will have our trucks equipped with RFID. This will facilitate gate control of trucks arriving and leaving our facility. The RFID has not been used on the product but on the trucks for tracking purposes. One of the problems we are addressing now is the interference of the steel products in the RFID transmission.

Future Issues

As far as future issues go, I anticipate having to address the implementation of CMMI, the possibility of moving our systems from the mainframe to servers, and resolving a unique Taiwan year reference problem.

The first issue, implementing CMMI, will help us develop a standard management approach to using information technology at China Steel. CMMI is the Capability Maturity Model Integration developed by the Software Engineering Institute at Carnegie Mellon University. The government of Taiwan has promoted CMMI for our software industry. The government would like a certain number of software companies to be appraised by 2007. Also, the government has committed to having government IT departments appraised by 2008. So, we at China Steel feel that we should support this government initiative. As a leading company in Taiwan, we will proceed to obtain CMMI appraisal. Our goal is to reach CMMI level 2 in an appraisal by 2006. We plan to engage a consultant who has experience in this approach.

One aspect of my past experience will help us implement CMMI. When I was the assistant general manager of another department, we introduced ISO 9001. I was in charge of the project and we completed the implementation within 1 year without employing any consultants. I appreciate the ISO system because I think it is a learning structure. I also think the CMMI is similar.

The second issue involves moving our systems from the mainframe platform to servers. This is a very interesting issue because there is always an argument about which is the better way to go. While the mainframe is a very stable environment it is very expensive. There is more competition in the server market because there are more suppliers. So, we will investigate moving our systems. But we will be cautious about which systems we move and how quickly we make the moves.

The third issue is unique to Taiwan. This issue is similar to the Y2K problem a few years ago. Well, in 1912, the Republic of China (ROC) started referring to that year as year one. So, by 2011, there will be our version of Y2K because we referred to the ROC year using two digits. Our effort will focus on the legacy systems for administration. We do not anticipate having many problems with the process control systems.

Final Comments

I do not think the title of CIO has been employed very much here in Taiwan. I do think that senior management needs to know more about information technology. If they know more they will be able to ask the IT department to provide more support for them. This would be very good for the company. I plan to promote the concept of a "war room." This will facilitate senior management coming together to plan a strategy not only for the company, in general, but how information technology can support the goals of the company. For instance, we could have information presented in the war room that would determine our production requirements based upon a prediction for steel products and in reference to our pricing policy for the near future.

Finally, we are supposed to provide a technology service for our users. If the users can tell me clearly what they want, then I will be able to provide the necessary level and quality of service. So, it all comes down to communication.

References

China Steel (n. d.). Retrieved January 30, 2007, from www.csc.com.tw

Section IV

United States of America

This section includes discussions with CIOs from the United States of America. Overall, the country has a wealth of resources and a well-developed knowledge economy. The population of the United States of America, as of 2004, was 293 million (Turner, 2005). However, in this book, the CIOs who participated reside and work in the Columbus, Ohio, area. The population of Columbus is just over 700,000, which serve a market area of over one million in Franklin County. The main industries in this area are retail, finance, and health services.

The individuals who were interviewed represent companies in the area in and around Columbus, Ohio. This geographic location is generally referred to as the "Mid-West." The following CIOs agreed to participate:

- Jonathan Dove, chief information officer, Worthington Industries
    - Jonathan was born in Pasadena, California. When he was eight, his family moved to a farm just outside of Pocahontas, Missouri, where he grew up. He has a bachelors in computer science from Coe College in Cedar Rapids, Iowa. He joined Worthington Industries in 1998.
    - Formed in 1955, Worthington Industries is a diversified custom metal processing company and manufacturer of metal related products.

- Gary Houk, vice president of Corporate Information Technology and Business Integration, Online Computer Library Center (OCLC)
  - Gary was born in Akron, Ohio. He lived in many different places growing up. He has a Bachelors in computer science and an MBA both, from Ohio State University. He joined OCLC in 1974.
  - OCLC was established in 1970 as a nonprofit member-run organization using computers to improve library productivity by creating and maintaining a shared catalogue database. OCLC also owns and maintains the Dewey Decimal Classification System.
- Marty Luffy, chief information officer, Installed Building Products
  - Marty was born and grew up in Pittsburgh, Pennsylvania. He has a Bachelor of Science in industrial management from Purdue University and an MBA from the University of Dayton. Marty is also a Certified Public Accountant.
  - Formed in 1991, Installed Building Products provides commercial and residential construction services such as insulation, waterproofing, gutters, shower doors, shelving, and mirrors.
- Angelo Mazzocco, vice president and chief information officer, The Dispatch Companies
  - Angelo was born and raised in New Castle, Pennsylvania. He has a Bachelor of Science in mathematics and computer science from Indiana University of Pennsylvania, and an MBA in marketing and information systems from the University of Dayton. He joined the Dispatch Companies in 1998.
  - In 1871, the Columbus Dispatch began printing and selling a daily newspaper. The company currently comprises 14 different entities in television, radio, newspaper, real estate, aviation, magazine, direct marketing, and professional sports.
- Cindy Sheets, senior vice president and chief information officer, Mount Carmel Health System
  - Cindy was born and grew up in Columbus, Ohio. She has a bachelor's degree in medical technology from Ohio State University and an MBA from the University of Dayton. She joined Mount Carmel Health System in 1989.
  - Mount Carmel was formed over 120 years ago by the Sisters of the Holy Cross. Today, it is a leading provider of general health care services in Ohio.

Table 1.

CIO Name	Company Name	City	Number of Employees	Sector
Jonathan Dove	Worthington Industries	Columbus	8,000	Manufacturing
Gary Houk	OCLC	Dublin	1,300	Library
Marty Luffy	Installed Building Products	Columbus	500 – 1,500 Seasonal	Manufacturing
Angello Mazzocco	Dispatch	Columbus	2,200	Communications
Cindy Sheets	Mount Carmel	Columbus	8,500	Health Services
Kathleen Starkoff	Limited Brands	Columbus	110,000	Retail
John Zarb	Libbey	Toledo	3,500	Manufacturing

- Kathleen Starkoff, chief technology officer and group vice president, Limited Brands
  - Kathleen was born and grew up in Port Clinton, Ohio. She has a Bachelor of Science in mathematics with minors in chemistry and business from Kent State University, and an MBA from Case Western Reserve with a major in policy. She joined Limited Brands in the late 1990s.
  - Formed in 1963, Limited Brands has over 3,800 retail stores carrying six retail fashion brands, including apparel and fragrance.
- John Zarb, chief information officer, Libbey
  - John was born and grew up in Highland Park near Detroit, Michigan. He has a bachelor's degree from Eastern Michigan University and an MBA from Michigan State University. He joined Libbey in 1996.
  - Libbey is the leading producer of glass tableware in North America. Formed over 185 years ago, the company produces glass tableware, ceramic dinnerware, metal flatware, and various plastic utensils.

References

Turner, B. (Ed.). (2005). *The statesman's yearbook: The political, culture and economies of the world.* New York: Palgrave Macmillan.

Chapter XV

Jonathan Dove
Worthington Industries

We treat our customers, employees, investors, and suppliers as we would like to be treated.

My name is **Jonathan Dove**. My most recent experience as a chief information officer was as Worthington Industries first CIO. I am also involved in volunteer work in the community. I am currently the president of the board of directors for Easter Seals of Central Ohio. Also, every year I participate in the Central Ohio CIO symposium. Along with Kay Nelson of Ohio State University and Angelo Mazzocco of The Dispatch Companies, we formed the CIO Symposium. I am the program chair this year. They are a great group of people. We learn a lot from each other.

Personal History

I was born in Pasadena, California.

Between the ages of five and eight, I was a child actor in Hollywood. I worked on television in My Three Sons and Mannix. I did commercials for Kool-Aid and Milky Way. I was also in a made for TV movie, "Wake Me When the War is Over." Even though I was very young, I think this experience has helped me to be comfortable speaking in front of people. I have always enjoyed being in front of a group of people.

When I was eight years old, we moved to a small farm in Missouri near a small town called Pocahontas. In my senior year of high school, I won a Rotary scholarship to be an exchange student in Denmark. This was an incredible experience and really opened my eyes up to different cultures.

When I returned from my exchange year in Denmark, I entered Coe College in Cedar Rapids, Iowa, in their premedicine program. In my junior year, I did a 1 month internship with a cardiologist. That 1 month experience made me realize I did not want to be a doctor.

I had been taking some computer science courses along with my medical courses. I had enjoyed the programming and had done well in the courses. So, I switched my degree to computer science.

When I graduated in 1985, my first job was with EDS at the Clark Street Cadillac plant in Detroit, Michigan. EDS has a very good training program and I was able to complete their systems engineering development program. I worked on the General Motors account in Detroit for 3 years. Then EDS assigned me to Portland, Oregon, to work for Bonneville Power for about 1½ years. I got my first taste of project management on the Bonneville Power account. Then, I was assigned to a General Motors account in Minneapolis, Minnesota, to help them build a regional support center. After 3½ years in Minnesota, I was assigned to manage an MCI account team in Colorado Springs, Colorado. We developed and managed a customer support system for trouble management. On all of these contracts, I was primarily a developer, getting the opportunity to develop into a leader.

Then, still with EDS, I transferred to Kansas City, Kansas, to manage on the Sprint account. While on the Sprint account, Sprint PCS was formed as part of a joint venture between Sprint and three cable providers. EDS had the contract to design the business processes, functionality, and organizational structure for this new business. I was given the opportunity to be the program director for this project. The project also included assisting Sprint build their call center and establishing a Program Office to manage all their projects, including the build out of their Wireless network. It was an enormous undertaking.

At the conclusion of this project, I was offered a senior vice president position at Alltel to help them build a professional services practice within one of their subsidiaries called Alltel Information Services. This company provides financial services systems mainly around banking and residential mortgages to the banking industry. I was in charge of the Strategic Technology Services Group in Little Rock, Arkansas. We specialized in project management, web system development, package implementations, and account support for our customers. This was a great opportunity for me to learn how to design and build my own consulting practice.

As it happened, Mr. John P. McConnell, CEO of Worthington Industries, was on the board of directors for Alltel. He had asked Alltel for help with his IT department. Through a series of phone calls, I was asked to offer assistance. At that time

Worthington Industries had six different entities. I assisted the various Worthington Industries IT organizations in developing an assessment and recommendation based upon the CMM maturity model. When I completed the assessment, I presented it to the executives of Worthington Industries and the directors of their IT organizations. From this assessment we set up a program to implement the recommended changes.

One of the recommendations regarding a new version of the organization structure involved the establishment of a chief information officer position. After working with Worthington for over a year by then, it was not hard to agree to become their first CIO in 1998.

Company History

The Worthington Industries group of companies is headquartered in Columbus, Ohio. It is a diversified metal processing company. Over 8,000 employees work in 63 facilities in 10 countries. Here is a brief history as reported on our Web site:

In 1955, John, H. McConnell, a young steel salesman, saw an opportunity in the market for custom processed steel. He purchased his first load of steel using his car as collateral and founded Worthington Industries. A company that later would be hailed for its financial success, business philosophy and employee relations, Worthington Industries has grown to become the country's leading intermediate steel processor and manufacturer of metal related products ... .

Mr. McConnell's business philosophy, which has been studied at Harvard University, led to Worthington Industries being named one of the top 100 Companies to Work For in America. At the core of the Philosophy is the company's Golden Rule: We treat our customers, employees, investors, and suppliers as we would like to be treated. The company's headquarters, located just north of Columbus, includes an onsite health and wellness center with three full-time physicians, pharmacy, barbershop, and other innovative employee benefits. In 1996, Mr. McConnell handed the leadership of the company over to his son, John P. McConnell, who now serves as the chairman and CEO.

My Company and Me

The reason I accepted the offer to join Worthington Industries as CIO was that I felt it was time to start practicing what I had been preaching, as a consultant, for so many years. I remember being asked after I presented my recommendations for their IT organizations,

"What can we expect three to five years from now if we implement all the things you say we need? We put in these program structures, standards, quality initiatives; we centralize what you recommend; what can we expect in three to five years? Should we expect that our IT costs will be reduced by fifteen percent? Do we expect that we should have a much better level of quality?"

I gave them an honest answer, "I do not know." I had only built and implemented solutions. I had never stayed around and managed them. It made me realize, "I had never eaten my own dog food!" I had preached for 10 years about how you should do things and I had implemented several different organizations successfully, but, I had never had to live with what I had implemented.

I think this move was a step forward from a career and professional perspective. In December of 1998, when I started at Worthington Industries, Mr. McConnell told me two things. First, "don't spend any money that absolutely does not have to be spent." Second, "Always spend just what you tell me you will" (aka. bring the projects in on time). Because each of the six businesses had their own IT departments, it was necessary to establish operating standards across Worthington Industries to ensure a high quality and level of service.

My first specific task was to address the Y2K program. We had about 85,000 items that had to be tested and remediated by October 1, 1999. By the way, this had to be done across our entire world wide operation, which at that time consisted of 57 facilities. Here again I was involved in another exciting 11 month project!

Initially, I removed the incumbent consulting company because of a lack of performance. Then, I established a program management office (PMO) and brought in two new consulting companies. I developed a new structure and method more appropriate to the organization. We got smarter as we went along. We had a very good mediation process. We accomplished the program significantly under budget. We spent about 60% of the original budget. But it was a difficult task. The common view of Y2K expenditures was that it was wasted money.

With the Y2K program underway, I then focused on the structure of the organization. I reviewed our existing policies, procedures, and standards to see where we could start, providing what I thought were value added services. I restructured our agreements with vendors and reduced the number we were working with. With the group of IT Directors, we identified the core competencies that our IT organization needed. If we did not need a specific competency we got rid of it. If we identified a competency that we needed but did not have we filled it. Then we established an organization to support this revised structure, including identifying specific leaders for each competency. We have centralized all of our telecommunications, including long distance, wide area networks, and cell phones. We consolidated all these services under one team and one set of contracts. We have also consolidated all the network technology such as switches, routers, and hubs. Now it is managed by one group.

Another interesting project was the implementation of an Oracle ERP system. We installed their e-business suite of financials, purchasing, and payroll and benefits in human resources. We took a very aggressive time line and implemented these systems along with major changes in functionality within 9 months. As a result of this project, we were required to standardize our security, infrastructure, web architecture, and wide area network solutions.

Implementing Oracle from a technology perspective was relatively straightforward. The difficulty came with implementing new business processes across three business units. Actually, we had very good cooperation from the business units. The difficulty came in deciding what the standard processes would be and then implementing these revised processes. We established a steering committee composed of representatives from each functional area. They were all very willing to work at changing their business model for the good of the organization. I think they were committed to this change because of the pain they were experiencing with their legacy systems. We had cross-functional teams working together. This project experience was a tremendous growth for me in understanding how to get business and technical teams to work closely together in one common vision, especially when significant change is involved.

There are two things that I find interesting about this position that I enjoy the most. First, we are a steel processor. We do not really leverage technology for strategic advantage in the marketplace like financial, insurance, or telecommunications companies. So there was a tremendous effort to only implement technology that truly added value to the business or protected our information. Second, I found it challenging to create an environment for the IT organization that allowed the IT team to believe they could have a technical career in a company like ours. It seems to be more difficult to create continual technical growth for IT employees in a company that does not leverage technology as a strategic advantage.

My Typical Week

A typical week, like most executive positions, is filled with meetings. I had Matthew shadow me one day and he told me, "Dad, all you do is go to meetings!" Most weeks start with executive meetings, followed by team meetings to cascade information and decisions. Then there is the various project meetings and individual employee meetings to discuss issues and drive decisions. The mix throughout the remainder of the week is meetings with various business teams to discuss needs to support their organizations. When I decided to take on this executive role, I made the decision to lead, not do. Everything from managing by "walking around" to selling the value of our solutions to the business teams. I guess it is fortunate I like people, because you deal with a lot of them during the course of a week.

Dealing with Users

Managing the expectations of a user is probably one of the most challenging aspects of being a CIO. As users become more and more technically aware, they become more demanding of their expectations of what an IT solution should provide. To help with this challenge, we hold facilitative sessions to attempt to understand the users' business needs. We look at the decisions they make and what information they need to make those decisions. We really have to try to learn their business. Then, we can help them understand how we can use technology to manage that information for their business needs.

We also have quarterly project "road maps" for all the business presidents and all the support vice presidents. This document identifies all the projects a business unit has identified to accomplish, the value to their organization, and the estimated cost to complete. It is a running 3-year time frame. So, every quarter we look out for 3 years and decide if projects should be initiated or postponed. It is not an authority to proceed with the project. It is just a plan. I consolidate all these plans up to the organization level and add in things like technology infrastructure to support these plans.

One of the IT core competencies I established during our IT restructuring was business information management. The business analysts in this unit work with the users on a daily basis. They are responsible to learn the business and how the users do their job. This helps the users feel more comfortable that we truly understand their business and needs.

We also use what we call a delivery framework methodology. Each individual project starts officially with a project charter. This is an official document that specifies the work to be done, the scope, how the project will be managed, and the cost. It is signed at the vice presidential level for the requesting business unit. The business analysts write the business requirements with the users. They participate in the business design and approve the business design before we develop the technical solution.

We are very interested in ensuring we have delivered what the users really wanted. This has to be accomplished in multiple ways. First, we have to have the business intimately involved in the design. We do this through the business analyst. Second, we get the users to validate their needs through a walkthrough of the technical solution. This can be done through a review of the information flows of the solution or by developing a prototype of the technical solution for them to use. Finally, and most importantly, we must manage their perceptions. What I mean is, we have to developed a trust relationship with the users and see how they are using the solution over an initial period of time. Based upon our observations, we may or may not make modifications, but they see that we continue to stay involved and ensure what we develop provides them the needed value they desire.

Finally, we established a single point of help, help desk, for more immediate type problems. We made sure that if a user had any problem they had one number to call and someone would help them solve their problems. We attempt to solve the problem on the first call.

Deciding on Technology Investments

Technology has a simple answer…it is used to automate and protect the integrity of your information. Technology decisions, for the purpose of technology, are usually a bad starting point. Technology decisions must have a business need or a risk mitigation purpose.

Technology solutions can be implemented to protect or secure your information. These projects can be in the form of security, infrastructure, or disaster recovery solutions. Deciding on these technology investments is a risk mitigation approach. What is the level of technology investment necessary to protect our IT infrastructure and information versus the cost of losing it? In several cases, we looked at the cost to the organization to be down without their systems. If Worthington Industries cannot ship steel, how much does it cost the company an hour? If the answer is $1M versus $100K, then you need to provide better recovery plans to ensure you are not down for a long period of time. The same type of decisions can be made for security or your network infrastructure.

For business needs, it is best to look at the return of investment. This is not always measurable by dollars and cents. Sometimes it is measured by customer satisfaction or organization efficiencies. These seldom have a direct measurable dollar associated to them. For these decisions, you develop a business plan that specifically defines the scope and cost of a project, including business costs, and determines the business benefit to the organization. As part of the technical design for the project, you establish the most effective use of technology to solve the business need and organizations capability. It is important not to take the organization too fast up the technology curve, because they will not have the ability to adapt the changes in the business with a large technology growth curve. Always move at the pace of the technology ability of the business teams.

At the end of the day, always remember the number one rule in technology decisions, "Only implement what the organization needs!" Anything else could be a quick path to the bread line.

Current Issues

One of our big projects now is the implementation of the second phase of our Oracle ERP application into Worthington Steel. This phase includes order management, customer service, and plant floor operations. It will allow us to provide better service overall to our customers and more on-time deliveries. This project will be a tremendous change management issue for Worthington Steel. Most plants within the company operated on their own process and procedures. For this project to be successful, you have to have the largest population of Worthington employees operate with the same procedures across the organization. This will be no small task.

Another important ongoing issue is the development of our response to Sarbanes-Oxley. We successfully implemented all necessary policies and procedures to be SOX 404 compliant. The continual challenge is to track, measure, and ensure continual compliance going forward.

Finally, there is the continued consolidation of business efficiencies. With four separate, yet similar companies, Worthington Industries faces the challenges of most large companies; "How and where can we leverage efficiencies to create greater shareholder return?" These efforts create similar change management challenges as described before, and cannot be easily solved overnight.

Future Issues

When I first started at Worthington Industries I was able to provide Mr. McConnell with my vision. I believe my job here at Worthington Industries is to own the company's information. I want to ensure the integrity, the timeliness, and the delivery of that information to the right people to make the right decisions at the right time. That is my goal.

In a July 2001 *Frontlinetoday.com* article, I was quoted as saying, "The biggest difficulty in overseeing a diverse organization like Worthington Industries is the number of different types of technologies that are in place. Worthington has grown by an acquisition strategy and by allowing individual units to build their own businesses. One of the biggest challenges for me is to get the diversity of the technologies to interact with each other."

Along with the Oracle project, we have also established a business intelligence solution, including the development of a data warehouse. We collect data, validate its integrity, and provide business intelligence solutions to the business units. The most critical aspect is the data. Actually, that comment applies to most information systems projects. Getting the data right is so critical.

The word "information" is in the middle of my title. I want a single location for all the information necessary for the organization to do its job at the highest level of integrity. Again, the Oracle ERP system will support this idea. Oracle provides us with the single location for all of our data.

You know the focus of my part of the organization is more on information management than on information technology. So, rather than discussing with users what packages they would like, we discuss what they need to support their business operations. Then I advise an information management solution. If they like it, then we implement it. Our users now recognize the necessity of information integrity and the value of that information to their business.

As I said in a September 17, 2001 *InformationWeek.com* article, "our biggest challenge is trying constantly to improve efficiencies on the operational side of the house."

Final Comments

I think taking on the role of a chief information officer was an incredibly eye opening experience. It puts you in the front line defense of IT, while constantly ensuring you are providing value to an organization. It is too easy to say what could be the right IT solution. However, until you see the results of IT decisions on a business, you truly cannot appreciate the importance of information technology and the role it plays in the business world. Even though I am no longer with Worthington Industries, I can clearly say that my 6 years as their first CIO was a very rewarding challenge. It taught me a lot about the importance of information, the role of IT in the business, the use of technology, and most importantly, myself as a leader. Being raised in IT from a consulting role taught me the "right way to do things," but being an actual CIO taught me the "right things to do" when it comes to IT and business.

References

Worthington Industries (n.d.). Retrieved January 30, 2007, from www.worthingtonindustries.com

Chapter XVI

Gary Houk
Online Computer Library Center

Furthering access to the world's information

My name is **Gary Houk**. I am the vice president of corporate information technology and business integration at the Online Computer Library Center (OCLC).

Personal History

I was born in Akron, Ohio. While I have spent most of my life in Ohio, I lived in a lot of different places growing up. For instance, I graduated high school from Parkway West High School in St. Louis, Missouri. In 1973, I obtained an undergraduate degree in computer science from the Ohio State University. Later, I went back and earned an MBA from Ohio State in 1984.

During my time at university, I had very interesting summer jobs. I started out majoring in mathematics. I really did not know what I was going to do with a major in mathematics. But, I enjoyed it and I was good at it. One summer I spent with my father in Oklahoma City. At the time he was working for a regional trucking company called Leeway Motor Freight. He managed to get me a job as a computer operator. The computer was an IBM 360 with a DOS operating system. I enjoyed this experience. So, upon my return to university, I switched my major to computer science.

Also, while I was attending university I was able to work for a local insurance company. I worked from 6 p.m. to 10 p.m. during the week and 12 hour shifts on the weekends. I was a computer operator on their IBM 360. I ran the longer batch jobs such as printing checks. In addition, on the side, I did some program language conversion. They had a lot of autocoder programs that I converted to COBOL. Remember, these were the days of limited memory and storage. So, we would desk check our code because we would only have one chance per night to compile the program. It certainly is not like that now.

After graduation, I worked for the North Electric Company in Delaware, Ohio. They were in the telecommunications switch business. It was a fun place to work as my first job because I got to work on a lot of different projects. Back then they were just inventing touch tone phones. I remember working with some of the scientists at North. They would give me algorithms to program so the computers could convert electronic signals into specific numeric digits.

About 13 months after I started to work at North they decided to relocate the computing staff to a data center in Galeon, Ohio. This is a very small town famous for Galeon tractors, big road graders. Well, this relocation would have meant moving to Galeon, or a 1 hour commute each way. So, I started looking for another job in Columbus. I soon found a position at OCLC and I have been here now for over 30 years.

Another key element of my career development has been my participation in various community related activities. I have served on the boards of various service organizations, including 1-year stints as president of the local Chamber of Commerce and president of the local Rotary Club. These activities have been rewarding on two fronts. First, they have helped develop my communications and collaboration skills. Second, they have allowed me to give something back to the community in which I work and live. Also, I am now serving on the board of an insurance company which wanted to retain someone with an IT background to diversify the makeup of that board. This has also been a very rewarding experience and one which I believe I learn from as much as I contribute.

Company History

OCLC is a nonprofit membership organization that was originally chartered as the Ohio College Library Center, serving 54 academic institutions in Ohio. Very quickly, by the mid 1970s, we were serving libraries outside of the state of Ohio. In 1977, the governance and name was changed to OCLC, Online Computer Library Center, Inc. We kept the same letters!

Now, we serve over 50,000 libraries in 109 countries. The founder of OCLC, Fred Kilgour, really had this vision of using computers to improve library productivity by creating a shared database rather than everyone working independently. We had a very interesting process for adding entries into our catalogue. If a library created a new entry we would give them credit. Then, everyone would have access to the entry through our system. This process really helped us increase the size of the database. Indeed, on August 11, 2005, the OCLC library community surpassed a major milestone when the Worthington, Ohio Public Library added the 1 billionth holding to the database.

In the late 1980s, OCLC took over responsibility for maintaining the Dewey Decimal Classification System. Most people think this system is in the public domain. But OCLC actually owns it, maintains it, and publishes it in both print and electronic formats. We even have an experimental Dewey browser tool now available which enables you to search and browse collections of library resources organized by the Dewey Decimal Classification (DDC). Try it out at http://deweyresearch.oclc.org/ddcbrowser/ebooks.

Currently, our Web site describes OCLC as follows:

Mission

OCLC exists to further access to the world's information and reduce library costs by offering services for libraries and their users.

Vision

OCLC will be the leading global library cooperative, helping libraries serve people by providing economic access to knowledge through innovation and collaboration

Quality Policy

OCLC will continually improve the processes used to deliver its products and services to achieve the OCLC Vision.

My Company and Me

I started at OCLC as a programmer analyst working on a Xerox Sigma 9. I was involved in two major areas. One area was applications, where we developed and maintained our online cataloguing system. The other area was operating systems.

We developed our own operating system that we called Ohio Bibliographic Monitor (OBM). My early work was to extend the capabilities of OBM so that development staff could test their programs. We also developed an OBM simulator that could run under the standard Xerox operating system, known as Control Program V (CP-V).

Our online system was initiated in 1971 with network speeds of 300 CPS. I realize that is very slow compared to today's standards. As part of that environment we had our own proprietary telecommunications protocol which was built into the terminals we sold to our customers. The terminals, by the way, were manufactured by Beehive. Not only did the terminals have to relate to our communications protocol, but they had to provide our specialized character set. We use the standard American Library Association (ALA) character set. It is an extended version with special characters.

For the first 6 years at OCLC, I was a programmer analyst, a senior programmer analyst, and eventually a section manager for a team of about seven people. In retrospect we seemed to be following the lead programmer model. I was part administrative manager. When I was part lead programmer, I would write some code. The rest of the staff would write some of the other routines.

Eventually, by the 1980s, we had 18 Sigma 9 computers running online. We built our own shared memory devices. Our databases were so large we required multiple computers to provide service to our customers.

Also, at this time Xerox was not building any more Sigma 9 computers. So, we would search out companies who were about to upgrade and we would buy their old Sigma 9 computers for spare parts.

After the first 6 years, I was given the opportunity to manage our Quality Assurance (QA) Department. This was a new area for OCLC. The company was growing and we needed to have a little more control in place on software configuration management and testing. We needed a better management approach to the overall process of moving systems from testing into production. So, for the following 6 years, I was manager of our QA Department. We introduced a formal systems development life cycle. I spent some time moving around the organization. In retrospect it gave me a broader understanding and appreciation for the overall enterprise. I think this movement is important for developing general management skills.

For the next 6 years, I managed our Systems Engineering Division, which included about 20 people. I was involved in vendor management, hardware selection, and the development of middleware. Our hardware included the Sigma 9 and Tandem Non-stop systems. We had our large data base on the Tandem computer. By the early 1990s, we removed use of our Sigma 9 computers. All of our main products and legacy systems were on the Tandem computers. We also started to introduce new products based upon IBM computers.

It was at this time that I was asked to take on the vice president role. I accepted and was assigned an interesting portfolio of business units. One unit related to managing our large private relay network. Another unit was a preservation operation in Bethlehem, Pennsylvania, where we were involved in high quality preservation micro filming and scanning services. The third unit was our contract services group. This is where we would perform cataloguing for libraries under a contract. There were about 200 people in this unit.

Over the years at OCLC, I have moved around in various management positions. But, I have always kept up on the technology side as well. Actually, here we have to be up to date with the technology because it is at the heart of what we do. As a user or sponsor, I met quite often with the IT folk. Because IT was my background, I found it easy to talk with them.

So, now I perform the CIO role for OCLC. Also, note that my title includes the words "business integration." I wanted this in my title in order to emphasize integrating not only what we do here in the main office, but also with the other offices.

When the CEO approached me about becoming the CIO, he was in the process of reorganizing the entire senior management team. The changes he was making were really part of an overall consolidation effort. He asked if I would be willing to run the information technology group. Remember, I had started at OCLC on the technology side. For the past number of years I had worked in the business management side, running some of our business units. I saw this as an opportunity to pursue the CIO path. So, I readily accepted.

The beginning of this assignment was a complicated time at OCLC. We were in the process of trying to align our costs with our revenues. Part of this alignment required that we reduce the size of our work force. So, one of the early challenges was to reduce our head count as well as reducing our corporate overhead and our total cost structure.

In the information technology area I created four functional units. The first group I will refer to as "governance." Here I combined our architecture function with quality assurance. The second group, "systems management," is responsible for managing such aspects as the data center, network, servers, database, and e-mail. They are also responsible for budgeting, capacity planning, and acquisition and implementation of systems. The third group deals with our online OCLC database. Their primary responsibility is World Cat, our primary database. The fourth group is our "enterprise applications" division. They have responsibility for all of our back office applications and data warehouse. Our ERP system is People Soft and our CRM is Siebel. This group also has responsibility for our e-commerce Web site, which is based on IBM WebSphere.

Also, when I became CIO, the major projects that were underway were the implementation of Oracle to replace our legacy database and also the implementation of our e-commerce Web site. Well, in both cases I went from each project's executive sponsor on the business side to the senior executive on the information technology side. I went from asking, "When are you going to have this done?" to "When do you want this done?" I felt comfortable with this change because I knew the systems from a business perspective and because of my earlier technology experience.

My Typical Week

First of all, I have too many meetings, but we are trying to be more effective at business meetings by having an agenda, taking notes, assigning action items, and most importantly, getting them done in less than 1 hour. Time is a valuable resource and I have found if you don't manage it, you end up taking too much work home. Each day I look at the daily production turnover report and see what transpired the day and night before. We have service level agreements for availability and response time of our customer facing systems, so we monitor and report on those daily. Another big time consumer is e-mail. I typically process over 100 e-mails per day. Not very glamorous, but it has become the primary mode of communications within the company.

Once each week, I participate in our strategic leadership team meeting, which is where our entire senior management team gets together and reviews new initiatives, opportunities, threats, and various activities of interest to the entire group.

I have several meetings per week reviewing major projects that are under way. Sometimes, these meetings have been scheduled in advance and other times they are spontaneous. I have an open door policy, so my staff knows they can bring issues to me at anytime.

When not in meetings, I tend to read industry publications in both print and electronic form. Technology moves so fast, it is important to spend 4-8 hours per week keeping up with the latest trends.

Finally, I usually find some time each week to brainstorm new ways we can do things as a company, both from a technology standpoint as well as from a business process standpoint. I start by looking at a specific business process and ask the question of how can we make this more efficient, and then I engage the appropriate staff to look at solutions. It is imperative that technology leaders start with the business process or business architecture before jumping into specific technological solutions.

Dealing with Users

We work with our users in a number of ways. Before we even decide we need to implement a system we engage the users on several levels.

One level relates to understanding the business. Some users will tend to tell us how to do something instead of describing what they need. We try to keep them focused on their requirements. They need to know the problems they are trying to solve and they need to be able to explain them to us. We want them to describe the business process and not a specific solution. So, as I have been known to say, "Tell me what, not how." In the past, we have implemented systems that simply support the current operation. What we should have been doing is investigating how technology could facilitate the improvement of our operations.

Another level exists in relation to customer membership governance. We have an elected members' council of 66 delegates that meets three times per year. We engage them in dialogues about the future. While we mainly discuss issues at the strategic planning level, we will also sometimes get down into some of the "nitty gritty." So, we may talk about current issues, ways to improve current operations, or aspects that are impacting our industry. All of this information is then fed into our development process to identify key objectives for the company.

At yet another level we are employing some of the concepts surrounding rapid development methodologies. Our development team will break a project down into relatively short "time boxes." The team members will sit with an "ambassador" user and develop requirements statements in a prototyping manner. Thus, we will have engaged the user from the very beginning and throughout the process. I think this approach has been successful because we are getting systems installed faster.

We also have a usability lab. We videotape users working with a particular system and then interview them. The data gathered this way helps us to identify aspects of the systems which we could improve upon.

Finally, every 6 months we conduct a customer satisfaction survey. Our marketing and sales group manages the survey of our external customers. We are somewhat more informal in obtaining feedback from our internal customers. But, in both cases, we are able to gain valuable input to possible ideas for improvement.

Deciding on Technology Investments

The actual decision process follows after some initial research. The adoption of a new technology may start in our research group. Someone will get an idea about a particular technology and they will develop a prototype. If it looks promising and we can identify a product idea, then our development staff will become involved and they will prepare a business case for review by senior management.

Eventually the idea, in the form of a project, comes before a finance committee charged with making decisions about proceeding with specific projects.

Current Issues

As I stated above, when I first became the CIO at OCLC we were in a cost cutting mode and we carried out a major reorganization. Now we are in an investment and growth phase.

The month of June this year is an important month for us. We will be implementing two major systems during that time. First, we will finally complete our Oracle implementation. This project has been active for some time. I think too long. But it is an important platform which supports our core business. The other major system is our resource sharing application.

{Well, the implementations went very well. We did both installations as planned. There were some minor problems. But overall we were very satisfied. We have turned a major corner with these two systems.}

Our e-commerce project falls under our key objective to improve the way we deliver products and services. This will allow us to reduce the number of manual touches between us and our distribution partners to process orders for services. It also puts in place a way for libraries to do self service. We are also automating the account management side.

We had a consultant involved in this project from the start who knew more about e-commerce than we did. This was a benefit at the start. However, now I want my staff to be knowledgeable about what we do in this area. So, we are terminating our contract with the consultant. We are pleased with the service from the consultant. We just want to affect a skills transfer in-house. This transfer is more difficult than I thought. We have had to hire someone from India. He was working on the project for our consultant. But, we want him to immigrate and he wants to move here. So, it is a win-win situation.

Another issue we are trying to address is our skill set. We are attempting to ensure that we acquire the necessary skills. This is difficult because our requirements seem to change quickly. Like most companies, our largest cost is labor. So, what we are trying is what I call a "three for two" approach. First, when we have an empty position we do not just fill it. We put it in a pool and try to decide where the position should be placed to best benefit the organization. Then, if we have a number of positions we might look at converting three positions to just two. This might permit us to increase the compensation available and allow us to acquire someone with a more advanced skill set. This approach is working well for my team and is accepted by our financial people. Other parts of the organization are also taking this approach. It is not on a massive scale. But, a few well-placed changes can really do wonders.

We are also making changes to our office automation environment. This involves Microsoft Outlook. We are looking at new ways to use technology to support our staff. Recently, I attended a conference where they gave out a free Blackberry to try for 90 days. After about 2 weeks of trying it, I realized that it might be useful. I had the Blackberry Enterprise server software installed and we integrated it with our e-mail system. Then, I recruited some of our senior managers to participate in a pilot project for a couple of months. I even used it on a trip to Europe and it worked very well. We have slowly expanded its deployment within OCLC to our second tier of senior managers and sales force. They all have reported a significant improvement in productivity. Another recent change is that we are now providing remote access to e-mail using Citrix Web access in combination with RSA Secure ID fobs. This allows us to provide secure access from public terminals through standard web browsers.

Future Issues

One of the issues we will continue to deal with in the future is staffing. We need to be able to have the right skill sets. So, we are doing some training of our current staff and we are trying to hire people who already have the skills we want. Both approaches have issues we must deal with. With training the internal staff there will be some casualties. Unfortunately, some people cannot or are not willing to change. So, when we run into certain situations like this we have to make some difficult decisions. The issue with acquiring skills is that we are competing with everyone else. There does not seem to be an abundant supply. I worry that in the United States we are not attracting enough young people into the IT field. There are some misconceptions among high school students and parents that all the jobs in IT are being outsourced to other countries and it is not a good field. But it is a good field for the same reason it was a good field when I was in high school 40 years ago. IT is everywhere there is a microchip in everything, so an IT graduate can find a job in almost any industry.

We are really trying to take advantage of newer technologies. But, we do not want to upgrade our technology for technology's sake. We really have to make a business case. We are exploring voice over internet protocol (VOIP) right now. We are looking at this technology from a cost reduction perspective as well as adding value to our customer service. After a lengthy analysis, we were finally able to justify this investment and are now in the process of converting to the new system. It was much easier to justify the conversion at home, as I have made the switch to VOIP 2 years ago and I am very satisfied with the quality of service.

I think it is important that, as we try to provide information technology services within our company, we avoid getting locked into a specific supplier or vendor. It is good to invest in technologies. But, I do not want us to become entrenched with a particular vendor. It is a constant struggle to keep the vendor relationship at an arm's length. There is this fine line that exists about having an objective vendor independent solution to a business issue. So, there may be some cost dividends available if we take an open standards or open source perspective.

An issue we have not yet started to deal with for our library services is mobility. People expect to have access to information anywhere and anytime. This expectation is perhaps more obvious with the younger generation. So, when we are designing systems, we have to take into consideration the possibility of providing the services on a mobile device. It is on our list of things to do.

Final Comments

In the Columbus, Ohio, area we have a CIO Forum. Once per month about 30 of us get together for a couple of hours over lunch. We will have a presentation which may be about technology or something else. It is a really good opportunity to interact with colleagues and find out how they may be dealing with certain issues. We really try to help each other out.

The role of the CIO has changed a good deal. I think it will continue to change. A lot of CIOs now have a broad understanding of the business. They are not just technologists. In my case, I worked on the business side for 12 years, interacting with the CFO, the CEO and other vice presidents. This gave me a good understanding of the business. I was involved in developing the business strategy. All of this experience was beneficial when I moved into the CIO role. It has been very helpful to have a broad view of the enterprise and to understand where we are trying to take the company in terms of our strategy.

References

Worthington Industries (n. d.). Retrieved January 30, 2007, from www.worthingtonindustries.com

Chapter XVII

Marty Luffy
Installed Building Products

Together to serve you better,

My name is **Marty Luffy**. I am currently the chief information officer at Installed Building Products.

Personal History

I was born and raised in Pittsburgh, Pennsylvania. I grew up in Pittsburgh and Columbus, Ohio. I attended Purdue University on a Naval Reserve Officers Training Corp (NROTC) scholarship, where I obtained a Bachelor of Science in industrial management (combination engineering and business degree). After several years experience working for Andersen and KPMG, I decided to attend night school at the University of Dayton for my MBA. I am a certified public accountant, and have many other professional certifications, including certified information systems auditor (CISA), certified data processor (CDP), certified systems manager (CSM), and certified production and inventory manager (CPIM).

I have worked for many employers in consulting, hardware, and software, as well as real estate businesses. These companies have included Andersen Consulting, KPMG Peat Marwick, Strategic Technology Integrators, Tandem Computers, Synon Software, Sterling Software, Exodus Communications/Cable and Wireless, and my current company, Installed Building Products. In these organizations, I have held various positions, from staff consultant to regional vice president to chief information officer.

I was at Andersen for approximately 5 years as staff and senior consultant. My responsibilities while at Andersen were mainly centered on systems development projects in exotic places like Plainfield, New Jersey, and Parkersburg, West Virginia. While at Andersen Consulting, I initially worked as a developer in the assembly and COBOL programming languages and after that performed systems analysis, design, project planning, proposal writing, and project management duties. In addition to beginning my career, learning methodology, and understanding the general business environment, my major accomplishments while at Andersen included the development of an IRA/Keogh system for a large local Savings & Loan and the modification and implementation of an order entry, inventory, and manufacturing system.

At KPMG Peat Marwick, I served as a manager and senior manager for approximately 5 years and I joined KPMG in order to help build and grow their Columbus, Ohio, consulting business. I was involved in helping to hire and train personnel, developed new consulting business in the Central Ohio region, and served the audit team as the primary person responsible for the review of audit clients in the systems controls area.

After a short 2-year foray into the real estate development business, I started my own consulting company (Strategic Technology Integrators), where my primary client became Tandem Computers. I eventually sold this consulting business to Tandem Computers, where I served as the general manager, Worldwide of Tandem Consulting Services for the America's and later as the managing director of the systems integration business on a world wide basis. While at Tandem, I was involved in managing teams that worked on the recovery of several significant projects and was also responsible for working with several large banking organizations in the creation, development, and implementation of one of the first large scale Web-based payment processing management systems.

As Tandem aligned the business for sale to Compaq computers, I moved to Synon Software, later Sterling Software, as vice president, Central Region. Based in Chicago, I oversaw the personnel in the major Central U.S. markets that supported the creation, development, and implementation of systems solutions utilizing the diverse and complex set of systems development tools created and supported by Synon.

After Synon was sold to Sterling Software, I joined Exodus Communications and held many positions of increasing scope and responsibility, including the senior vice president of the Central and Southeast North American regions. While at Exodus and during a period of over 40% growth for multiple consecutive quarters, I was responsible for the build-out and operation of several large scale Web hosting facilities (over 100,000 square feet each) and the professional services staff that assisted customers in the build-out of network, systems, and operations infrastructure. My accomplishments while at Exodus included the profitable growth and management of a revenue stream of over $200 million in the combined Austin, Dallas, Atlanta, Miami, Washington, Toronto, and Chicago markets. I was also heavily involved and responsible for the development and installation of the first major Web initiative for one of the world's largest brokerage houses. I left Exodus Communications shortly after the company was sold to Cable and Wireless Communications.

Currently, at Installed Building Products, I am the chief information officer and have been responsible for recruiting and building an IT organization that has been and is responsible for the integration of many new businesses into the organization, creation of an enterprise-wide Internet-based application to support the business, design, and deployment of the network and operations infrastructure to support the significant compounded annual growth of the business.

Company History

Installed Business Products provides construction services to commercial and residential builders in the areas of insulation, waterproofing, gutters, shower doors, shelving, and mirrors. Formed in 1991, the company now serves customers in almost every major market in the central and eastern U.S. As stated on our Web page:

At IBP, our success is built on a commitment to hard work, respect for individuals and the constant delivery of superior customer service. We're the type of company that people can get excited working for, and working with. IBP is a division of Edwards Companies, a family-owned enterprise that operates as a residential builder, commercial developer and contractor in land development, property management and numerous other operating companies."

The company mission is to grow the business in a profitable manner, providing the world's best products in the installed products market while providing our employees with personal and professional development opportunities. Over the past few years we have been able to significantly increase our market share and establish a number of new locations. Our goal is to continue to expand our presence in this industry.

My Company and Me

I was initially attracted to the CIO role at Installed Business Products because it offered me the opportunity to work in a small and growing organization where I could add significant value in creating an organization to support the business, utilizing my technology and management background, and be involved in the early stages of growth. I think the following discussion will highlight that I have been able to accomplish this in a short period while simultaneously completing many successful projects, building a strong team of personnel, and creating a platform to support the future growth of the company.

Prior to my arrival, the company's senior management team had experienced varying degrees of success (many of them bad) in relation to the development and implementation of information systems. For this reason, my mission and responsibilities early on in my tenure included the creation of a credible IT organization that was able to respond to the change and growth while successfully and economically delivering mission critical applications systems and infrastructure. To measure our success, we have consistently documented, tracked, and reported critical operational metrics that enabled us to see the increases in productivity and reductions in costs that we were able to effect in practically all areas of the business. Most important to our success has been the need to clearly define expectations and commitments prior to the beginning of projects and then to clearly report on the results.

Because we are a small organization I have always had an increasing number of direct reports. My direct reports currently include eight people, including the IT operations manager, network manager, and the application development, support, and implementation teams.

Perhaps the most interesting aspect of my involvement at Installed Business Products has been the amount of change that continues to occur and how we need to always consider the impact that the growth has on every aspect of the support that we provide to the business. The changes have been driven mainly by the expanding employee and geographical base and the ever increasing need for personnel in all areas of the business to adapt their operating practices, procedures, policies, and standards to provide the appropriate support required to build a strong and agile enterprise.

At Installed Business Products, we are growing at over 30% per year. I am continually occupied with the selection, hiring, and development of a team capable of working in this dynamic environment. We have built a world class Internet-based application and implemented it in over 50 branch offices located throughout the United States during the last 2 years.

At the beginning of my tenure with Installed Business Products, I dealt with issues relating to staff, infrastructure, and the prioritization of projects.

Staff

This issue relates to the development of staff to facilitate continued growth of our business. Because the business was very small when we started, most employees had to wear many hats, but as we have grown, personnel have had to not only learn to be more productive in the areas they are responsible, but have had to grow their communication, management, and technical skills as the systems, networks, and organization has become increasingly complex.

Infrastructure

When I began work at Installed Business Products, I found it necessary to change, reinforce, and replace major portions of our infrastructure in order to provide a more resilient and cost effective operating environment. The continuous significant growth of the company has required that we provide an environment that is scalable, but which because of the economics of the industry and the capital requirements for growth, also allowed us to build-out the infrastructure utilizing far fewer resources than would normally be expected. Several areas where we have had to make changes included the need to expand facilities, networks, applications, and end-user support, while dramatically improving the measurements metrics for the organization. A prime example of this is the re-architecting of the network infrastructure to support more than twice the number of users and five times the number of geographical locations at a reduced cost.

Prioritization of Projects

As we have grown our operations, the number, scope, and complexity of projects has continued to grow. To avoid creating a monster that would continue to consume an increasing amount of resources and budget dollars, we early on recognized the need to establish a process for setting project priorities. As the organization has grown, we have continually transitioned this process into a more mature state and we currently have a variety of priority setting groups, including the most senior management personnel from both the field and corporate functions, functional users groups, and regional field management.

My Typical Week

As many of you know, in a growing business and today's continuously changing business world, there is no typical week, and personally I would not have it any other way, because change is important. However, there are three common weekly rituals and several periodic chats that I feel are important to the well being of the business. While these rituals and periodic chats are not embraced by everyone in the business, nor are they ever exciting events in and of themselves, I have found from previous experience that the lack of information exchange will end up contributing to organizational failures that have never been imagined and the completion of them provide opportunities for the discovery, identification, and creation of new and different ways to do business that will have profound impacts on the business. This is especially true in a continuously changing and growing environment. These rituals include:

1. **Scheduled weekly meetings or touch bases with direct reports:** These are typically one-on-one type meetings that provide an opportunity to gauge how well someone is doing and to determine their current mindset and priorities. While many readers of this are thinking that "Geez, I cannot believe that mindsets or priorities need to be checked each week," I would respond that in a high-growth, high-stress environment they do, and those that ignore this need will someday be surprised. And, like anything else, the earlier an issue is identified and addressed, the more productive life becomes. So, these meetings are utilized to help set priorities, look for issues, and develop plans for addressing problems and issues.
2. **Scheduled weekly leadership team meeting:** Because we are not a large company, our IT leadership team consists of four people, plus me. I chair a joint leadership team session where each member of that team has the responsibility to communicate and share the status of ongoing projects and issues with the other members of the leadership team in order to provide others with the knowledge of what is going on in other areas of the business. But, more importantly, it is an opportunity for everyone to come together to address any issue(s). And, periodically, for a change of pace, I will hold this meeting over a lunch, at an extended off-site session, or in an otherwise hospitable place, like our favorite hamburger stand.
3. **Scheduled weekly acquisition integration status calls:** Regardless of what is going on in my world, regardless of where I am, and except for weeks where I am on vacation, I have blocked out Wednesday and Thursday afternoons to attend, chair, and help referee individual conference calls with each branch that is new to our environment. The purpose of these meetings is to address our ongoing systems integration and implementation efforts with the business leaders (operational and administrative) at those branches, identify and plan for resolution of their concerns and issues to help these new business leaders, and communicate outward to other parts of the organization where the issues and concerns are beyond the scope of our authority. I view these meetings as the most critical weekly discussions because we oftentimes are the sole department in the business who have made it our business to be on-site and in the line of fire with the acquired business leaders as this is a critical time

for the acquired businesses to have a regular forum with the corporate support group management. These meetings not only allow us to identify issues that may have been smoldering and to put out the potential fires before they really get started. I believe these calls are one of the reasons we have been able to be extremely productive with an implementation team that currently has an average of 5 months tenure with the company and which last year alone completed 24 branch integrations on-time, on-budget, and on-scope.

My Nontypical Week

So, with all these meetings, what else could there be time to do, you ask? Well, very little time, but lots to do. With branches in three time zones, a very lean management team, and many critical and sometimes emotional issues, we have forced ourselves to make the time to further communicate the mission, priorities, and direction of the business and the IT support organization to the company. In these not so typical weeks, I find myself involved in a number of activities focused around providing field reconnaissance (i.e., visiting our branches to build relationships with the branch personnel and setting integration direction), planning, and support that will enable a more productive environment for the IT personnel as they carry out their duties in the organization. Besides the typical daily barrage of issues that fly across e-mail, phone, and internal issue tracking systems (help desk), during these nontypical weeks, and in addition to the meetings held during typical weeks, I participate or chair the following:

1. **Periodic operations committee, user group, and cross functional management team meetings:** These meetings include the senior management team, the application end-users and the various corporate department managers, respectively. For the operations committee meeting I am an attendee and provide input to the other senior executives regarding current issues and status of the department. I am the chair of the user group and cross functional management meeting. The function of these groups is to receive and provide input as to the status of project issues, development of ideas for improving the operations, and the creation of conceptual designs for system modifications.
2. **Regional presidents' roundtable:** The regional presidents are the key operations personnel responsible for field operations in our regions. They are responsible for the sales and delivery of services to our customers, and every branch reports to them. This meeting is held periodically, on an as needed basis, to determine the relative priority of development requests and to establish an IT commitment to the regions for project delivery.

Besides these meetings, I get involved in a variety of operational issues from dealing with vendors, negotiating contracts, screening resumes, interviewing personnel, completing personnel reviews, and all the other things required by the business in order to keep the lights on. Some weeks, I find myself on the road, fulfilling my personal objective to visit the newly acquired branches. In fact, one week during January 2003, I drove over 2,500 miles, visiting over 10 branches in upstate New York, Massachusetts, New Hampshire, and Maine.

Dealing with Users

We interact with users in a number of ways and depending on their responsibility and authority. In addition to the user group and regional presidents' roundtable discussed previously, the most widely used method for communicating with our users is through the use of a system called the help desk. This system was developed in order to help us more productively gather, catalogue, track, assign, and disseminate information from our users on issues, problems, questions, and requests for modifications. The system is available to all users, providing them with a single place to log their requests and allowing us to assign those to the appropriate analysts, technicians, and developers for resolution. The help desk system also provides the IT department with a means for tracking outstanding requests by category (application, network, hardware, software) and by individual. Our personnel use this system to track, manage, document, and prioritize their daily work.

In cases where users have requested a modification to the application software or a new system project, the help desk issue is the beginning of a process that requires the development of a business case. The business case process continues to change as the organization changes, and currently requires the users to document their requirements in a number of ways depending on the extent of the project requested. During this process, especially for development that will require significant design, development, and testing effort, users are requested to complete a one-page business case analysis, which along with their design requirements documentation, requires that they document the return on investment (ROI) in quantifiable terms when applicable and that they record the nonquantifiable benefits to the organization. This business case analysis is then utilized by the operating committee to approve and prioritize the requests. During the completion of the business case analysis and design documents, we conduct regular one-on-one meetings to ensure that users and designers/developers are fully cognizant of user requirements. These meetings are typically carried out at the direction of the business analyst/designer and usually include the review of design documents, white board discussion and documentation of issues, concerns, and questions that need to be resolved.

Upon the completion of all projects, we conduct a follow-up investigation in detail with the users. We review the initial requests and compare them with the specifications and the final results. We also compare the final costs with the initial estimated budget and determine if variances exist. These variances are then determined to be either estimating or staffing variance and are used by the analysts and developers in the creation of future project estimates and commitments in addition to being reviewed by management.

Deciding on Technology Investments

The entire investment process is based on the operating requirements for supporting the current and future security and control, supportability, reliability, and availability of the systems to the user community. The addition of personnel is based on productivity measurements. Tools, techniques, and methods are applied as required to increase short term and long term productivity, while productivity is generally measured by the number of issues (by type) processed during each quarter. User satisfaction is gauged by discussions with the regional presidents, users group, and the types and quantities of help desk issues received during the quarter. At the end of each quarter, each application area and the network and infrastructure areas complete a quarterly operations review report that is shared with the CEO and the operating committee members after it has been reviewed with the IT department during a quarterly off-site meeting.

Current Issues

Tomato Plant Problem

We have more requests for projects than we can respond to with our current resources. It is like having too many tomato plants and not enough water. The gardener must decide to either attempt to water all the plants, putting an entire crop at serious risk or must decide which plant will get watered and which will be ignored. Due to our growth and the limited number of resources, we must react in a similar way. Our plan for addressing this issue is to create an environment where we will apply project management office (PMO) techniques to track and report to senior management on the portfolio of projects. The expected outcome will be the creation of a balance between supply and demand by either constraining demand or increasing supply. Demand may be constrained through the process of project approvals. Supply may be addressed through increasing the availability of appropriately skilled personnel. Another important result will be senior management's better understanding of project scope, complexity, and operational requirements.

Overworked Staff

Because we are faced with the tomato plant problem as described above, and with all user's and management's desire to improve operations, the staff is continually faced with pressure from all facets and levels of the business to produce more. Because the staff has significant personal pride, a desire to please, and because we encourage them to interact with our users, the volume of calls naturally has increased as we have grown. This has required personnel to work longer and harder, including nights and weekends, to keep up with the workload. Our plan for addressing this problem is complimentary to the prioritization of development requests, regular communication of the work completed with senior management, communication and review of IT commitments, implementation of monitoring and management tools to improve productivity and allow staff to more pro-actively address issues, and the use of users to assist in the design and testing of system functions and features. Because we are staffed only during the typical business day, we have also engaged the management team in setting response time service level agreements with the user community to eliminate the expectation of a 24 by 7 by 365 response expectation.

Organizational Education

We need to provide educational opportunities to the rest of the organization about how to adapt technology to their functional areas and recognize the value information technology can provide to the organization. This is probably the most elusive and difficult issue that we currently face, as every part of the organization is stretched due to the tremendous and continuous growth and by the fact that many of our users have never worked in any organization that provided the technology resources we have available. Thus, we do not oftentimes have the experience to review their operations and determine how they can best apply technology to improve the value of their operations to the business. As with the other current issues we face, the plan for resolving this one is to increase interaction and communications with all levels of the user community through many of the aforementioned design reviews, prioritization, and discussions. However, we expect that this issue will take much longer to resolve because our population of users continually increases and new technology continues to be requested and developed into the environment. Not to mention, that even in a static environment, it can take years to educate personnel on the methods, techniques, and analysis required to review their processes and determine where to best apply technology.

Future Issues

Slot Machine Management

Slot machine management can be best described as the phenomenon where a staff continually faces a changing direction due to inconsistent focus and frequent directional changes from managers. This frequently occurs in fast growth environments where priorities are continually changing and where staff does not have the wherewithal to focus on various aspects of the business so that a consistent process or processes are put in place, communicated, and absorbed by the culture of the organization. The effects of this phenomenon are that the organization feels like it is always fighting fires, processes are never fully developed and communicated, and productivity and morale suffers. Due to our tremendous growth, we continue to have this issue. However, to date, we have been able to deal with these issues because we were small enough that individual contributors (with Herculean efforts) were able to overcome and conquer the issues. I expect that as we get larger, the ability for individual contributors to adapt their work to adequately respond will diminish and the outcome will be the failure of various operational aspects of the business. While these failures may or may not be critical failures that will hurt the business, the possibility exists that such failures will create a downward spiral in productivity, control and management of the business, and employee morale, and could create situations that eventually absorb significant amounts of attention that could have been applied to more productive activities. Further, our operational requirements are driven by an uneven flow of acquisitions, and although the volume of acquisitions can be throttled back, it is extremely difficult to plan the timing of such acquisitions. Thus, we have an ever increasing size and changing functionality requirements. This issue will be addressed by the education of the user community and continued review of priorities for future projects with senior management, as discussed previously. We will need to develop, document, and present more detailed project designs and plans and become more formalized in assigning specific resources or we will need to reduce the change to the technology environment as the user base grows and the support requirements increase. Also, we will need to continue to conduct the quarterly operational review activities and possibly expand those reviews to include other departments.

Information Technology Governance

As discussed previously, we have begun to establish a review process for our technology, application, and infrastructure investments. However, to date, the focus has been on functionality that the users actually see (new systems, new reports, and the like). As we mature, senior management will need to be better educated on the complexities of the systems environment, and in addition to increasing their involvement in the review of applications and major functionality requirements, they will need to begin to understand the intricacies of regression testing, systems monitoring, security, and performance testing. We will address this issue by continuing to conduct regular operations meetings with senior management regarding IT issues, where management will be asked to review, prioritize, and approve business cases developed by the sponsoring department's most senior manager. But, we will likely need to expand the frequency of such meetings and the depth of the discussion required.

Final Comments

Within our organization, a young, maturing, and growing one, my role as chief information officer is continually changing and evolving. During the past year, I have moved from reporting to our executive vice president for strategic planning to reporting to the chief executive officer. I now sit on the senior management operations committee and attend regular meetings of this group. I continue to work closer and closer with the senior management team on operational issues due to the lack of a specific defined chief operating officer role in the company. I continue to take on an increasing role for the revision and creation of business processes, definition of overall priorities, creation of business vision, and prioritization/governance over human and financial resources.

In order to weather the storm and keep from falling off a cliff during my many experiences, I continue to live and work by a few simple rules:

- Never believe what you are told, read, hear, or see; prove it to yourself. Trust, but verify.
- Be prepared to embrace change and encourage change in all things.
- Plan your life and then live your plan.
- Be sure to consider all aspects of your life and strike a fair balance between work and play.

References

Installed Building Products (n.d.). Retrieved January 30, 2007, from www.ibpteam.com

Chapter XVIII

Angelo Mazzocco
The Dispatch Companies

The number one source of information in Ohio and Indianapolis.

My name is **Angelo Mazzocco**. I am currently vice president and chief information officer at the Dispatch Printing Company and Affiliates.

Personal History

I was born and raised in New Castle, Pennsylvania, just 50 miles northwest of Pittsburgh.

I obtained a Bachelor of Science (Magna Cum Laude) in mathematics and computer science from Indiana University of Pennsylvania in 1979, and an MBA (marketing and information systems) from the University of Dayton in 1981.

Before joining The Dispatch Companies, I gained valuable experience working for the following companies. My first job was at National Cash Register (NCR) in 1979. I was a programmer/analyst assigned to develop a number of systems, including an order/billing system. I was also responsible for production support. At the same time I was working on my MBA at the University of Dayton. Most nights I was either fixing production problems or working on my courses. NCR introduced me to my profession and I will always be grateful for that. It was a great place to learn how to work hard and get rewarded for your results. Management had no problem with involving the newer employees with very significant assignments and projects.

After NCR, I joined Nationwide Insurance in 1982 as a systems manager. Here, I was responsible for information technology support for all departments and related businesses within the Nationwide Life Insurance companies. I lead the team that converted the Group Life and Health business to a new technology platform. At this time, I was also instrumental in the development of strategy and systems for the first Health Maintenance Organization (HMO) and Preferred Provider Organization (PPO) health insurance systems at Nationwide. Subsequently, we established partnerships with five other insurance companies for PPO processing. I also participated in the conversion team responsible for the integration of seven other insurance companies into the Nationwide Insurance group of companies. Nationwide taught me how to be an entrepreneur. You may ask how this could be since Nationwide is such a large company. I worked in the Group Life and Health lines of business and we operated like our own little company. This afforded me the opportunity to see the business as a whole from a customer service, sales, actuarial, legal, underwriting, medical systems, human resource, and financial point of view.

Then I moved to Andersen Consulting (now Accenture) as a consulting manager, in 1988. I was generally responsible for the financial performance of a number of Financial Services projects in the Ohio region. I was also involved in many large systems development consulting projects. These projects included new metering systems for American Electric Power, new credit card applications for Bank One, new workflows for Nationwide Insurance, and a new workers' compensation system for the state of Ohio. The opportunity to work at Andersen was extremely valuable. Not only were you taught about designing and developing new systems and technology, but you were also shown how to serve clients and create profits.

In 1991, while I was still working for Andersen Consulting, I was given the opportunity to teach in the MBA program at the Ohio State University as part of the adjunct faculty. Although what started out to be a favor to the department head of the Accounting and Information Systems department, eventually became my second career. I was so excited about the opportunity that at my first class, I brought my "personal computer," which was an IBM AT that weighed about 20 pounds, an overhead projector, and VGA Board, which allowed one to connect to the computer and show presentations via the overhead projector. The only problem was that buildings were not equipped to handle all of that output, so needless to say, the electricity in the business building shut down as a result of the overload. I seemed to do everything wrong that quarter, so I was so sure that this would be my first and last quarter teaching. However, much to my surprise, 2 weeks after the end of the quarter the department head called me to ask which classes I would be willing to teach in the subsequent quarter! I have taught at the graduate school level ever since.

In 1997, I began teaching at Otterbein College. Teaching has taught me to plan, research, and prepare. It is also a great way to "sharpen the saw." MBA classes are very difficult to teach because there are usually a wide variety of people with varying backgrounds and degrees. It has not been unusual for me to have students with a PhD in engineering, BS in nursing, BA in business, and an MS in mathematics in the same MBA class!! I teach an MBA information technology course. I like to start each lecture with a discussion of current issues, such as security or viruses. I encourage my students to relate stories about events in their experiences. I always try to direct the discussion to what they would do about an issue in their workplace. Each time I teach this course I think I learn as much as the students. They are business professionals who bring a lot of experience to our discussions. In a number of areas they know as much as I do.

The next move was to Network Compatibility Group as chief operating officer in 1994. I was involved from the time when this company was relatively new as we grew a start up professional services company from 25 people to over 125. Eventually, we became the professional services division of CompuCom. The division grew to over 800 employees. Most of my previous career allowed me the opportunity to work in consulting and software/system development. NC Group/CompuCom allowed me to gain a better understanding of the hardware and network aspects of the information technology business. In addition, I had a significant profit and loss (P&L) responsibility, so I got to put my entrepreneur hat back on.

Since 1998, I am the vice president and chief information officer for The Dispatch Companies.

Company History

The Dispatch Companies are family owned and operated. They comprise 14 different entities whose industries include television, radio, newspaper, real estate, aviation, magazine, direct marketing, and professional sports. The largest component is the newspaper.

In the late 1800s, most newspapers focused on discussing political matters. In June 1871, the idea of a newspaper, which provides general news items, came to fruition with the formation of The Columbus Dispatch. The first edition, consisting of four pages and costing three cents, was printed on July 1. By the end of the first month of operation, the daily circulation reached 2,000 easily surpassing the other daily newspapers in the area. Of note at this time is the idea of an "Extra." This is a short one-page report of late breaking news. The concept of the "Extra" continued until radio became the more accepted vehicle for reporting current news items. Over the years, the Dispatch expanded circulation, merged with other newspapers in the area, and incorporated new printing technology. In 1984, a new color press was installed with a capacity to produce 50,000 papers per hour. In 1980, the newspaper was published online for the first time. In late 1993, the Dispatch inaugurated is own Web site (*Dispatch.com*) for $6,000. Today, the Dispatch Printing Company's *Columbus Dispatch* is one of the largest privately owned (the Wolfe family) newspapers in the United States. The Daily circulation is more than 250,000 with a Sunday circulation of over 360,000. These circulation numbers put The Dispatch in the top 10% of newspapers in the country. There are over 1,200 employees. Everyone is committed to publishing and distributing the best newspaper possible.

ThisWeek Community Newspapers, founded in the 1980s, are a group of award-winning suburban weekly newspapers serving 300,000 homes throughout more than 20 communities in central Ohio. ThisWeek's commitment to excellence has been recognized time and time again by Ohio-based press clubs as the most decorated of any community newspaper group in Ohio. ThisWeek also produces the Columbus Parent Magazine, which is devoted to parents, mothers-to-be, and young families.

Dispatch Consumer Services, founded in the 1970s, provides a number of services, including distribution, telemarketing, direct marketing, and specialized printing. Distribution includes delivery of the Wall Street Journal, Investor's Daily, and the New York Times throughout Central Ohio. Telemarketing is provided to companies for a number of niche industries and markets. Direct Marketing is served through OnTargetMarketing and TheBag, which allows corporations to microtarget advertising inserts to the specific households that are requested.

The Ohio Magazine and Ohio Publications create magazine and brochure products to all of Ohio. Ohio Magazine is the most read magazine in Ohio of all the magazines produced there.

Another major component of the Dispatch companies is Dispatch Broadcast Group. The group includes WBNS-FM, WBNS-AM, and RadioOhio radio interests and WBNS-TV, ONN, WTHR, and Sky-Tracks television properties.

Founded in 1949 by the Wolfe family, WBNS is the most-watched television in central Ohio. Since its inception, WBNS has continually employed cutting edge technology to broadcast high quality news and entertainment programming. In 1997, WBNS broadcast the first high definition TV show when it televised the West Virginia University vs. the Ohio State University football game. WBNS is a CBS affiliate and broadcast to most of the central Ohio community via air, cable, and satellite.

WTHR is an NBC affiliate and the most watched television station in the Indianapolis area. Its Sky-Tracks affiliate provides weather information to viewers 24 hours per day.

In the 1990s, the Ohio News Network (ONN) was formed to serve the cable television viewers of Ohio. The 24 hour, 365 days-per-year, news service provides up to the minute news to all areas of Ohio.

WBNS-FM, WBNS-AM, and RadioOhio are some of the top radio sources in central Ohio. WBNS-AM is totally focused on sports and is nicknamed "The Fan." Besides being one of the premier sports talk radio stations in Ohio, "The Fan" broadcasts all Ohio State University football and basketball games. WBNS-FM delivers music. RadioOhio brokers radio programs and advertisements to other radio stations.

Capital LTD manages the enterprise's real estate, Ohio Partners performs venture capital investments, Wolfe Aviation supports the Dispatch Companies' and other companies' travel needs, and the Wolfe Enterprises and Wolfe Associates deliver community investments and services.

The Dispatch Companies continue to leave their mark on Central Ohio, Indianapolis, and the media industry. At a recent technology awards banquet, the Dispatch Companies was voted as a finalist in the "Technology Team" category. I have included the evaluation criteria and justification in an appendix to this chapter.

The Columbus metropolitan area is in the heart of Ohio and is the state capital. The population of the metropolitan area is 1.6 million, making it the 15th largest municipality in the United States. Columbus is a cosmopolitan city with high employment. The city has consistently grown since the mid 1940s, yet has been able to retain its small-town midwest charm.

My Company and Me

As the vice president and chief information officer my mission is, "to provide information technology vision and leadership for developing and implementing information technology initiatives that creates and maintain leadership for the enterprise in an environment of constantly changing technology and a competitive marketplace." Our information services department provides the right information and technology solutions to the right people at the right time.

As chief information officer I am, "accountable for directing the information and data integrity of the enterprise and its divisions and for all information service functions of the enterprise, including all data centers, technical services, production systems, help desks, communication networks (voice and data), computer program development and computer systems operations." I am, "responsible for managing the information technology affairs of the companies while balancing technological and operational needs with financial and marketing needs. This is to be accomplished with the use of computer and communication technology that supports both self generated growth and growth through acquisition. Seamless integration of data and information from the customer through financial statement and management reporting is one of the primary challenges of this position."

I report directly to the chief executive officer. All information systems staff at The Dispatch Printing Company and Affiliates reports directly to me.

In a recent publication of the local Columbus Technology Council newsletter, I explained my involvement with The Dispatch Companies.

When I joined The Dispatch Companies in 1998, the Internet was hastening news cycles, Y2K loomed, and none of the systems within the 14 privately held subsidiary companies worked together. Today, I oversee systems that allow these companies to rush breaking news and advertisements to their many readers, viewers, and listeners.

As the company's first CIO, I was eager to take on the challenge of integrating 14 stand-alone companies. These included the following:

- The Dispatch Printing Company's daily newspaper (*The Columbus Dispatch*)
- 22 "This Week" community newspapers, *Columbus Parent Magazine*
- Dispatch Consumer Services' distribution, printing and telemarketing
- WBNS AM, FM and RadioOhio radio stations
- WBNS, WTHR (Indianapolis), and ONN televisions stations
- Ohio Partners venture capital
- The Capital Ltd., real estate
- Wolfe Enterprises community relations
- Wolfe Aviation aeronautical services
- Ohio Magazine and Ohio Publications operations

Dating from the late 1970s through the late 1990s, FCC regulations prevented one company from owning multiple media outlets. The Wolfe family's holdings had been grandfathered in since their ownership dated from before the 1970s. But managers kept the operations separate. Some of our companies even competed with one another. Regulatory change allowed the companies to consolidate. I approached Y2K and systems integration as a single project across all 14 companies. After identifying redundancies, my team began to unite back-office functions such as human resources, finance systems, and Internet and intranet services. We also unified the network infrastructure for telephone and data communications and Internet service. Our success early on gave us credibility with business managers and allowed us to continue.

As the clock rolled over to 12:00 a.m. on January 1, 2000, I waited downtown while systems came online without a glitch. I stayed until the Indianapolis systems tested out an hour later, and then visited The Dispatch printing operation. I remember driving home at 4:00 a.m. and feeling grateful to see all the lights twinkling in the city skyline.

Technology generates rapid change in the news industry. Our greatest challenge is that we operate 24/7, 365 days a year. Today, our companies operate with 2,400 employees using 2,000 desktop computers in 41 different buildings. A team of 100 information technology workers and broadcast engineers supports systems and infrastructure.

With the convergence of different media, breaking stories can be posted on Web sites, aired on ONN TV, and delivered via WBNS TV and radio news breaks almost simultaneously. So, Eyewitness News carries a fresh angle on the 11:00 p.m. news. Then, the next day, The Dispatch newspaper offers in-depth analysis.

Technology that was undreamed of only a few years ago now shapes the way reporters gather and deliver news. From the early 1900s until the mid 1980s, the technology was virtually unchanged. Not all that long ago, many of our people were still using paper and pencil. We are 90% more dependent on technology today as compared to 20 years ago. Wireless communications allow sports reporters to upload stories and photos from the sidelines at high school football games in time to report final scores in the next morning's newspaper.

I am a strong supporter of the Columbus Technology Council and the technology community in Columbus. In preparing for Y2K, I joined with four other central Ohio CIOs to compare notes. The CTC was involved from the start in creating what is now the 34-member Information Technology Leadership forum, now known as the CIO Forum, which organizes the CIO Symposium. Annually, we bring together many technology leaders from the area. We use the group as a sounding board on strategic, technical, and process issues. It's amazing how we can take ideas from food production or insurance and apply them to our business.

My Typical Week

My typical week is to spend Monday's in internal staff, project, and executive meetings. This allows for a fresh weekly update of what is important to our customers and executives, as well as to review how well we are delivering to those expectations.

Tuesday's are normally spent with key vendor partners. In today's information technology age, some vendor partners are absolutely integral and vital to services that we provide end users. Without them, we would fail. It is very important to work with those key vendors and treat them as you would treat key staff.

On Wednesday and Thursday, I like to get out and meet with our end users. These are typically the heads of our companies and major departments in those companies. This is when I find out how well we are doing from the viewpoint of end users and customers. I usually like to ask what issues, accomplishments, and plans are on their agenda. From this discussion, I can normally get a feel for problems, concerns, victories, and desires.

Fridays are usually spent doing administrative tasks such as status reports, evaluations review (I review the evaluations for everyone of the nearly 100 people in our department), and budget review.

Dealing with Users

The communications process that the Dispatch Companies has defined is important to information services' dealing with users.

Every 2 weeks, the executive committee meets to discuss and decide issues, plans, and accomplishments. All vice presidents of the major business units are represented on the executive committee as well as the president and owner. Major decisions are approved or declined at the executive committee meetings. This means that approved items do not need to be approved again at the department level.

Every week the operating committee meets to discuss and recommend issues, plans, and accomplishments. All directors and vice presidents of the major business units attend the operating committee meetings. Major and tactical decisions are reviewed. Most items decided by executive committee are also reviewed.

Each week I meet with my direct reports (six directors and managers). We review the executive and operating committees' minutes, as well as the issues, plans, and accomplishments that are unique to information services and broadcast engineering. Meetings are also held between information services, broadcast engineering and the major business units on a regular basis.

All of this communication keeps information services and the users on the same page. Because of this, dealing with the users is much easier.

In a recent article in *Computer World* (Leading change: 12 steps to get your organization from here to there, by Mary K. Pratt, January 10, 2005), I was quoted about leading organizations through change. "Seek out leaders within other departments to champion changes. 'If we can get those [business] people on our side, we'll get everything to work,' says Angelo Mazzocco, vice president and CIO at The Dispatch Printing Co. in Columbus, Ohio. Mazzocco, who oversees the IT departments of 14 affiliate companies with more than 2,000 employees, holds monthly meetings with senior IT and business managers so he can notify allies when changes are proposed." Getting the users to see change as theirs is very important to the success of that change.

The article goes on to say, "Mazzocco also recommends tapping colleagues in other industries for advice, which is something he does at a CIO forum he started six years ago. 'It's helped us in implementing major initiatives,' he says. "We can help influence our users' acceptance of change with advice from other organizations in the community. Also, if our companies make the commitment for change, we need to make sure that we go at it 'all out.' The article concludes, "We're all doing more with less these days, but when it comes to change, Mazzocco says it's best to devote the necessary people to the project by freeing them from their day-to-day duties."

Deciding on Technology Investments

The users and information services recommend technology investments to executive committee on an annual basis. This process is part of the budgeting process. Executive committee approves or declines the budget.

During the course of the year, each approved investment is re-reviewed with executive committee when it is due to be designed or implemented.

Current Issues

Three strategic directions have evolved for the Dispatch Companies; Convergence, Digitization, and Personalization.

Convergence attempts to combine the strengths of the different companies of the enterprise into a common power. News, information, advertising, distribution, and administration can be dealt with by employing economies of scale. We are using the convergence of the powers of our media companies for greater public awareness, better information to our customers, and an optional single marketing and sales approach.

Digitization attempts to transform all the assets of the enterprise into digital format. We are digitizing our assets, including video, audio, print, and photo for greater work flow efficiency and public access and purchase. The newsrooms are able to access all assets immediately for news purposes. The Internet allows the public to access many of the assets that can be offered for value or cost.

Personalization puts news and advertising closer to the clients who need and want it. We are personalizing our news and advertisement offerings. Vehicles for doing this include media types such as the Internet, radio, TV broadcast, cable, newspaper, magazine, telemarketing, and direct marketing.

Future Issues

Some of the future issues that the Dispatch Companies need to address include sustainable financial growth, increasing revenue sources, and adding new services to meet customer needs.

Financial growth is difficult when an enterprise is a "David" among "Goliaths." The Dispatch Companies is a relatively small enterprise in comparison to other media giants in the industry. Economies of scale do not occur at the Dispatch Companies from having many TV stations or daily newspapers. Instead, economies of scale occur with the Dispatch Companies by combining the assets of multiple media companies. This approach can be more difficult in growing the companies financially.

Increasing revenue sources is finding ways to increase the sales of our companies. This can be done at the individual companies or through combined company efforts. One such example is an online auction that was sponsored by the daily newspaper, weekly newspapers, TV stations, and radio stations. The effort was a huge success in creating a local "e-bay" type revenue source.

Adding new services that exceed the needs of customers means to be sensitive to what customers want. A recent effort by the newspaper called preprint zoning permits advertising customers to choose the areas of central Ohio where they wish to offer preprint ads for sale in the newspaper.

Final Comments

Being a CIO in today's business environment is truly exciting and rewarding. The past 10 years has seen CIO's go from being the lead techies to being invited to the Executive Board Room. So much of this is because of how dependent on technology businesses have become.

The biggest responsibility we have today is to ensure the business gets what it expects out of technology and the change it causes. In the business world today, change almost always means technology impact. That is why we, the CIO's, have become so integral to the change process.

At the Dispatch Companies, I have seen much change during the 7+ years that I have been here. The challenge is keeping technology relevant to the business. Implementing technology for technology's sake is not a good thing. However, implementing technology for the business' sake is a good thing. And it is the CIO's role to make sure of that.

References

The Dispatch Companies (n. d.). Retrieved February 5, 2007, from www.dispatch.com

Appendix. Technology Award "Technology Team" Finalist

Innovation

- First Media organization to introduce high definition TV in Ohio, third in the nation.
- Created "State of the Art" Radio Broadcasting facility in 2004.
- Voted "best color" in publishing by IFRA, the international media publishing association.
- Developed "Convergence" concept for its entire media companies to integrate news, information, and advertising, which are considered the model in the industry.
- Fully automated the ONN-TV station programming delivery.
- Developed political polling process that is viewed as one of the best in the U.S.
- First completely computerized mailroom in the newspaper industry.
- First adopter of computer to plate newspaper technology.

Speed to Goal/Market

- Reengineered the entire distribution process to 600,000 locations in 18 months.
- Digitized text, photos, graphics, audio, and video back to the year 1985 in 24 months.
- Gained penetration to over 250,000 viewers daily to online Web sites in 2 years.
- Reduced size of daily and weekly newspapers in 12 months.
- Designed and implemented "State of the Art" radio station in 14 months.
- Converged news and advertising across all media companies in 18 months.
- Implemented advertising zoning in 18 months.
- Implemented enterprise business intelligence system in 11 months.

Accomplish Extraordinary Mission

- Integrated 14 stand alone companies into a single enterprise.
- Implemented shared services and convergence to accomplish mission.
- Supports 14 delivery systems that include TV, radio, newspaper, Internet, magazine, real estate, direct marketing, distribution, venture capital, agri-business, community service, and aviation.
- First Media organization to implement high definition TV in Ohio, third in the nation.

Raised the Bar Criteria

- Never missed production of a newspaper since 1905 (longest time period in the industry).
- Created a radio station viewed by the industry as the most "State of the Art" in 2004.
- Dispatch.com is the most viewed local Web site in central Ohio. 10TV.com is second. The Dispatch Companies combined Web sites are the most viewed of any set of Web sites in the state.
- First high definition television station in Ohio.

Positive Effects of Working Together as a Team

- Developed Enterprise Technology Group in January 1999 that brought all the technology leaders of the Dispatch Companies together on a regular basis to resolve issues, understand accomplishments, and develop plans. The group continues to exist today.
- Developed the Technology Forums in April 1999 that brought all the technology leaders of central Ohio together on a regular basis to discuss nonconfidential issues, understand accomplishments, and develop plans. The group continues to exist today. The Dispatch Companies benefit much from the Forums.

Chapter XIX

Cindy Sheets
Mount Carmel Health System

Honoring every soul with loving service.

My name is **Cindy Sheets**. I am currently the senior vice president and chief information officer at Mount Carmel Health System in Columbus, Ohio.

Personal History

I was born over four decades ago in Columbus, Ohio, where I have lived my entire life. I majored in medical technology at the Ohio State University and graduated from the 5 year program in 1980. I worked for several years before returning to graduate school in 1988 for an MBA at the University of Dayton.

My first professional job was as a medical technologist at Ohio State University Hospital and a private laboratory. I also worked as a Medical Technician at a community hospital, St. Anthony Medical Center, where I made the transition into information systems. I was hired as a systems analyst to oversee the laboratory implementation with no experience, other than laboratory operations. We successfully implemented a Technicon Data Systems (TDS) system which was state of the art at the time with a very small information systems staff but a lot of heart. What I mean is by all standards, the staff should not have been able to successfully complete the project, but they did! It was at this time I returned to graduate school. I held progressive levels of responsibility within information systems, leaving that facility as the manager of information systems.

Company History

Mount Carmel Health System is a leading provider of health care services in central Ohio. It consists of three acute facilities with over 1,000 beds, home care, hospice, home medical equipment, HMO (Health Maintenance Organization), physician practices, and other ancillary business segments. Mount Carmel is over 120 years old and was founded by the Sisters of the Holy Cross at the request of local physicians. The mission of Mount Carmel is service, particularly to the poor and underserved. It is a beacon in the Columbus community of a caring and competent institution. I find the mission compelling and lived authentically throughout the company.

Our Web site presents our culture and values as follows:

At Mount Carmel, we're a family, and as old-fashioned as that might sound, we're as proud of our family orientation as we are of all the state-of-the-art technology we've introduced during the one hundred-plus years we've been around.

At Mount Carmel, we believe it's not enough that we care. We want to make certain that we show that caring in everything we do, to everyone we meet, every day. That's why, at Mount Carmel, we have some guidelines that we live by. We call them our CARE values—Compassion, Acceptance, Respect, and Empathy:

***C**ompassion for others, whether they're our patients or our co-workers*

***A**cceptance for all: young and old; men and women; rich and poor; black, white, Asian, and Hispanic. We welcome and honor everyone here, both as patients and as employees.*

***R**espect for those with whom we work and to whom we give care.*

***E**mpathy that not only understand that everyone's life holds challenges, but goes a little further and helps to shoulder the burden.*

We believe it is our cause—honoring every soul with loving service—that really makes Mount Carmel, Mount Carmel. It's posted all around our hospitals, clinics, health centers ... everywhere Mount Carmel is.

But best of all, it's posted in the heart of each and every one of us. Its part of a leadership philosophy called Higher Ground that serves as the underlying foundation for all we do at Mount Carmel. Working according to the Higher Ground philosophy means being ourselves, and giving of ourselves to others. It means living and working by the principles of authenticity, truth-telling, and love.

We want to create a workplace that people love going to every day, a place where each individual can find meaning, fulfillment, and inspiration.

My Company and Me

I came to my current employer as a systems analyst for clinical systems in 1989. The hospital system was in the process of implementing a new hospital information system, including clinical applications, which was new for the facility. After the implementation was complete, I was promoted to systems manager, then director, then vice president of information systems strategic planning. The department and application portfolio grew exponentially during this time.

I accepted the role of senior vice president and chief information officer in 1999. I asked the CEO what he expected me to accomplish, and he said simply, "make the doctors happy."

I decided to meet with the physicians' one-on-one and ask them what they were unhappy about with the computing environment. I did about 20 interviews with the elected medical staff leadership and also the informal leaders, whose names I procured from the secretaries who *really* know what's going on. There were two universal themes that percolated from the interviews: they did not like signing onto multiple clinical and administrative systems to get information and they wanted the information to be presented in a uniform manner, not different screens for different applications. I summarized the information I learned, took it back to the Medical Executive Committee, and asked for further input, asking, are these the right problems we need to work on? I received a resounding YES.

At that time we had no technological solutions for the problem. Most of the applications were proprietary and turnkey from vendors. I began to think, literally in the middle of the night, that we had all the pertinent data electronically, and we just needed a way to access it and unite it in a logical way. Why couldn't we do this with the Web and present the information in a browser? I met with our technical team and challenged them to find a development vendor we could work with and figure out a way, even without access to underlying databases, to get the data. We formulated an request for information (RFI) and found the list was short, very short, of potential vendors who had developed anything like this in the health care space.

Again, the industry includes many turnkey applications, and typically the only road to integration is a single source vended product. I understood that what we wanted to do was new, and had some inherent risk in that it had not been done before, but I decided we had nothing to lose. We couldn't buy on the open market what we needed, so the solution, in my mind, required new thinking and solutions.

We found a small company in Alabama that had done some work like this but it wasn't their core business. They were, however, interested in working with us (Mount Carmel is a large, prestigious hospital in the information systems' space) and would contractually commit to the deliverable. The cost was relatively low, about US$250,000, in relationship to what we typically would pay for clinical applications. It took nearly 12 months to fully develop and implement what we called the physician portal, or "AccessMC." It was available both in house as well as remotely over a secure connection. It was an immediate hit with the medical staff.

The physicians liked the format, response time, and logical organization of data and immediately began to give more feedback on what else they would like to be included in the portal. Six years later, the product continues to evolve and has anecdotally become the gold standard in the physician community for physician access to information.

In the late 90s, with the Y2K crunch, staff retention was a critical issue. We were experiencing turnover as high as 47%, but today it is 4%. We focused on competitive salaries (hospitals had not kept pace with technology companies), work life balance, education, and simply asking the staff (via surveys and focus groups) what we can do to improve their job satisfaction. We implemented casual dress code, associate directed division meetings, staff recognition, and formal development plans, among other things. In the most recent Gallup survey conducted at Mount Carmel, the Information Resources Division scored the highest in the company in employee engagement and satisfaction, 4.25 above the top quartile of the Gallup database.

My Typical Week

Monday

- Meet with leadership team to do a mission discernment over possible sale of health plan
- Meeting to review status of Six Sigma projects and how we might increase cost savings
- Teleconference with home office on status of system wide clinical system project
- Meeting for long range financial plan for care continuum businesses

- Dinner meeting with physicians to discuss practicing at Mount Carmel

Tuesday

- Executive committee meeting of the Foundation Board
- Orientation meeting with home medical equipment company (recently started reporting to me)
- Meeting for long range financial plan for health plan and corporate health businesses

Wednesday

- Bi-weekly status meeting with vice president of Care Continuum businesses
- Annual chili cook off in honor of football rivalry Ohio State vs. Michigan
- Orientation meeting with Home Infusion

Thursday

- Weekly leadership team meeting
- Information System Leadership Council Teleconference (Trinity Health)
- Interview candidate for open position in IT
- Ohio CIO Symposium committee meeting

Friday

- Meeting with physician regarding health plan payment
- Meeting with home office to discuss roll out of physician office systems nationally
- More Six Sigma project reviews

Dealing with Users

We have three full time people. Their job is to be out in the facilities talking with the physicians each and every day. They also cover off hours call support. So, a physician can reach one of my staff 24 hours per day. The physicians will be able to see them in the hallway during the day or on the phone at night.

We also have employed on a part time basis a practicing physician as our director of medical informatics. It is very important that this individual be respected more from a clinical perspective than as a computer expert. He is the "go to guy" for the other physicians. He is well respected as someone who knows about medicine. This has really helped us to provide service to all of the physicians.

We also have various user group support teams. We have a clinical systems user group which provides support to areas such as patient accounting. We have an installation and technical support group which provides desktop support. If it's broken, this group comes and fixes it. We also have a customer support function that people may call. It is actually used quite a bit.

For the budget cycle we coordinate all of the requests for information technology. Our director of project management initiates the budget cycle by distributing guidelines for the use and cost estimates of information technology.

Our user community is very engaged. They have absolutely no problem in calling anyone in my area, including me, for whatever it is they would like. Based upon our customer satisfaction scores I am confident they are very happy with the service they are receiving. I do not see any disconnect between our user community and our shop.

Deciding on Technology Investments

We do not have an information technology council that approves investments. We used to have one but we dissolved it because it was not providing any value to the organization. Now, our senior management team, as the ultimate overseer of capital expenditures, can approve or disapprove at that level. So, our user community will propose projects to this senior management team. My area provides a coordinating service for this process.

For hardware, we have an operating budget for routine processes for dealing with replacement, replenishment, and obsolescence. Our proposals here are not usually challenged. I think this is because we provide good service and, as I stated above, our user community is very satisfied with our service. The same applies to software upgrades and maintenance.

As far as acquiring people, this is a challenge. Everyone is the health care field is trying to do more with less. Our managers spend a lot of time on metrics regarding workload and trying to determine whether we are applying the right skills. We are also constantly aware of providing service to our customers and ensuring they are satisfied. Within Mount Carmel, I am treated the same as all the other departments when it comes to skill acquisition. There is no preferential treatment for any one specific area.

Recently, we created a new position called executive support analyst. This person will be investigating productivity tools for executives such as smart phones. We would be looking to provide some kind of tool for an executive to use that may allow them to gain say, 15 minutes, out of their work day.

We will calculate an ROI for our user-based applications. But for our basic information technology infrastructure, we view it more as a utility. I like the example of when we are constructing a building we do not do an ROI on the elevators.

Current Issues

With the health care cost crisis in full swing, probably the biggest challenge is obtaining capital to support and expand the technological environment and cost control. Much of the operating budget is driven by past investment in the form of maintenance contracts. Trying to reduce operating costs is an ongoing chore. To reduce capital, we're implementing blade servers and looking to consolidate systems onto virtual servers. We discontinued 411 information service (saved $20,000 US) and made phone books available online.

Future Issues

An important issue that we will have to address in the future is the use of clinical information systems by physicians. In the United States today, with the Washington agenda there are several bills before Congress that will hopefully fund some national infrastructure for electronic health records. With a view to patient safety a large component is supposed to be computerized physician order entry. I expect a lot of funding for this initiative. But, there is a dilemma. The approach will be good for patient safety. However, it will take physicians longer to do and they will resist adding more work to their current heavy work flow. Time is money to the physicians. So, we are going to have to figure out the best way to engage the physicians. We have to make it seem like the extra effort is a good thing for them. We will have to provide support for the physicians to an extent that they will buy into the effort and actually use the system. What I plan to do a Mount Carmel is ask the physicians how they think we can engage their colleagues. We are getting some good ideas. Overall, the prevailing idea is that the approach will not be the same for everyone. We have different hospitals and physicians with different specialties, all of which will require different ways of engaging them in the process. So, we may constitute a committee or work with physicians one to one. Some hospitals may already have standard orders and it will just be a matter of automating them. But, we realize that one size will not fit all.

Another issue relates to the overall contention for capital. Health costs for employers have been increasing significantly over the past few years. On our side we have been experiencing cost pressures. I foresee in the future there will be less capital available within the health care system to fund information technology initiatives. This is unfortunate because it is happening at the same time as we are realizing that information technology could also be used to address the cost pressures throughout the entire health care system.

There is a lot of conversation about pay for performance as a form of funding in the future. But, we do not yet know how the business model will function. However, we do know that information technology will have a role. We will have to develop some metrics to measure performance and some way to report the results. The quality indicators and how they are reported and reimbursed will have to be consistent across all hospitals nationally.

Yet another issue relates to our work force. We cannot find enough people with the right skills. We need skills in project management, networking, and business analysts with knowledge about clinical operations. So we need people who know how the clinical process works. They should be good in work flow analysis. We have the technology. It's just deciding how to utilize the tools in the most efficient way to decrease costs and produce the best outcomes.

Final Comments

I do not think that CIOs are going to go away. I have long held the belief that CIOs are not technical officers. They should understand the business. They should be able to support the business and even improve the business. As a role, I see it evolving into a more expanded role. They must bring the normal business skills to the table, such as leadership.

References

Mount Carmel Health System (n.d.). Retrieved January 30, 2007, from www.mchs.com

Chapter XX

Kathleen Starkoff
Limited Brands

Building a family of the world's best fashion brands.

My name is **Kathleen Starkoff** and I am the chief technology officer and group vice president for Limited Brands Technology Services.

Personal History

I was born in Port Clinton, Ohio. I attended local Catholic elementary and high schools that were walking distance from home. I obtained a Bachelor of Science with a major in mathematics and minors in chemistry and business from Kent State University. I also have an MBA from Case Western Reserve with a major in policy.

Out of college, I went to work for Parker Hannifin in Cleveland, Ohio. They make fluid power components. I was an engineering administrator, which was a good combination for my technical undergraduate degree and the MBA. As part of the position, I became involved in the division's introduction to the Material Requirements Planning system. This involvement led to further responsibility and a new role of inventory control manager; in these roles, I worked closely with the technology organization.

I was with Parker Hannifin for about 5 years, when I got a call! It was from the placement office at my alma mater, Case Western Reserve University. They told me IBM was hiring and that my resume was a perfect fit for their requirements. My first response was to decline because I was happy with the challenge of my current position. Fortunately, Case's placement office was persistent and convinced me that it was an unusual situation for IBM to be hiring and I was an unusually good fit. I agreed to meet them for lunch. IBM is, of course, great at sales and they convinced me to join the company.

So, in 1983, I moved to IBM. I enjoyed a very extensive training program in technology and subsequently worked marketing and account representative positions. My favorite and final position was in the financial services area as a financial consultant at domestic headquarters in White Plains, New York. My team creatively solved complex financial problems with large IBM customers.

I was with IBM for about 6 years, when I got a call! It was from a gentleman I had worked with in Cleveland, Ohio. He was the CIO of National City Corporation. He was frustrated that his management team would not take the proliferation of PCs in the organization seriously. There were solely focused on "big iron" (mainframes), despite his best attempts to convince them otherwise.

So, in 1989, I moved to National City Corporation in Cleveland, Ohio, reporting to the CIO, to manage personal computers and networks. From there, I was given great opportunities in systems development. This included managing the development organization responsible for business consulting and all critical projects, including ERP (e.g., PeopleSoft) implementations. I was at National City Corporation for about 5 years, when I got a call!

Next I moved to KeyCorp, which was a competitive bank in Cleveland. They were most interested in my PeopleSoft experience because they were anticipating a similar but larger installation. I joined as senior vice president, development and support. The bank was aggressively consolidating administrative functions like purchasing, human resources, and financial functions as part of a bank consolidation effort. My team was established to deliver large scale client server initiatives, like PeopleSoft, HR, and Oracle. I also designed and established an organization to manage the relationships between the services organization and bank. This team did strategic planning with the business units to establish a 3-year plan for systems and operational processes, as well as to deal with day to day matters.

Then, right around Christmas I got a call! This time it was Bank One Corporation in Columbus, Ohio. This opportunity was a difficult one to consider because relocating would impact my husband's position as managing partner of a law firm in Cleveland. After many long conversations, he decided he was ready for a change and joined a large law firm in Columbus. I was appointed senior vice-president of integration and conversion for Bank One, which was rapidly acquiring and consolidating banks. I managed the technology integration team for these consolidations. Later, I was promoted to chief technology officer for one of the bank's groups. The group did high risk financial lending; at the time it was focused on establishing multiple Web businesses. The technology group needed to be reenergized to keep the pace of the organization. This was done and the Web businesses were quite successful. Unfortunately for me, Bank One sold the profitable group, and this time there was no call.

As the Bank One group's sale was being finalized, I had a serendipitous meeting with the head of strategic planning for Limited Brands at a social function. During our conversation he saw a correlation between my experience and the needs of Limited Brands. Initially, the relevance was difficult for me to see but further conversations convinced me. As vice president of direct marketing systems, I aligned the somewhat maverick IT organization with the rest of the enterprise's IT organization. I was promoted to chief technology officer for Limited Brands. The responsibilities of this position change often and change dramatically depending on the needs of the business. It has included the definition and implementation of enterprise architecture, IT organizational success metrics, enterprise system implementations, and strategic system planning. The current focus is on the consolidation and implementation of an ERP system that will replace nearly all of the legacy systems and enable the company to materially change its operational construct, from distributed to federal. My team designed the enterprise architecture and will drive the implementation.

Company History

Limited Brands was founded in 1963. From one store in Columbus, Ohio, it has grown to over 3,800 stores carrying six retail fashion brands. Our brands include the following:

- Victoria's Secret
  - World renowned for intermit apparel, beauty products, sleepwear, hosiery, and fashion
- Express
  - A fashion leader for high quality work and casual wear for young men and women
- Bath & Body Works
  - A modern apothecary of beauty and well-being providing a holistic approach to the care of skin and body
- The Limited
  - Sophisticated fashion for women
- The White Barn Candle Co.
  - Products that add fragrance and ambiance to the home
- Henri Bendel
  - Fashion that reflects youthful New York glamour

In the March 3, 2003, issue of FORTUNE Magazine we were voted "World's Most Admired Companies" in the specialty retail industry. The receipt of this award is a reflection of our values. We want to do what's right for our customers and our suppliers. We are involved in and support our communities where we live and work. We are committed to being a responsible member of the global community.

My Company and Me

The issue that first required my attention at Limited Brands was alignment of the direct systems IT organization with the rest of the enterprise's IT organization. This group did not have an established direction, the staff was not effectively engaged, and the business did not believe it was being effectively supported. This required a focus on the business, translating its goals into technology objectives. I helped the team establish a communication process to align technology to the business and keep it there.

To be more specific, we established a monthly operational plan. The document outlined the business goals and correlated supporting technology projects and service levels, with a focus on relative priority and progress to date. To complement the plan, we established an executive (business) board to review, update, and change plans as the dynamic business changed. The operational plan and executive board synchronized the business and the application of technology.

Another issue that required attention was the lack of technology investment methodology at the enterprise level of Limited Brands. The issue was that many technology projects were approved and initiated without priority. With business partners from many diverse organizations wanting to know their project was starting immediately after approval, the limited technology work force was diluted over many projects; without resource focus, projects took much longer than necessary to finish.

The technology organization needed to understand project priorities to determine appropriate start times and resource allocations. This dynamic process determined relative project priority and impact to other projects with each addition. The process rules were devised, communicated, and incorporated into the technology organization's operational model.

Addressing the above issues has helped the communication between the technology and business functions of the company. The application of technology is more appropriately aligned with the business goals.

Another issue relates to the development and realization of enterprise architecture. What I mean by that is it is critical for an enterprise to have a strategy for technology solutions that fulfill the needs of the business in a holistic way. This was particularly difficult in our company because of its history of distributed organizations. Prior to 2000, each of the 20 or so organizations had its own independent technology organization. Consolidations of these systems resulted in a diverse portfolio that would not enable the new federal model of business operations.

The selection of an ERP solution was confirmed, with a multi year implementation strategy. Processes, including an architectural review board, were established to make sure that investments made in the interim are consistent with the future state strategy.

My Typical Week

My typical week varies dramatically week by week based on business needs. I find the variety to be refreshing. There are several things that seem to remain a constant challenge, and the week includes too many meetings and not enough time for staff development or strategic thinking.

Dealing with Users

The approach for our ERP implementation was a significant decision. There were two main options: to roll out by function (i.e., finance, planning, etc.) across businesses, or to roll out complete functionality by business. The function-focused approach decreased the risk to a given business but required heavy expenditures for temporary interfaces and caused a given business to be part of the transition for several years. The by business-focused approach increased risk to a given business but minimized temporary interfaces and required shorter (but more focused) interaction of the business. The by business-focused approach also minimized the risk to the enterprise, and it is the strategy that was chosen.

To assure business appropriateness of systems, subject matter experts were dedicated by the business to work on the process and system design. These individuals play an important role of enabling functionality that addresses the requirements of their business and ensuring that the functionality is appropriate for all enterprise businesses. They have to check their business unit biases at the door.

We involve the users throughout the entire process. They are involved in defining the requirements for any revised business processes. Process owners act as the independent review of the configured systems. When the system is ready for implementation, they "test drive" it by developing "what if" scenarios. They are directly involved in integration testing and ensuring the system will operate as they anticipate. They are the ones who give the nod of approval for us to proceed.

Deciding on Technology Investments

A portfolio view of technology investments was developed to assure a balanced investment across infrastructure, tactical, and strategic investments. A board of investment directors acts to align the business strategy with appropriate investments.

Current Issues

Currently, I have two main areas of focus. One area involves the implementation of an ERP system. The other area relates to ensuring our current technology organization is ready to facilitate organizational change.

The first issue involves the design and implementation of systems to support the change in business strategy. Actually, we see this as an opportunity rather than an issue. We are in the process of changing the business from a decentralized model to a centralized model. Our information systems must support this enterprise view. We are implementing a number of software applications, including SAP, over the next couple of years. The challenge is to remain focused on the tactics of a successful set of implementations but to retain a strategic perspective with all of our other design and development activities.

The other issue relates to the IT function's organizational change, including cultural and process change. First, we are trying to more clearly recognize leadership within the organization. We want to identify those individuals who clearly contribute with a positive attitude and a customer service orientation. These are the cultural aspects of the people we want to invest in. They are going to be our leaders of the future. We have a process where these individuals are identified so that we can make investments in their future via opportunities or training. We want to be sure they have a role on the future of our organizations and that they know they do.

The second aspect here relates to business processes. We have identified that our current business processes are not sufficiently integrated to support our strategic systems, which are highly complex. As we integrate our business processes through technology, our risk increases. We are cognizant of this change and are taking action to implement industrial strength processes.

Future Issues

One of the issues we will have to deal with in the near future relates to how much change an organization can tolerate. We are wrestling with the question, how big is too big? Technology is easy to design and implement, and the challenge which we believe has a limit is how much and how quickly change can be assimilated by individuals in the organization. The company is bullish about the future and wants to drive to a dramatically different model quickly. Aligning the change necessary for the people and the systems is a point of focus which must also be assimilated with a corporate environment of merger and acquisition possibilities.

Staffing is another important issue. The enterprise transformation program has created a bubble of demand for staff. We need many more people than we normally employ. We need different skills than we currently have. But, we will only need these skills for 2 to 3 years. So, the issue relates to how we balance our financial commitments, the values of the company, and getting the project completed. It is very important that we get this right. For instance, the financial perspective would suggest hiring a large number of staff with the appropriate skills and then let them go when the project is complete. However, this is contrary to our company values, which suggests acquiring the services of contractors or consultants for the necessary period of time. This approach seems more palatable from our company values perspective. We do not want to be known as one of those companies that hires and lets people go based upon project activity.

Offshore staffing is an important consideration in the staffing conundrum. We are working with outsourcing services in India, using both onshore and offshore coordination points. Our experience has been very good.

Final Comments

The personal challenge of synchronizing technology with business strategy is most rewarding.

References

Limited Brands (n.d.). Retrieved January 30, 2007, from www.limitedbrands.com

Chapter XXI

John Zarb
Libbey

My name is **John A. Zarb**. Until recently, I was the chief information officer at Libbey.

Personal History

I was born in Highland Park, Michigan, which is right by Detroit. After high school, I joined the military. Because I expected to end up there anyway, I joined. I thought I could get a trade, grow up a bit, and see the world. All that happened and more! Because I had joined I was given 15 minutes to convince someone where I should be assigned. I had worked part time during high school at a grocery store with two young men who were studying computers. So, during my 15 minutes I said I really wanted to be a computer guy and that I thought I had the aptitude. Well, instead of being assigned to Fort Polk, Louisiana, and shipped off to Vietnam, I was sent to the computer department at Fort McArthur, California.

In September, 1969, I met Sally Nowinski. Her first comment was, "John Zarb, how wonderful to see you. We have been waiting for the experienced computer operator to show up." After a tour of the facility I said, "Sally, I have never seen any of this stuff before. In fact, I have never seen a computer before." She looked at me with tremendous disappointment. I was thinking about where I would be shipped. So, I told Sally I was a quick learner and asked for 2 weeks before she made a decision about me. It all worked out and I was there for 4 months. Today, 36 years later, we are still very dear friends.

My next assignment was at CINCPAC in Hawaii. This is where all the logistics and planning was coordinated for Vietnam. It was also the headquarters for all activity in the Pacific region. I was stationed here for 2 years in a state-of-the-art computer centre working with what was considered at the time very modern computers. Also, during this time I was taking programming courses at Chaminade University in Hawaii. Before I finished, I was shipped home and released from my military service.

So, I returned to Detroit, 20 years old, with a great resume, including 2 solid years of computer experience. As any young Detroiter would want to do, I set out to work for an auto company. I got my $18 sports coat and my $6 pair of pants and headed out to Ford with my resume in hand. In the personnel department, I was promptly told they would not even consider me because I did not have a 4-year university degree. I was heartbroken. But I was not going to give up. I finally got a contract programming position with Computer Services Corporation. My first contract was at Ford! A few months later they offered me a position.

I found myself working with state-of-the-art computers again. At the time Ford had the largest nongovernment data centre in the country. In the evenings I was working on my degree, first at community colleges and later at Eastern Michigan University. I graduated in 1977 and had 8 years experience by then in computing. I remember a conversation I had with my boss at the time. While I was enjoying programming, I wanted more. I wanted to get into the factories and I wanted to see our operations in the rest of the world. My boss thought I was crazy. He told me that if I played my cards right I would have his job, programming manager, in 15 years. It did not take me long to figure out that as one of 2000 information technology professionals at Ford, this was not going to fit into my long term plans. Ford is an institution in Detroit and few people leave. But, I started nosing around a little bit.

I started reading Fortune, Wall Street Journal, and Business Week to search out companies that I would like to work for. This is where I found Bill Agee, who was, at 36, the chairman of Bendix, a supplier to the automotive industry for brakes, filters, and spark plugs. I was drawn to the company and was lucky to get an interview and job offer in September 1978 to join their management development program.

I started at Bendix in the audit department. Because a lot of the accounting systems were now automated, the auditors needed a way to look into the computer files of payables and receivables. So, the plan was to form an EDP audit department. The timing really worked in my favor. Within 2 years, I was leading this department.

Bendix was purchased by Allied Chemical in 1983 after a lot of takeover activity. I was given the assignment as the director of information planning for Allied Automotive. So, I was back in the mainstream of information technology. I started to get more operational, office systems, and planning experience. I was learning the business at a managerial level. I worked with vendor contracts and procurement of services. I also had the chance to explore an "intrapreneurialship," where the company invested in a high tech consulting company, and I co-managed the Detroit office. This was a real exploration and one which taught me a lot. Then, in 1986, I went to work for the Bendix Safety Restraints Division of Allied Automotive. It was a 450 million dollar seatbelt company. Airbags were just starting to be used in cars and we expanded enormously over the next 5 years. I was involved in installing my first ERP system. At the senior management level, I was heavily involved in building plants from the ground up, joint ventures, mergers and acquisitions, and due diligence work. Also, at this time I was working on an Executive MBA at Michigan State University. Both my work and this educational experience helped me to realize that this was what all those years of training were leading me to do. It was a wonderful place to be at a wonderful time of growth. This 5 year assignment was absolutely priceless in learning how to become a CIO. Every decision I made had a direct impact on the bottom line.

Along with this phenomenal growth came expansion in Europe, among other places. I was traveling there to oversee the installation of information systems. In 1991, I was asked if I would take on the role of director of information technology for Europe. After some discussion, and it was a family decision, we moved to Brussels. I found myself in charge of 19 operating units in 12 different countries. I found the best way to learn a culture is to live in it. Over the next 4 years, I learned how to work with the different groups of people from different countries of Europe. We installed SAP in all of our operating divisions. About 2 years into this assignment, we moved to Paris. I had a fabulous team and it was a wonderful tour of duty. But for family reasons (our children were approaching high school age) we decided to move back to the United States.

I was lucky enough to get an assignment as CIO for the automotive aftermarket for Allied Signal in Rhode Island. Now, I had the title of CIO. But you know, even as difficult as it is to move to a new culture, it is even more difficult to return to your own culture. Things change, people change, and you change. So, the Rhode Island assignment became a stepping stone. My wife, Connie, and I decided we needed to be closer to Michigan and we needed to downsize. Also, at this time, my father was seriously ill and I was regularly flying back to Detroit. On one of the flights I read in the Wall Street Journal that Libbey was looking for a CIO in Toledo, Ohio. After some investigation, I thought this is the company for me. It fits what I would like to do and it fits what my family would like to do. I applied for the position and beat out 200 other candidates. So, I started as CIO of Libbey.

Company History

Libbey is the leading producer of glass tableware in North America. This 185-year-old company, with head office in Toledo, Ohio, has operations in the U.S., Portugal, and the Netherlands, is building in China, and is involved in a joint venture operation in Mexico. Products include glass tableware, ceramic dinnerware, metal flatware, and various plastic utensils. These products are distributed to food service companies and through retail establishments in more than 75 countries. According to the Web site, Libbey's corporate culture is reflected in the following statements:

Vision

World-Class, Second to None.

Mission

To expand Libbey's tabletop leadership
in a growing world market

Values

Libbey has five core values.
These values form the basis for how we work together to achieve results, and describe the five most important elements of the Libbey culture.

Teamwork

- *Get involved*
- *Involve others*
- *Challenge with respect*

Change

- *Embrace it*
- *Promote it*
- *Make it happen*

Performance

- *Exceed challenging goals*
- *Have a sense of urgency*
- *Quality throughout*

Respect

- *Listen*
- *Value others' opinions*
- *Treat people fairly*

Development

- *Learn*
- *Encourage*
- *Coach*

Through a series of acquisitions and cost efficiencies, Libbey provides exceptional service to its customers in the food services industry and retail distributors. Based upon its corporate philosophy Libbey provides technical advice to glass tableware manufactures throughout the globe.

My Company and Me

I started at Libbey in 1996. The first issue that I became involved with was the implementation of an ERP system. About 2 years before my start we had made a decision to acquire JD Edwards ERP system. By the time I started, the implementation was underway with the financials and purchasing modules already installed. Also, just before I arrived, Libbey had made a strategic acquisition. So, they were looking for someone who had ERP implementation experience and they needed someone to hit the ground running. It was certainly something I was prepared to do and enjoyed doing. But, it is almost like jumping on a moving locomotive. The jumping part may not be that difficult but you sure have to catch up quickly.

Well, I started in April of 1996, when we were looking to install the manufacturing and sales order modules, along with integrating the new company, by September 1. This date was imposed because it represented the start of our busy holiday season. Unfortunately, we did not make the date. But, we did complete the installation by the end of our first quarter of 1997.

This project was a very tough implementation. The first 6 months of duty at Libbey for me was lots of hours and lots of immersion. I spent a lot of time getting to know the people, customers, processes, and products. All at the same time we were really at a crescendo with the implementation of the ERP system.

A lot of the issues that I had to deal with regarding this implementation were similar to those that I had to deal with when working overseas. There is usually resistance to change and this project was no different. An ERP system by its very nature changes processes quite dramatically. People may have been doing something one way for quite some time and now the software insists that they do it another way. It is difficult to convince many users of an ERP system that the software is smart enough to do their work in a better way. But, over time, by mid 1997, about 1 year into the job, we had manufacturing, sales order processing, and distribution systems up and running, and running well. But, it was a difficult first year.

Another major issue that I initially had to deal with was relating to my experience in this industry. Remember, I spent 24 years in the automotive industry, first at Ford and then the automotive supplier, Bendix. So, I needed to learn an entirely new industry. I had to learn about the customer base, the product set and the way in which people operated. Also, closely related to the new industry was a new culture. Remember, I had been working overseas and on the east coast of the United States. Well, the midwestern culture is different.

The way we would oftentimes get things done in the automotive industry is just look you straight in the eye and say, "here's what we need and here's when we need it. I am expecting you to do it. I'll be taking measurements on a regular basis. If you make it, that is going to be wonderful. But, if you don't, I suppose you won't be around." So, that was really my mindset.

It is a little more family-oriented here at Libbey. While I quickly embraced this approach, my instincts took some time to change. I was just more direct and much more quick and succinct about making things change organizationally. But, I changed a lot. Also, the company began to see accountability as being an important attribute. So, I think it was mutually beneficial. My adjustment to the corporate culture here at Libbey was not unlike my adjustment to the culture when I worked in Europe.

My Typical Week

I average about 10 hours per day at work. The first thing I do each day is coordinate my calendar. I review what will be happening that day. I line up my appointments and ensure all the prework is done and that I have all the necessary files. Next, I check out how things are running simply by clicking on a series of icons that show me the status of various important system functions. If there are any problems I need to deal with, I will know right away. If there were any problems overnight I will receive an e-mail, known here as a problem corrective action report (PCAR).

Meetings take up about half of my day. They may be internal, vendor, customer, or overseas conference calls. The items may range from the very specific issues to long range strategic planning.

I spend some time on administrative tasks such as budgets, organizational issues, planning, and reporting. I will also have face-to-face discussions with my team members. One hour of my day may be taken up by doing e-mail, interactive messaging, phone calls, writing memos, or doing spreadsheets.

The remainder of my day is devoted to the future.

My daily routine may be altered due to traveling, training, facilitating strategic planning meetings, or attending bi-monthly or annual budget meetings.

I am a firm believer in allocating equal time to three important things.

- Keep the business running well
- Continuously improve the business
- Define and aim for the future

Dealing with Users

You know, users come in many different flavors. There are the day to day, heads down people who are using IT solutions. The people in my department are constantly working with this user base. I spend more time with their managers and the senior people in the company.

I think there are three fundamental levels to this position. The first level is about keeping the business running well. This is the kind of day to day interaction between the users and the IT staff. The second level relates to continuous improvement. Here, the relationship with the users is more projects-oriented. We may need to set up a project to replace 30% of our PCs this year so that we can provide people with more computer power on their desks. We may need to install a preventative maintenance system in our mold shop. We might want to establish connectivity with our bank so that we can eliminate the need for faxing. That's the second level, which is about improving existing processes. The third level relates to defining and aiming for the future. This is directed more at the strategic level and is the level where the CIO must spend most of the time. So, I might discuss a scenario with senior management to see if there is a creative way to address any issues they may anticipate requiring resolution in the future.

Deciding on Technology Investments

We make technology investments in the same way as any other important investments here at Libbey. Whether it's a decision to acquire new Blackberries or a decorating machine for glass, it is a given that we will determine the return on investment. We will also consider such aspects as cost avoidance and how the investment might make us look to our customers. That is, will it make us more competitive in the marketplace?

The problem with technology investments is the extremely short life span. If you buy a warehouse or a piece of factory equipment, you can expect it to last 30 years or so. This is certainly not the case with technology investments. We are currently upgrading our e-mail system. But there will be a new level release in just 3 months. I have to wonder why we are putting our customers through this change when we will probably ask them to do it again so soon.

Current Issues

Libbey was formed in 1818 as a private company in the state of Massachusetts. It later moved to Toledo, Ohio, because of the access to natural gas, sand, and workers, all the components necessary to make glass. Then in 1993, we went public and over the next 7 years performance was very positive. We delivered good results to our shareholders. It seemed that each quarter we established a new record for revenue, income from operations, and earnings per share. In the world of publicly traded companies, that is the formula. The year 2000 was a particularly good year because of the millennium. The millennium created an artificial one-time event with parties going on all around the world. Sales in 2000 were particularly strong for us because of the demand for glass. Then along came 2001 and September 11th, which is still having a ripple effect in many industries, including the hospitality industry. The downturn of the hospitality and airline industries affected our sales. Also, the SARS situation even further affected travel and tourism.

We started to have performance issues because we had developed a certain capacity which was not being utilized. It becomes a slippery slope quite quickly. Because of the kind of process industry we are in, our furnaces must run continuously. We cannot switch them off and go home. So, we made some major adjustments to cut back on our capacity.

In conjunction with our cutbacks, our overseas competitors saw an opportunity to expand their production. They slowly became forces to reckon with. They found U.S.-based partners and became known here. Many of the large retailers here in the

United States have become large importers of glassware products. In the past we could have counted on them to consider buying U.S. made products.

So, these major events have changed the principle players in the industry and have also changed the business model. We have changed as a result. For instance, we have established a plant in China so that we can be a local supplier to that country. In the past, we would have expanded a U.S.-based plant and exported to that country. We have entered the European market with the purchase of companies in Holland and Portugal. We are building up our European thrust not only in terms of sales but also in terms of local manufacturing.

We are also attempting to deal with and respond to a number of cost factors. We are faced with extremely high natural gas process. That is the most costly raw material that goes into our process. So natural gas has become a very huge part of our cost base. Also, our workers form another part of our cost base. Currently, we are attempting to deal with cost issues related to medical and pensions. As pension investments in mutual funds receded, we have had an increased exposure to our pension liabilities. As a publicly traded company we have to respond to this issue. I realize we are not alone in having to deal with this issue.

In summary, we have been making glass for a 185 years and we really know how to do it. The manufacturing process at this company is considered a core competence. It is considered a strategic advantage because we have a tremendous engineering department. We have a very good manufacturing department that really knows how to make glass. But it's the external forces that are changing the rules of how we conduct our business. It is a continual struggle to try to keep up.

So, given this environment as CIO, I participate along with other senior management in attempting to respond. There are a number of initiatives related to employing technology to support this response.

We are becoming far more cost conscious than ever before. I spoke at a conference recently at the University of Toledo. The conference was about open source vs. proprietary systems. There were vendors in attendance from Microsoft, Sun, IBM, HP, Dell, and Novel. I was introduced as still having the first nickel my mother ever gave me. Apparently, I have this reputation with the local vendors. This certainly does not embarrass me because at the end of the day our biggest job is to keep the costs controlled. I continually try to chip away at the costs in this company.

We are also trying to help the company move forward without a great deal of lead time. We must develop solutions faster through more rapid development and execution. So, we do a lot more benchmarking. We learn more from listening to customers who have already purchased and installed a product than we learn from the actual vendors. Now, we do not proceed unless we have talked with four or five other companies that have already installed the product. We are not installing unique, first generation solutions. It just is not practical at this time when cost is such an important business driver.

Furthermore, I am also making my services more available to the rest of the company. I assist with strategic planning and I provide project management services. Because of the size of the company, I am able to work a lot closer to the business. That certainly suits me.

Future Issues

Let me refer to the first issue here as "organizational utility." What I mean by this is that the computer is becoming a commodity tool in many businesses.

I sit on the board of a local hospital and I see the computer being as important to the patient as the doctor. There may be a dozen processors attached to a patient checking up to 50 different readings. That is the way our factories operate today. We need computers with speed capable of controlling such business aspects as thermal temperatures, piece counts, rejects, and quality inspections.

Furthermore, people are coming out of university these days with a significant amount of computer literacy. Perhaps a few years ago they would have called their IT person to help them restart a control unit or computer. Now they are capable to do those themselves. So, the first level support can be accomplished by the person themselves on the factory floor or in the hospital room. The second level, if they cannot do it themselves, could then be done by their supervisor. Finally, the third level is IT. So, we need fewer IT specialists. Their role will change to be more tightly coupled with the business requirements. Eventually, we may even reach the point where IT as we know it today may not even exist.

A second issue relates to cost control within IT. The cost of IT is very complicated and in some cases misunderstood. It is difficult for many who are not in IT to relate to costs associated with software maintenance, telecommunications, networks, long distance charges, and annual maintenance fees. It used to be that the head of the IT department would simply say we need the money and it would be approved. Now the CIOs, if they are going to maintain their role, must be prepared to justify the expenditure and will be tested about how they are controlling costs.

Another aspect of cost control relates to using IT to reduce expenditures throughout other parts of the company. The concept of the lean enterprise basically means taking the waste out of the major business processes.

The last issue here relates to incorporating IT into our products. That is, what can we do to our product to make it easier for our customer? Can we do something that will differentiate our product from that of our customer? Perhaps we could use technology to make our products a little bit more sophisticated to reduce our customer's cost of placing our product in inventory. We could use radio frequency identification (RFID) tags and our product could be ready to go onto the shelf when it arrives at the customer's premises.

Final Comments

I started in this field as a 17-year-old computer operator in 1969. I have been involved and watched this industry grow. To be involved in an industry that has changed so much has been an absolute privilege. But, I am saddened and a bit frustrated that we are still somewhat misunderstood. We are still quite young in the field of business. We are still the little brother with milk on his chin.

The appropriate use of technology can really accelerate the pace of any business process. But, it requires all senior management, especially the CEOs, to understand how the contribution may be made.

I think some interesting things are going to happen over the next 10 to 20 years. I want to be part of that.

References

Libbey (n. d.). Retrieved January 30, 2007, from www.libbey.com

Section V

Conclusion

The goal in creating this book was to document issues identified by the CIO and to explore these issues relative to various corporate and national contexts. In-depth exploratory interviews document major issues addressed by the CIO. Issues are identified based on a chronological discussion of the CIO's career. In general, the role of the CIO is to manage information technology for the benefit of the firm. The activities performed by the CIO will have a direct impact on the firm's bottom line. It is thus incumbent upon the CIO to ensure that the use of information technology is aligned with the business goals and objectives of the firm.

This section consists of three chapters which describe how the results of the interviews were initially reviewed and then analyzed. There is also a discussion of the content of the themes that were identified.

Chapter XXII: "Reviewing CIO Comments" presents a discussion of the content of the comments offered by each CIO in response to the general categories of questions in the interviews. To begin, the first section presents summary data about what the participants did before they became a CIO. This section discusses their early life and education, provides an overview of the types of positions held before the participant became a CIO, and outlines some of the comments made about why the participant accepted the position of CIO. Following this initial discussion, the chapter presents sections related to the major category of questions asked during the interviews. These major categories are as follows:

- Dealing with Users
  - How the CIO interacts with various levels of users within the organization
- Deciding on the Technology
  - What aspects surround the decisions about the acquisition of technology for the corporation
- Initial Issues
  - Categories of issues that required the CIO to take action upon, assuming the CIO position
- Current Issues
  - Issues the CIO is dealing with now (or at the time of the interview)
- Future Issues
  - These are issues the CIO foresees having to deal with in the future

Chapter XXIII: "Analyzing CIO Comments" presents an analysis of the comments made by the CIOs. Mintzberg's managerial roles framework is introduced and the components are described. The themes identified within each of the major categories of the CIO interviews are then mapped into the roles described in the framework. This process supports a discussion of the analysis of the CIO comments about their management experiences. The final section of the chapter presents some concluding remarks.

Chapter XXIV: "Final CIO Comments" presents an overview of the final comments made by the CIOs. At the end of each interview, the CIO was asked to provide an overall comment from a general perspective about how they interpret their role within the context of their company. These interpretive comments are divided into three main categories. The first category presented in the chapter includes comments about the internal operations of the CIO's business unit. The second category relates to the CIO's interpretation of how the information systems business unit should relate to the corporate user community. The third category discusses how the CIOs view their role in relation to senior management. A brief conclusion section ends this chapter.

Chapter XXII

Reviewing CIO Comments

Introduction

This chapter presents a discussion of the content of the comments offered by each CIO in response to the general categories of questions in the interviews. To begin, the first section presents summary data about what the participants did before they became a CIO. This section discusses their early life and education, provides an overview of the types of positions held before the participant became a CIO, and outlines some of the comments made about why the participant accepted the position of CIO. Following this initial discussion, the chapter presents sections related to the major category of questions asked during the interviews. These major categories are as follows:

- Dealing with Users
    - How the CIO interacts with various levels of users within the organization
- Deciding on the Technology
    - What aspects surround the decisions about the acquisition of technology for the corporation

- Initial Issues
    - Categories of issues that required the CIO to take action upon assuming the position of CIO
- Current Issues
    - Issues the CIO is dealing with now (or at the time of the interview)
- Future Issues
    - These are issues the CIO foresees having to deal with in the future

The data in Table 1 will be referenced in the following sections. Because of the very small sample size relative to the overpopulation of CIOs in each country, it is not possible to make a generalized statement about gender differences or preCIO role experience. However, it is interesting to note the gender differences across the countries of those who volunteered to participate in this book. Two of the five CIOs in New Zealand are females. There were no females who participated from Taiwan. Of the seven participants from the United States, two are female. It is also interesting to note that the majority of CIOs from both the United States and Taiwan had technical experience before they became a CIO. However, in New Zealand the majority came from a business background.

Table 1. CIO demographics

	New Zealand	Taiwan	United States	Total
Gender				
Male	3	6	5	14
Female	2	0	2	4
Education				
College		1		1
Some Uni	2			2
Bachelor	1	3	2	6
Masters	2	1	5	8
PhD		1		1
PreCIO Role				
Technical	2	5	6	13
Business	3	1	1	5

Before Becoming a CIO

All of the participants indicated that they were born and grew up in the countries in which they now hold the position of CIO. A few mentioned that they are children of parents who immigrated to the country. Some individuals traveled or studied in another country for some period of time. But, all were drawn back to their country of origin in order to progress in their respective careers or for family reasons.

As shown in Table 1, almost all of the participants have obtained either a bachelor's or master's degree. The bachelor's degree was either in business or some subject area related to the products and services offered by the company. In all cases, the master's degree is a Master of Business Administration.

Positions held before becoming a CIO were either technical- or business-oriented. Only two of the CIOs progressed through the company from a business perspective. Both had only worked for their respective companies and are thoroughly knowledgeable about the company and its industry. The remaining CIOs have more technically-oriented career paths. These career paths reflect the normal progression from programmer or software developer through more senior positions such as systems analysts. Eventually, the CIO would move into management and advance to the position of CIO. Some CIOs before they assumed their role were consultants providing advice to many different organizations about the use of information technology. Most CIOs worked in the industry in which they became a CIO. Very few have moved from one industry to another. In the case where this has transpired, the CIO has indicated a very steep learning curve with regard to acquiring the knowledge of how the business functions in this new industry.

The final general comment for this section is about the reasons the participant accepted the CIO position. In the majority of cases the participant was approached about assuming the position. If the participant was already employed by the company, they were either asked or assigned to the position. Some of these situations arose due to a major reorganization of the company and the consequent recognition of the importance of establishing within the company a senior position responsible for the management of information technology. Also, with the recognition of the importance of information technology, some companies found that they had to look outside to find someone who could fill the position and relate to the type of business processes involved with the specific company or industry. In the case where the CIO position was filled from outside the company, most individuals were contacted by a senior manager of the company. Very few actually responded successfully to an advertisement.

It is interesting to note that a number of the CIOs indicated that they accepted the position because of the opportunity to respond to the challenge of such a position. They indicated that there was the challenge of helping the company to adopt information technology for overall benefit. They also recognized the challenge of establishing a new position on the senior management team and the opportunity to develop a reputation both for themselves and the position. They felt they were contributing to the formal recognition of the importance of information technology to the company.

Dealing with the Users

This section presents the themes that were identified in the interviews that relate to how the CIO established processes to deal with the users within the company. Themes that were identified include such aspects as perspectives presented by different levels of groups within the company, help desk service as an initial point of contact for the users, and client services for the resolution of more long term issues.

A factor that affects all aspects of dealing with users has to do with change. Any time a user involves the services of the information systems area, the result will be a revised process. Thus, it is incumbent upon those individuals who work in the information systems area to realize how change and resistance to change may affect the attitudes of users to the resolution of an issue. Many implementation efforts fail due to user resistance (Joshi, 2005). The information systems professional must continually strive to ensure that users recognize there will be change and that they are committed to work toward a revised business process for the benefit of the work unit and the overall company. The CIOs who were interviewed indicated they emphasized open and ongoing communication with all levels of users. As shown in the next subsection, CIOs will focus their interaction with members of senior management. The CIOs also stated that they established a process to facilitate communication between their staff and other department's members. These processes may include such vehicles as newsletters, as well as regular and frequent meetings.

Alternative Perspectives

There are users who work at different levels within the organization. The range may extend from the senior management board members to an accounting clerk in the payroll department. The CIO will spend most of their time with senior management. When interacting with senior management, the CIOs indicated that they try to create opportunities to have one-on-one meetings where they would discuss issues related to the direction of the company and the issues surrounding potential use of information technology to support future corporate plans. Further, at this senior level, the dialogue should focus on the future. Issues should be discussed at the strategic planning level. The focus should be on ways to improve operations, or aspects that may be impacting the industry. The results of these discussions will support the identification of key information technology objectives for the company.

Help Desk

The Help Desk or Service Desk is the users' first line of contact with the information services function. The CIOs noted that this fact should be reinforced as often as possible. This is where the information systems function captures requests for service. Most requests for service are resolved during the first phone contact. However, if this is not possible the request is escalated. This escalation may result in one of two possible outcomes. First, a more knowledgeable technician may respond to the request and resolve the issue. Second, the request may be more of a systems performance issue and should be directed to a Client services function. This function is discussed in the next subsection of this chapter.

The CIOs reported that calls to the Help Desk provide valuable information. An analysis of the types of calls and their content provide input to future training plans (Casey & Doverspike, 2005). The training may be designed for the user community or for those information systems professionals involved in the development and implementation of information systems. Also, the establishment of a Help Desk is another way the CIO can promote communication between the information systems department and other functional areas within the company.

Client Services

The description of the client services function in this subsection deals with identifying users' needs and determining information systems specifications to address these requirements.

Some of the CIOs interviewed identified a gap which exists between the users and the information systems department. The establishment of the Client services function will serve as a bridge between these two groups. Individuals within this group will be able to understand the business requirements and to interpret these requirements into an information system capable of responding to these user requirements. Another function of this unit is the consolidation of requests for service. Because the staff members within this unit are knowledgeable of both business functions and the capability of information technology, they will understand how some requests may be resolved through the development and adoption of one solution.

Some of the CIOs who were interviewed work with the user departments to develop a long range information systems plan. These plans identify applications which may prove beneficial in the future. Further, the information systems plan must be aligned with the business strategy (Clarke & Doherty, 2004; Rathnam, Johnson, & Wen, 2005). Further, these plans are eventually identified as budget items. To become a budget item, a business case must be developed which documents the requirements based upon a gap analysis of what exists and the needs to be addressed. Thus, before the project is initiated agreement must exist between the two parties. This agreement, in the form of a project charter, will facilitate the management of expectations. Finally, as part of a continuous improvement process, a review at the conclusion of the project will identify any variance between the business case and the final product. This variance may necessitate further action for the project or the revision or improvement of skill sets of the project participants.

Each individual project should start with a project charter. This is considered an official document which outlines the work to be done, the scope, how the project will be managed, and an estimate of costs. The project charter documents expected outcomes and forms the basis for project related decisions (Hayes, 2000). Agreement must be signified by a senior manager in the user department.

When a request for service is initiated, a meeting will be held between the Client services unit and a user department representative. This meeting is used to ensure both sides understand and agree upon the requirements. Based upon these requirements a new system may be developed or an existing system may be modified. Alternatively, the solution may be as simple as modifying a manual process. In all cases, other areas of the company must be considered. That is, the functional requirements of another area of the company may impinge upon the resolution of an issue in the requesting area. Further, a solution of an issue in one area may provide an applicable solution in another area. All of these associations should be considered in the development of solutions. An overall benefit to the entire company should be paramount in addressing user requests.

The CIOs also commented on the use of some version of a work breakdown structure. At the detailed project level, a method should be employed which is acceptable to everyone involved. The method may include breaking down the project into small identifiable action items and the employment of such techniques as prototyping. Whatever method is employed, it should facilitate the engagement of the user from the beginning of the project and throughout the remaining activities of the project. The CIOs commented about their desire to facilitate this engagement in an ongoing manner.

User participation in systems development will contribute to the success of the system. McKeen and Guimaraes (1997) investigated levels of user participation in systems development projects. They determined that users should be more involved in information systems development when the complexity of the tasks to be incorporated into the system is high. They further proposed that the nature of the participation should relate to specific activities, including team membership for feasibility, identifying and approving requirements, interface design, and team member for installation. Participation in other activities neither contributed to nor hindered the successful outcome of the system development effort.

The CIOs also mentioned another function performed by the Client services unit which is project management (Gillard, 2004; Gowan & Mathieu, 2005) through the establishment of a project management office (Hill, 2004). Service requests are used to identify action items, which in turn become projects. A standard set of operating procedures are then employed to conduct the project. Regular project meetings are held with the user department to discuss progress at each stage of the project. Both the user department and the client services unit must sign off at each stage to indicate their agreement that the delivery of services matches the original plan for the project as approved by the user and the Client services unit. From a longer term perspective, the CIOs are working toward improving the probability of project success through the acquisition of appropriate skills and providing experience (Kanter & Walsh, 2004). Another initiative of the project management office is user satisfaction. On a regular and frequent basis, user satisfaction surveys are conducted. Feedback is employed to analyze current operations. Also, information is obtained about future issues that should be addressed.

Outsourcing is another alternative approach considered by CIOs to address the needs of users. This service may be employed for two different situations. First, outsourcing may be initiated to provide service for noncritical information systems. This approach will allow internal staff to focus on those systems that are considered important for the company. Second, projects may be outsourced which require specific knowledge or a skill set that is not available internally. A decision must be made in this situation that this knowledge or skill set will not be necessary in the future after the completion of the specific project.

Some of the CIOs took the approach that users should be encouraged to describe what they need rather than how an issue should be resolved. The users should focus on identifying their requirements by describing the business process. Ensuring a thorough understanding of the business process will assist in the development of a solution. A further consideration here relates to the solution perspective. It is not sufficient to simply implement a solution to support current operations. In the long run, it will be more beneficial to the functional work unit and the company to investigate how technology can be employed to facilitate the improvement of operations. Further, the information system must respond to the shared values and expectations of the users (Martinsons & Chong, 1999).

Summary: Dealing with Users

In summary, the CIOs felt it was important to establish a positive relationship with the users. When working with users at any level, all employees of the information services function had to be cognizant of a general resistance to change. Users need to be guided from a comfortable situation in their current operations to a somewhat uncomfortable experience of implementing and working in a new work environment with a new or modified information system. Both the users and information systems professionals, under the guidance of the CIO, have to understand how information technology may be employed to improve business processes. It is not sufficient for only the information systems professional to know this. The information systems professional cannot force the user to adopt an unknown technology which will change their own business process. Thus, the information systems professional and the user must work together. It is necessary, however, for the information systems professional to ensure that requirements are documented as early as possible in the development of a new information system. Indeed, the information systems professional may consider challenging the user to ensure the appropriate identification of requirements. The information systems professional must attempt to deliver what the user really needs, not necessarily what the user may want. Also, the information systems professional must guard against adopting an appealing technological response to a business problem which may not be necessary. The focus should be on the improvement of a business process for the benefit of the overall operation of the company.

Deciding on Technology Investments

The themes presented in this section relate to how decisions are made within the company about acquiring various forms of technology.

Committees

The use of management-oriented steering committees leads to investment decisions being made based more upon a business perspective rather than from a technological perspective. Karimi, Bhattacherjee, Gupta, & Somers (2000) determined that steering committees enhanced the sophistication of the management of the information technology within the company. They further suggested that steering committees contributed to the alignment of both business and information technology strategies. In turn, this alignment facilitated the appropriate selection and utilization of information technology resources for the company.

Standard Procedures

The annual budget process documents future plans for all business units. The plan includes a discussion of any new information system development that may be necessary to support the business unit plans. Budgeting for information technology is part of the overall corporate budgeting process. The corporate budget is derived from long term company direction and business plans.

A business case is prepared by the business unit at the start of a specific project. If it is deemed necessary to acquire some new hardware the business case is employed to justify the funding. However, the final decision regarding funding rests with the senior management team. So, the focus of the decisions is on the business processes rather than technology. Also, during the year, a budget adjustment may be necessary. If a change can be identified within the purview of a business case that will be beneficial to the company, then project priorities may have to be revised.

The company should develop a standard procedure for making specific technology investment decisions. To begin, evaluation criteria must be developed. If the information technology will be for infrastructure purposes, then the information systems area will develop the criteria. However, the user area will be involved if the information technology will be required for a functional application. Once the criteria have been developed, external resources should be contacted to provide responses to be evaluated.

The CIOs identified some investment decisions which can be difficult to analyze from a financial perspective. For instance, it is difficult to determine the return on investment on the acquisition of a new server. In this situation some of the CIOs reported that they base the decision on the provision of a service level to users. In many instances, the users are not interested in the details of these kinds of investments. They seem more interested in whether the infrastructure is in place to provide the desired level of service in the form of response time and availability. General hardware investments relate to replacement, replenishment, or obsolescence. Specific evaluations may not be carried out in these situations. The main evaluation criteria relates to the provision of service that satisfies the users.

People

There were many comments about the effort to develop the necessary individual skills to work with the information technology. Staff in general must possess the necessary skill sets and these skill sets must be kept as up to date as possible. The skill sets must be aligned with the requirements of the projects currently underway and those planned for the foreseeable future. These skills sets may be developed within the organization or acquired through outsourcing.

External Resources

Hardware and software vendors and systems consultants should be treated like partners. They too can help to add value when making information technology investment decisions. In order to create a win-win situation, the decisions should create value for the company and the external resource provider.

Summary: Deciding on the Technology

The adoption of new information technology should facilitate existing or planned business operations. A technology should not be implemented simply because it is new.

An interesting approach identified by some of the CIOs interviewed for this book relates to differentiating the evaluation of investment decisions. Thus, a different approach is taken depending on whether the investment is for infrastructure or an information systems application in support of a revised business process. If the investment is for infrastructure changes, the decision should be based upon improvement of service to users. Examples of infrastructure components are telecommunication services or servers. The improvement of service to users may be measured by user satisfaction surveys which could include questions about information system availability and response time.

The development and implementation of information systems in support of a business process should be evaluated in a similar way that any other company investment would be made. Thus, a business case should be developed. Alternative solutions may be considered within the purview of the company's use of return on investment calculations.

Initial Issues

This section presents a discussion of the themes which emerged about the issues that the participant initially had to deal with upon assuming the position of CIO. The major topic areas include management of the function which relates to actions taken within the direct area of responsibility for the CIO. The next major topic relates to management issues that related to the overall company. Issues in this instance relate to various forms of establishing recognition for the CIO within the company. Finally, issues related to the technical theme are presented.

One initial and nonrecurring issue related to Y2K. Many CIOs were hired at a time when the issue of Y2K was being addressed, which required unique one-time solutions. The important aspect of this issue is that it allowed the CIO to demonstrate their capability to contribute successfully to the resolution of a major problem for the company. This initial success would go a long way to establishing a positive reputation for both the CIO and the information systems services function throughout the company. This positive reputation would be very beneficial for subsequent initiatives in the employment of information technology for the company.

Management of the Fuction

Upon initial appointment, the area of responsibility for the CIO may require some reorganization. The CIO may have desired to have the right people in the right places. There may have been the necessity to set a new direction because of the establishment of the CIO role within the company. So, it was necessary to realign the information systems area and put in place new managers who could support the new direction.

The CIO not only will change the department, but also the jobs employees perform within the reorganized department. In the long run, the CIO must feel comfortable with the people in place and with the organization structure. Sometimes it might be necessary to help individuals realize it is time to move on or to retire. These can be quite agonizing decisions both for the individual as well as the CIO.

Another aspect which may be encountered upon the initial appointment of the CIO is a demoralized work force. Here again, the CIO may have been appointed because the information systems staff is overworked or underperforming. Further, they may not be receiving the recognition for their efforts. Thus, it is incumbent upon the new CIO to celebrate performance and to attempt to obtain company-wide recognition for the efforts of the information systems staff. There are a number of ways to celebrate the performance of information systems staff. One of the main ways is through financial rewards. While this approach may work in some situations, it may raise other issues. To begin, financial incentives are short lived. Also, the use of financial rewards can create (warranted or not) jealousies and potential conflict. Another way to celebrate performance involves different approaches to publicly recognizing individuals for their efforts. One example is a department newsletter.

The decision whether or not to outsource is another major issue (Fish & Seydel, 2006; Rao, 2004). To begin, it is necessary to decide what functions will be outsourced. Some CIOs preferred to retain their core competencies. Thus, what may be outsourced would be functions that the company is not directly dependent upon. If the decision is made to outsource a function, then a service level agreement (SLA) will be negotiated and signed. This agreement should clearly document the priority of service, price, and scope of the service. There should also be a clause related to costs for extra services. If, however, the decision is made to develop and retain the competency within the company, then a job description will be developed and recruitment activities initiated.

Many of the CIOs indicated that initially there was a requirement for them to deal with the issues surrounding system integration. Recall that the CIO was usually hired because of the recognition that information technology was becoming an important vehicle for improving the business. Also, in some cases, the company was expanding through sales growth or the acquisition of other entities. This meant also that systems may be acquired that were not originally designed to interact with each other. So, issues of incompatibility arose. It was therefore necessary to develop a plan to ensure that these systems could be integrated. This plan may have included a process of revising and updating the legacy systems. Alternatively, a completely new approach could be taken with the implementation of a cross-functional enterprise resource planning (ERP) system.

A project management office could be established with standard operating procedures for conducting projects. The project office could manage the requests from user departments and the conduct of feasibility studies. The project manager could be either from the project management office or from the functional area. In any case the project manager must take the lead of the project. At every stage the user department representative must sign off before the project may proceed further. Project managers must strive to ensure the quality and accuracy of the service delivered. Very early in the operation of the project management office, a process should be devised to help set priorities for projects. Both senior management and the functional areas should agree upon this process. There should also be a process in place that facilitates the revision to the established project priorities. This revision process will be necessary as the environment changes and new aspects come to light about the necessity to change business processes. The guidelines for establishing project priorities should also take into consideration a portfolio approach. That is, in a similar fashion to an investment portfolio, the company should be aware of which projects may be of higher risk than others. Information system projects may be designated as high risk because they involve the adoption of a new technology and incorporation of an approach that has not been employed by the information systems professionals involved in the project. As far as possible, multiple high risk information systems projects should be avoided. At a minimum, senior management should be informed that certain projects are higher risk than others.

Management of the Company

Some companies will initiate the CIO role as a way to change how they operate. Thus, the CIO role may be established to facilitate major revisions to the business processes of the company. Changes of this magnitude require the use of information technology, as well as a revised attitude about how to carry out business operations. The CIO is usually involved in both aspects and may be expected to provide the leadership necessary to facilitate both kinds of change. It was noted by several of the CIO participants that the cultural change requires significantly more effort than the technical change.

Communication with the users was also an initial issue that CIOs had to deal with. The CIO may have had to establish or improve the communication link with the users. In many instances this was accomplished through many face to face discussions about current requirements or future needs.

Initially, some CIOs encountered a dissatisfied user community within the company. This dissatisfaction may have been the result of poor performance or simply poor communication. In either case the response should be more and improved communication. It is important that the user community is knowledgeable about what the information systems function can provide in support of the business functions. If the dissatisfaction is the result of poor performance, the communication outlined above will provide information about areas that need improvement. It will then be necessary to take specific and direct action to make improvements in performance. One example was the installation of a help desk to respond to users' immediate needs.

Some of the companies are in regulated industries, such as telecommunications and media. This involvement necessitated the CIO to become knowledgeable in working with the appropriate regulatory bodies to ensure any new application of information technology would not contravene any established industry rules. In some cases, the CIO may be required to petition the regulator to attempt to have an existing regulation changed in order to facilitate the beneficial implementation of information technology for the company.

Governance was also an initial issue. The CIO may have found it necessary to demonstrate to senior management that they would have to take responsibility for the decisions about the implementation of information technology.

Technical

Issues in this section relate to initiatives of a technical nature that the company was in the process of implementing upon the arrival of the CIO. These technologies that may have been new to the CIO could include networks and infrastructure. In a number of instances, the CIO had to quickly become knowledgeable about the technology. Based upon their past experiences, the CIO may have not had to deal with technology in general or a specific aspect of technology. This situation resulted in a steep learning curve or the necessity to ensure someone was hired with the appropriate knowledge. Another technology which may have been new to the CIO could be the company Web site. On one hand, a technical specialist may be required to ensure the appropriate level of performance is attained from the Web site regarding responding to a specific volume of transactions and response time. On the other hand, the Web site may require the assistance of a marketing expert to ensure the appropriate type of content is developed and maintained in an up to date manner.

One major technology which may be employed to significantly change the culture of an organization is the implementation of an enterprise resource planning (ERP) system. If an organization is large enough to establish the role of CIO, then it is also probably large enough to consider the implementation of an ERP system. Indeed, the establishment of the CIO role and the implementation of an ERP system may occur in a similar time frame. Both aspects relate to the senior management recognition that information and information technology are important resources contribute to the overall performance of the company.

Another technical issue relates to standardization. There may be standardization issues for the internal operations of the information systems area, as well as issues for the overall company that may affect or be affected by the information systems area. Within the information systems area, there should be standards adopted for computers. Thus, there should perhaps be one type of laptop and one type of desk top. In both cases, the same operating system should be employed. This common approach will facilitate establishment of contracts with vendors. It will also make the initial imaging and maintenance of computers a great deal more efficient.

Summary: Initial Issues

It was extremely important that the CIO, very soon after accepting the position, met with success. This success must be recognized by both senior management and the rest of the company's user community. The CIO has to demonstrate how the new position can add value to the company. The CIO must initially develop a credible organization structure for the information system function capable of providing appropriate and satisfactory service to the rest of the company.

Current Issues

This section discusses issues that the CIOs identified that they are currently addressing. Again, these issues have been organized by the major categories of questions asked during the interviews.

Management of the Function

As companies change and adopt information technology to support current or revised business processes, the skill sets necessary to support these initiatives must be kept up to date. New information systems staff may require some time and training to become familiar with the corporate culture. From a management perspective, there are many "soft" skills that may be necessary. Communication skills will always remain important. Further, information systems professionals may be required to learn how to manage people, how to work as a team member, and to take responsibility in performing their duties. The acquisition of technical skills may require specific training unique to the company. Each company will have a unique mixture of legacy systems and cross-functional systems. Further, the company may have a Web site which could vary in complexity from simply providing static information to one that accepts payment for the provision of products or services.

Management of the Company

Governance is an issue that is currently attracting a lot of attention. It is currently being deemed necessary for senior management to be thoroughly knowledgeable about and involved in the decisions surrounding the implementation of information systems. They must retain responsibility for these types of decisions. Senior management must be cognizant of the value that these decisions may make to the company.

At the user level, within the company the gap between the users and information systems must be managed. Usually, information systems professionals are knowledgeable of the technology, while the users are more knowledgeable about the business processes. Thus, the information systems professionals should know how to lead the business professionals to learn about the capabilities and use of various information systems. This engagement period may be quite long because of the resistance to change. But, time must be taken to ensure the users realize the benefits of change and with the implementation of the new information system. Also, the information systems professional must be prepared to learn about the business process.

Several companies, whose CIOs participated in this book, are currently implementing or have recently implemented an ERP system. These systems are being employed to facilitate the cross-functional capability desired by organizations. Their implementation is a result of the senior management team recognizing the importance of information to the organization. Not only are these systems being used to facilitate decision making within the firm, but they are also supporting the intercompany sharing of information with business partners in the form of, for example, production plans. The implementation of ERP systems will support change in business strategy. Some companies see this as an opportunity rather than an issue. They want information systems to support the change in enterprise view from a centralized model to a more decentralized model. It is recognized that the implementation of an ERP system will facilitate a cultural transformation. Organizations are taking a more customer service orientation. Thus, it is important for all those involved to know what their role will be within the revised approach to conducting business.

The implementation of an ERP system will facilitate the evolution of the business processes to support a revised corporate perspective.

Some of the CIOs involved in this book are promoting the concept of business intelligence to allow managers to analyze vast amounts of data in a simple and easy way. To begin, employing the concept of business intelligence requires the existence a corporate database in the form of an ERP system. Then various data mining techniques may be employed to support the business intelligence effort. This is another situation where early success is important. The implementation of business intelligence should focus on a small number of high profile areas. This success should be communicated throughout the company. The communication will facilitate cooperation for subsequent implementation efforts. One approach to implementing the business intelligence concept described above is through the use of a "war room." A meeting room for senior management may be fitted with state of the art hardware and software. This will allow the provision of company-wide and up-to-date information for effective decision making. The business intelligence software will be supported by the data warehouse which is the major part of an ERP system.

Technical

An example of a technology issue that a company may be implementing currently is voice over internet protocol (VOIP). This facilitates the integration of telephone and Internet access and provides efficiencies with regard to economies of scale and mobility within the company offices.

Some companies are addressing a plethora of issues related to supply chain. These initiatives are related to the endeavor to more effectively manage inventory. Data is shared with suppliers relating to production plans which allow suppliers to ship the necessary inventory just before it is required in the manufacturing process.

Wireless communication supports mobility and constant communication. If the organization requires workers to be in touch with data as they move around the office or the plant, then some form of wireless facility may be considered.

radio frequency identification (RFID) is being employed to keep track of items that are important to the company. These items could be products or customers and their baggage. In all cases, it is anticipated that the use of RFID tags will ensure complete accuracy of items and their movement.

Summary: Current Issues

Currently, CIOs are working to ensure their team has up-to-date skills and possesses the necessary approach to dealing with the many initiatives of the company.

The CIOs continue to work at establishing and expanding their influence with the senior management team and throughout the company. They work with all levels of users to explain the capability of information technology in general and the specific services offered by the information systems department. Further, innovative initiatives are being employed such as ERP systems, business intelligence, and a "war room" approach to decision making in order to attempt to take full advantage of the benefits of information technology.

Future Issues

This section presents the themes which were identified regarding issues that the CIOs expect to deal with in the future.

While this subsection presents a discussion of common themes for the future, there is one unique issue that will prove very interesting. This issue is unique to Taiwan and is similar to the Y2K problem. In 1912, the Republic of China implemented a year numbering system with the number 1 representing 1912. When computers started to be used, this unique year numbering system was incorporated into the information systems that were being developed. Like the Y2K problem, due to space limitations, only 2 digits were set aside for this numbering system. So, in 2011, Taiwan will have its own version of the Y2K problem. While there may be some legacy systems which will have this problem, most systems being developed now have addressed this issue in the design stage.

Management of the Function

One of the internal issues that CIOs plan to deal with in the future relates to establishing performance standards for the information systems function. One approach to developing these standards is to adopt an industry standard. The Software Engineering Institute has developed a large number of capability maturity models for the assessment of performance of a company's information systems function. One such model is the Capability Maturity Model— Integration. This approach provides an independent assessment of the standardized management approach to using information technology within the company.

It is important to have the right skills mix. So, staffing will be an ongoing issue. But, as the company evolves, so to does the necessary information technology skills mix necessary to support the new direction of the business and the revised businesses processes. In the future, the CIOs will find it necessary to develop their own company specific combination of hiring new employees or training existing employees to ensure the acquisition or development of appropriate skills mix. Further, the necessary skills mix will evolve over time as information technology in general changes and new business requirements are identified.

Management of the Company

As the profile of information technology and the CIO rises in the company, there will be more interaction with the external environment. The CIO must be willing and able to deal with suppliers, customers, and regulators. The concept of vendor-managed inventory (VMI) means that the supplier will hold the inventory until the company needs it for the production process. Where the results of an information system directly interface with customers, it becomes very important to identify their requirements and expectations. A good example is the introduction of e-commerce. Thus, Web sites must be able to facilitate, with ease, the interaction of the customer and the company through the appropriate level of sophisticated technology.

As companies expand internationally with the support of information technology, there arises the need to ensure that the company complies with local regulations. This applies not only to dealing with workers and customers, but to the use of data gathered and held within information systems. It is incumbent upon the CIO to ensure the company does not contravene the laws of the country in which they operate.

In the past, the review process for information systems focused on ensuring the functionality was required and delivered in an appropriate manner to the users. It is now more necessary to involve senior management from a governance perspective. That is, the senior management team must be made aware of the ramifications of the decisions they are making regarding the implementation of information systems. Companies and their senior management team may be held legally responsible for the use of erroneous decisions resulting from inadequate information systems. Thus, senior management will have to be involved in reviewing, prioritizing, and approving business cases which propose the development and implementation of information systems.

An overall company approach to addressing the issues surrounding staffing and the skills mix is off-shore outsourcing. A way to attempt to improve the success of off-shore outsourcing is to have a resident information technology person at each location. Thus, if a U.S. company outsourced a development project to India, it would be beneficial to have an Indian speaking coordinator in the US and an English speaking coordinator in India. This approach to coordination will contribute to improved communication and interpretations of requirements and specifications. Further, this approach may also address the inefficiencies caused by wait times resulting from lack of decision making initiatives at either end of the process.

Cost control of information technology is complicated. It is now necessary to justify costs associated with such aspects as software maintenance, network access, and annual maintenance fees. Another aspect about cost control relates to employing information technology to reduce expenditures in other parts of the company. The concept of the lean enterprise means removing waste for business processes. The business manager must be able to understand how information technology can support such efforts.

Technical

People now expect to be able to access information from anywhere and at anytime. Thus, the design of information systems must now take into consideration the ability to provide the service on a mobile device. This desire for mobility is not just an individual preference. There are now business processes that require the ability to support employees who are very mobile. The company, for instance, might want to be able to provide current product information, including pricing, to sales staff while they are in the field.

The opportunity to upgrade equipment occurs when current leases expire. Because technology changes so quickly, this opportunity should be addressed regularly and as frequently as possible. Further, the adoption of current technology will facilitate various infrastructure aspects such as server consolidation, back-up integration, and business continuity planning.

A data warehouse may be employed to support the establishment of the concept of business intelligence. Data must be collected and its integrity validated as it is entered into the data warehouse. Getting the data right is a very critical process if it is to be used to support the business intelligence concept and facilitate decision making by senior management.

Just a few years ago, security was not a large issue. However, now and certainly in the near future security will become very important. With the prevalent use of the Internet it is now necessary to be able to deal with spam and antivirus requirements.

Companies are currently investing in RFID technology. While this technology will provide valuable assistance in dealing with products or small shipments, there is one potential concern about its use. RFID may be employed to keep track of employees or customers. Airlines are considering employing RFID tags in boarding passes. Also, RFID tags may be implanted in employee badges. In both cases, it will be possible to track individuals at all times. This raises the concern for privacy which has yet to be resolved. It is interesting to note that although this technology is available, it is a decision to be made by the company along with employees and, indeed, society in general, about the appropriateness of employing such a technology.

Another issue with the use of RFID tags relates to integration. If a company uses one or more shipping, forwarding, or distribution companies, there will be a necessity to develop and employ a common standard interface among the trading partners throughout the value chain.

Summary: Future Issues

The future entails some exciting times for the CIO. For their business unit, the CIO will be investigating the implementation of standards in the performance of duties. Staffing will continue to be an issue. Finding individuals with the necessary skills and ensuring they retain those necessary skills will require continual vigilance as business requirements evolve. Further, as the CIO is recognized within the company as a full fledged member of the senior management team, there will be more of a requirement to contribute to the overall goals and direction of the company. The contribution to be made by the CIO and the information systems function will be in the appropriate application of technology in support of the company goals. It will still remain the purview of the CIO and the information systems function to be the source for ideas on the application of new technology. Again, it will be incumbent upon this area to show leadership in the appropriate use of any new and emerging technologies.

Conclusion

This chapter discussed the description of the emerging themes from the comments included in the transcripts as presented in the CIO interviews. Initially, some demographic data were presented. Then major issues were discussed. These issues were presented and organized by the major question categories of the interviews. In general, the emerging themes as presented by the major categories related to either management issues or technology issues. The management issues included such aspects as governance, growth and change, supply chain, staff and skills requirements, user relations, project management, and performance evaluation. The technology issues related to system integration, security, data warehouse, and wireless or mobility. Specific applications of radio frequency identification (RFID) were also discussed as one example of the potential application of leading-edge technology.

References

Casey, M.S., & Doverspike, D. (2005). Training needs analysis and evaluation for new technologies through the use of problem-based inquiry. *Performance Improvement Quarterly, 18*(1), 110-124.

Clarke, S., & Doherty, N. (2004). The importance of a strong business-IT relationship for the realisation of benefits in e-business projects: The experience of EGG. *Qualitative Market Research, 7*(1), 58-66.

Fish, K.E., & Seydel, J. (2006). Where IT outsourcing is and where it is going: A study across functions and department sizes. *The Journal of Computer Information Systems, 46*(3), 96-103.

Gillard, S. (2004). IT project management: A conceptual view. *Journal of American Academy of Business, 5* (½), 381-384.

Gowan, J.A., & Mathieu, R. (2005). The importance of management practices in IS project performance. *Journal of Enterprise Information Management, 18*(½), 235-255.

Hayes, D.S. (2000). Evaluation and application of a project charter template to improve the project planning process. *Project Management Journal, 31*(1), 14-23.

Hill, G.M. (2004). Evolving the project management office: A competency continuum. *Information Systems Management, 21*(4), 45-51.

Joshi, K. (2005). Understanding user resistance and acceptance during the implementation of an order management systems: A case study using the equity implementation model. *Journal of Information Technology Case and Application Research, 7*(1), 6-20.

Kanter, J., & Walsh, J.J. (2004). Toward more successful project management. *Information Systems Management, 21*(2), 16-21.

Karimi, J., Bhattacherjee, A., Gupta, Y.P., & Somers, T.M. (2000, Fall). The effects of MIS steering committees on information technology management sophistication. *Journal of Management Information Systems, 17*(2), 207-230.

Martinsons, M.G., & Chong, P.K.C. (1999, January). The influence of human factors and specialist involvement on information systems success. *Human Relations, 52*(1), 123-152.

McKeen, J.D., & Guimaraes, T. (1997, Fall). Successful strategies for user participation in systems development. *Journal of Management Information Systems, 14*(2), 133-150.

Rao, M.T. (2004). Key issues for global IT outsourcing: Country and individual factors. *Information Systems Management, 21*(3), 16-21.

Rathnam, R.G., Johnsen, J., & Wen, H.J. (2005). Alignment of business strategy and IT strategy: A case of a fortune 50 financial services company. *The Journal of Computer Information Systems*, *45*(2), 1-8.

Chapter XXIII

Analyzing CIO Comments

Introduction

This chapter presents an analysis of the comments made by the CIOs. To begin, Mintzberg's (1973) managerial roles framework is introduced and the components are described. The themes identified within each of the major categories of the CIO interviews are then mapped onto the roles described in Mintzberg's (1973) framework. This process supports a discussion of the analysis of the CIO management experiences. Further analysis is presented which attempts to determine if there is any variability of issues across the chronological stages of the CIOs' tenure in their position. This section investigates whether the emphasis of the management experiences might change over time as the CIO gains company specific experience. The next section analyzes the comments from a cultural perspective. The seminal work by Hofstede (1980, 1983, 1993, 2001) is introduced and is then employed to compare the comments of the CIOs representing New Zealand, Taiwan, and the United States of America. The last analysis section included in this chapter reviews the concept of leadership and its impact on the role of the CIO. The final section of the chapter presents some concluding remarks.

Managerial Roles

The data obtained from all the interviews was analyzed in reference to Mintzberg's (1973) framework of managerial roles. The framework was adopted here because it represents a comprehensive approach to analyzing the roles of senior managers. Tsoukas (1994) has suggested that Mintzberg's (1973) framework results from the documentation and analysis of the observable practices of managers. Further, Lamond (2004) suggests that Mintzberg's (1973) framework documents management as it is, which is a reflection of the Argyris and Schon (1974, 1996) *theories in action* vs. *espoused theories*. In a similar vain, the data gathered for this book represents the self-reporting of CIOs of their actions carried out in the performance of their duties. Also, other research (Kmetz & Willower, 1982; Martinko & Gardiner, 1990; Sproull, 1981) has shown that the roles outlined in the framework apply across functional areas and hierarchical levels. This further supports the decision to compare the themes that have emerged from the discussions with CIOs with the roles that form a part of the Mintzberg (1973) framework.

To begin this section, Mintzberg's (1973) framework is described. Next, the themes that have emerged from the interviews are mapped onto the framework. The results of this process are presented organized by relative chronological stages. That is, in the interview the CIO was asked to describe issues that were addressed at three different chronological stages. The CIO described issues which were addressed initially upon taking the role. Then, current issues were described. The third stage included issues the CIO anticipated dealing with in the future. This presentation highlights the CIO management experiences for each stage within the framework and then proffers some conclusions.

Table 1 presents Mintzberg's (1973) framework for managerial roles. The framework includes 10 highly interrelated roles which are grouped into three categories. One category of role is titled "interpersonal". This category relates to the performance of duties of a more ceremonial nature. Thus, while interaction with others is based upon company-related aspects, the emphasis of this category is more of a personal nature. Another category is "informational." Here the manager collects information relative to company performance and subsequently distributes that information to the appropriate stakeholders. Both the collection and dissemination activities may involve internal and external sources and recipients. A third category is "decisional." This category relates to the plethora of aspects related to making decisions. Thus, the manager will search for opportunities, respond to issues, negotiate when necessary, and make or approve decisions resulting from these efforts.

The next subsection describes the process which was employed to map the themes identified in the interviews onto Mintzberg's (1973) framework.

To begin, the data presented in each CIO chapter was reviewed to identify themes. This review focused upon distinguishing those themes relating to issues that arose

Table 1. Mintzberg's managerial roles

Role	Description	Example
Interpersonal		
Figurehead	Symbolic head; required to perform a number of routine duties of a legal or social nature	Ceremonies, status requests, solicitations
Leader	Responsible for the motivation and direction of subordinates	Virtually all managerial activities involving subordinates
Liaison	Maintains a network of outside contacts who provide favors and information	Acknowledgement of mail, external board work
Informational		
Monitor	Receives wide variety of information; serves as nerve centre of internal and external information of the organization	Handling all mail and contacts categorized as concerned primarily with receiving information
Disseminator	Transmits information received from outsiders or from other subordinates to members of the organization	Forwarding mail into organization for informational purposes; verbal contacts involving information flow to subordinates such as review sessions
Spokesperson	Transmits information to outsiders on organization's plans, policies, actions, and results; serves as expert on organization's industry	Board meetings; handling contacts involving transmission of information to outsiders
Decisional		
Entrepreneur	Searches organization and its environment for opportunities and initiates projects to bring about change	Strategy and review sessions involving initiation or design of improvement projects
Disturbance handler	Responsible for corrective action when organization faces important, unexpected disturbances	Strategy and review sessions involving disturbances and crises
Resource allocator	Makes or approves significant organizational decisions	Scheduling; requests for authorization; budgeting; the programming of subordinates' work
Negotiator	Responsible for representing the organization at major negotiations	Contract negotiations

Source: Adapted from Mintzberg (1973).

upon initial appointment of the CIO, those the CIO is currently dealing with, and finally those issues the CIO anticipates having to deal with. Recall that the structure of each interview followed a discussion of issues relating to these three chronological phases. The data for each CIO has been summarized up to the country level for each of the three chronological phases and presented in the following tables.

Note that the data gathered regarding initial issues may be mixed due to the range of duration performing the role of CIO. The range of in-position experience in performing the role of CIO varied from a few months to several years.

The numbers in the above three tables are small and represent the count of the occurrences of the themes that emerged and could be mapped onto the roles of

Mintzberg's (1973) framework. This count represented by the numbers in the tables may be used to represent their relative importance. Note that those roles with low counts or zeroes do not necessarily mean they are unimportant. It simply means they were considered less important than those themes which were discussed more by the CIOs.

Table 2. Initial issues

	Role	NZ	TW	USA	Total
	Interpersonal				
1	**Figurehead**	0	0	0	0
2	**Leader**	6	1	3	10
3	**Liaison**	1	0	0	1
	Informational				
4	**Monitor**	0	0	0	0
5	**Disseminator**	3	1	1	5
6	**Spokesperson**	0	2	0	2
	Decisional				
7	**Entrepreneur**	11	6	13	30
8	**Disturbance handler**	0	0	0	0
9	**Resource allocator**	9	4	8	21
10	**Negotiator**	1	1	0	2

Table 3. Current Issues

	Role	NZ	TW	USA	Total
	Interpersonal				
1	**Figurehead**	0	0	0	0
2	**Leader**	2	0	5	7
3	**Liaison**	1	0	0	1
	Informational				
4	**Monitor**	0	0	0	0
5	**Disseminator**	0	3	1	4
6	**Spokesperson**	0	0	0	0
	Decisional				
7	**Entrepreneur**	20	10	9	39
8	**Disturbance handler**	0	0	0	0
9	**Resource allocator**	6	4	6	16
10	**Negotiator**	3	2	0	5

Table 4. Future Issues

	Role	NZ	TW	USA	Total
	Interpersonal				
1	**Figurehead**	0	0	0	0
2	**Leader**	1	2	3	6
3	**Liaison**	0	0	0	0
	Informational				
4	**Monitor**	0	0	0	0
5	**Disseminator**	1	0	1	2
6	**Spokesperson**	0	0	0	0
	Decisional				
7	**Entrepreneur**	14	11	8	33
8	**Disturbance handler**	0	0	0	0
9	**Resource allocator**	5	0	10	15
10	**Negotiator**	1	1	0	2

The more prevalent themes that were identified relate to Mintzberg's (1973) roles of Leader, Resource Allocator, and Entrepreneur. In order to provide some elucidation of these roles as described by the CIOs, some of the specific aspects mentioned by the CIOs are listed below.

Leader

- Respond to demoralized staff by creating a positive environment
- Establish a business focus
- Establish guidelines to measure and improve performance
- Form a steering committee to encourage the concept of governance on the part of senior management

Resource Allocator

- Provide funding for staff recruiting, skill set development, and retention
- Establish standardized mechanisms to identify cost items and to determine priorities for resource allocation
- Develop an organization structure to support carrying out assigned unit activities

Entrepreneur

- Investigate the adoption of new technology
  - Mobility
  - VOIP
  - Robotics
  - E-commerce
  - E-learning
- Adopt innovative processes
  - Paperless office
  - Business continuity planning
  - ERP
  - Help Desk
  - Scalability for growth and acquisitions
  - ITIL
  - Vendor Managed Inventory

Stephens (1993) employed Mintzberg's framework and coding scheme to observe five CIOs. The findings of this research are that the roles of Resource Allocator and Entrepreneur are where the most time was consumed by CIOs in the performance of their duties during the observation period. While there is no standard guideline for the allocation of time to specific CIO roles, the Stephens (1993) results show a level of relative importance to these two roles. This finding is supported, in general terms, by the data presented above.

The following paragraphs describe research projects which have employed Mintzberg's (1973) framework to analyze the activities of CIOs. The first series of paragraphs discuss the data relative to the chronological stages of the CIOs in their positions. Then, aspects related to the culture of the CIOs and the findings of the interviews conducted for this book are reviewed.

Stages

The above tables may also be employed to present the profiles that emerge when the themes identified in the interviews are mapped onto Mintzberg's (1973) framework. Recall that the profiles are organized in Tables 2, 3, and 4 by the CIOs' comments regarding initial, current, and future issues. As the CIOs gain more management experience in performing the duties of their position, and as the CIOs establish a reputation throughout the organization, it would be expected that the emphasis of the roles would change. That is, as the importance of a role is elevated within the organization and it matures, it would be expected that the focus of the role would change. However, the data presented in Tables 2, 3, and 4 show that the emphasis across the three chronological stages has not changed. This result may be explained by reviewing some previous investigations and relating those conclusions to the results of the interviews conducted for this book.

Grover, Jeong, Kettinger, & Lee (1993) also employed Mintzberg's framework to investigate the perceived role of the CIO. They employed a proven survey instrument where CIOs (71 responses) and information systems managers (40 responses) were asked to rate the importance of certain items outlined by Mintzberg's framework. Their study investigated three aspects related to the management experiences of the CIO. These aspects are as follows:

- How the CIO roles differ from other senior managers
    - The conclusion here was that the unique aspects of information systems influenced to some degree the role played by the CIO. In terms of relative importance of managerial roles, the CIO was different from those managers responsible for manufacturing and sales. However, the CIO role was similar to that of the senior financial manager. Grover et al. (1993) suggest this similarity is the result of the common historical information support function played by both of these positions.
- How the CIO roles differ from other lower level information systems managers
    - Both similarities and differences were determined for the investigation of this aspect. In general, similarities occurred where the lower level managers were playing a support role for the CIO. The differences were identified with regard to those activities related to organizational level. That is, the lower level managers took a more internal perspective because they focused on the daily operations of the department. The CIO, however, adopted more of an external perspective because of the requirement to deal with other parts of the organization and external entities.
- The effect on the CIO roles of the maturity and centralization of the information systems function
    - The emphasis of the CIO role changes relative to both maturity and centralization. With maturity the end user takes on more of the activities of the information systems department. Thus, the CIO takes on more of a strategic leadership role. Similarly, with more centralization, the CIO is able to take a more environmentally interactive role.

In their investigations Grover et al. (1993) reported that CIOs rated the "entrepreneur" role as the most important. The investigation reported in this book also found that the CIOs continue to consider this role to be important. Across the three chronological issues stages the managerial role of "entrepreneur" remains relatively important. That is, the CIO will continue to investigate opportunities to improve business operations which inevitably result in change.

Another conclusion by Grover et al. (1993) relates to the relatively low ranks for the role of "liaison" and "monitor." At the time of the Grover et al. (1993) study, it was suggested that this result is because of less of an emphasis being placed on environmental scanning and interorganizational relationships. Based on the interviews included in this book, these roles continue to be considered relatively less important.

A further comment by Grover et al. (1993) concerns maturity of the organization regarding the use of information technology. They suggest that as the organization matures the end users take on more of the activities of the information systems department. This suggests that the role of the CIO is influenced by the environment in the overall organization. This is supported by the research above (Grover et al., 1993; Pearson & Chaterjee, 2003).

Grover et al. (1993) then conclude that, "… the roles of the CIO are contingent on organizational and environmental variables…" (Grover et al., 1993, p. 19).

Gilbert, Pick, & Ward (1999) identified a series of issues considered important by a sample of CIOs. Their analysis identified three underlying factors directing the performance of the CIO. These factors include "leadership," "advocacy," and "software." It is possible to map these three factors onto specific roles identified by Mintzberg (1973). So, the Gilbert et al. (1999) "leadership" factor maps directly into Mintzberg's (1973) leadership role. Both of the Gilbert et al. (1999) roles of "advocacy" and "software" map into Mintzberg's (1973) Entrepreneur role. This result provides further support for the conclusions presented in this book.

Further, Dearstyne (2006) commented on the relationship between CIOs and managers of a major functional area of records and information management professionals. Dearstyne (2006) suggests, "… CIOs used to be primarily IT experts and managers; now they are called on to be leaders, managers, and entrepreneurs" (Dearstyne, 2006, p. 46). Dearstyne (2006) also suggests that CIOs strategies for success should include strategies related to "leadership," "understanding the organization," and "managing expectations." The first item in this list has been discussed above. The second and third items relate to the discussion about the CIOs carrying out their roles within and influenced by the organization context and in direct interaction with the CEO to whom they report.

In summary, the emphasis of the management experiences across the chronological stages is relatively consistent. This is a reflection of the CIOs adopting strategies that are consistent with the organization's culture and that coincide with senior management expectations. This cultural aspect is discussed in the following section.

Culture

Based upon the numbers in Tables 2, 3, and 4, there does not seem to be any variability in the emphasis of the roles when different cultures are taken into consideration. In general, because of cultural differences, variability should be expected. In Hofstede's (1980 & 2001) research, cultural variability was identified based upon five dimensions, as defined in Table 5.

Table 5. Hofstede's dimensions of national culture

Dimension	Description
Individualism/Collectivism (IC)	Individualistic societies expect people to be independent and look after themselves. Collectivist societies consist of a tightly knit framework of mutual dependencies and obligations.
Power Distance (PD)	High Power Distance societies accept unequal distribution of power within society. Low Power Distance societies strive for power equalization and participation.
Uncertainty Avoidance (UA)	Strong Uncertainty Avoidance cultures control uncertainty by strict rules and codes of behaviour. Weak Uncertainty Avoidance cultures are not as strictly controlled and deviance is more accepted.
Masculinity/Femininity (MF)	Masculine cultures emphasize achievement, success, and assertiveness. Feminine cultures emphasize caring, close relationships, and harmony.
Long/Short Term Orientation (LS)	Long Term Orientation cultures focus on building relationships. Short Term Orientation cultures focus on immediate results.

Table 6. Cultural dimensions indexes

Country	Cultural Dimensions				
	IC	PD	UA	MF	LS
New Zealand	79	22	49	58	30
Taiwan	17	58	69	45	87
United States	91	40	46	62	29

Based on these five dimensions, Hofstede (1980, 2001) proposed that it is possible to distinguish cultures.

Table 6 shows the values for these dimensions for the cultures involved in this book.

For the most part, New Zealand and the United States are similar across the cultural dimensions. The Taiwan culture tends to be either higher or lower on all dimensions. So, it would be expected that while New Zealand and the United States would have similar cultures, that of Taiwan would be different.

A general conclusion was reached by Grover et al. (1993) that how the roles played by the CIOs are dependent upon the specific organization and its environment. This conclusion is supported by the following investigation and the work by Hofstede (1980, 1983, 1993). Pearson and Chatterjee (2003) support this conclusion. They investigated the relevance of Mintzberg's framework to general managers in the Asian culture. While their findings identified the same roles as the framework, the operationalization of these roles was carried out in a manner more reflective of the specific culture and contextual nuances of specific local practices. However, the specific management practices may vary depending upon the culture. In relation to Mintzberg's framework, then, while the roles may be the same, how the roles are performed may be influenced by such environmental aspects as culture.

Research related to the information systems profession has attempted to address this issue of cultural variability. Hunter and Beck (1996) investigated cultural variability of how information systems professionals are perceived. They compared perceptions held by business professionals in Canada and Singapore. They concluded that there was evidence for both convergence and divergence for this perception. The convergence perspective was supported by the common education and training of information systems professionals. The divergence perspective suggested there was a difference in how the roles were played which represented a reflection of the culture. These results have subsequently been supported by more recent investigations (Pearson & Chatterjee, 2003; Pearson, Chatterjee, & Okachi, 2003) which have identified commonality of the Mintzberg (1973) roles, but variability in how the roles were carried out. Thus, the roles are similar and consistent with those identified by Mintzberg (1973). However, the way the roles are performed may be culturally dependent. In the research by Hunter and Beck (1996), the information systems professionals in Canada were viewed as "coach," while in Singapore they were regarded as an "expert." An example from the CIO interviews provides support. For instance, in Taiwan one of the CIOs indicated that the IT area provided leadership, expertise, and direction (expert) for the company. In New Zealand, however, the comment was more about how the IT area must attempt to work with (coach) the users.

Thus, organization culture, as a reflection of societal culture, will to a large extent influence how a role is played. However, as shown in the above discussion, the role itself, as depicted by Mintzberg's (1973) framework, will remain consistent. Further, the CIO role will be influenced by senior management expectations. Thus, it is incumbent upon the CIOs to assess and manage how their peers interpret the deployment of information technology within the organization. This last comment relates to the concept of leadership which is presented in the next section.

Leadership

Leadership involves the interaction between at least two people where one individual influences the behaviour of the other(s). A leader establishes goals and then strives to ensure the followers understand the goals, are committed to reaching the goals, and are adequately performing the necessary tasks to accomplish the goals. So, what does this mean for the CIO? The answer to this question should be addressed from two perspectives, unit and corporate.

The unit refers to the business area over which the CIO has direct control and responsibility. This unit includes such functions as information systems development and maintenance, hardware acquisition and operation, and telecommunications. Individuals within the unit who perform the duties related to these functions report directly to the CIO in a subordinate relationship. In this situation, the CIO performs the traditional leadership role as outlined above.

Aspects of leadership of the business unit gleaned from the CIO comments include the following:

- Hiring and training to develop the appropriate skills mix
- Skill set alignment with the current requirements of the company
- Development of soft skills such as communication or working as a team member
- Acquisition of technical skills related to the functions of the business unit
- Establish performance standards
- Implement procedures to celebrate performance

The corporate perspective on the CIOs leadership role is more complex. While the CIO represents the unit and provides the necessary technical expertise at the corporate level, a subordinate relationship does not exist. When working with other members of the senior management team, the CIO will be dealing with peers. Further, when working with users (subordinates of the CIO's peers) there will be even further distance involved in this working relationship. Also, in both cases the CIO may possess more technical knowledge than the other individual and perhaps less business knowledge. Thus, the CIO will be in the difficult position of explaining a technical response to a business situation where both parties are not fully cognizant of the others domain of knowledge.

For the most part, the CIOs included in this book have taken a contingency approach to this situation. In some instances, the CIO has had the benefit of having worked within the company in another capacity for some period of time. This management experience has provided valuable exposure to the business processes and knowledge of the specific company. Alternatively, CIOs with relatively little company experience have had to work at developing a corporate level reputation and trusting relationship. An approach adopted by many of the CIOs in this situation has been to work with individuals on a one-to-one basis. Each has been able to get to know the other and this interaction has facilitated the development of a positive relationship.

Conclusion

This chapter has analyzed the CIO comments about their role from different perspectives. Analysis of the emerging themes was based upon Mintzberg's (1973) managerial roles framework. Some differences were noted in comparison to earlier investigations of CIO management experiences. Further, role differences emerged based upon the chronological stage of the CIO position. The cultural perspective did not determine as much variability as would have been expected. This result is perhaps based on the level of western culture education and training that is found related to the use of information technology. Finally, the concept of leadership was employed as a lens to view the results. The difficult aspect of leadership for the CIO is not relative to subordinates, but more associated with peers and their subordinates.

References

Argyris, C., & Schon, D.A. (1974). *Theory in practice: Increasing professional effectiveness.* San Fransisco, CA: Josey-Bass.

Argyris, C., & Schon, D.A. (1996). *Organizational learning II: Theory, method, and practice.* Reading, MA: Addison-Wesley.

Dearstyne, B.W. (2006, January-February). CIOs: Information program leaders in transition. *Information Management Journal, 40*(1), 44-50.

Gilbert, A.H., Jr., Pick, R.A., & Ward, S.G. (1999). The role of the CIO: Enduring MIS issues. *The Journal of Computer Information Systems, 40*(1), 8-16.

Grover, V., Jeong, S., Kettinger, W., & Lee, C.C. (1993). The chief information officer: A study of managerial roles. *Journal of Management Information Systems, 10*(2), 107-131.

Hofstede, G. (1980). *Culture's consequences: International differences in work-related values*. Beverley Hills, CA: Sage Publications.

Hofstede, G. (1983, Fall). The cultural relativity of organizational practices and theories. *Journal of International Business Studies*, 75-89.

Hofstede, G. (1993). Cultural constraints in management theories. *Academy of Management Executive, 7*, 81-94.

Hofstede, G. (2001). *Culture's consequences: Comparing values, behaviors, institutions and organizations across nations.* Thousand Oaks, CA: Sage Publications.

Hunter, M.G., & Beck, J.E. (1996). A cross-cultural comparison of "excellent" systems analysts. *Information Systems Journal, 6*, 261-281.

Kmetz, J.T., & Willower, D.J. (1982). Elementary school principals' work behavior. *Educational Administrative Quarterly, 18*, 62-78.

Lamond, D. (2004). A matter of style: Reconciling Henri and Henry. *Management Decision, 42*(½), 330-356.

Martinko, M.J., & Gardner, W.L. (1990, May). Structured observation of managerial work: A replication and synthesis. *Journal of Management Studies, 27*(3), 329-357.

Mintzberg, H. (1973). *The nature of managerial work.* New York: Harper and Row.

Pearson, C.A.L., & Chaterjee, S.R. (2003). Managerial work roles in Asia: An empirical study of Mintzberg's role formulation in four Asian countries. *Journal of Management Development, 22*(7/8), 694-707.

Pearson, C.A.L., Chaterjee, S.R., & Okachi, K. (2003, March). Managerial work role perceptions in Japanese organizations: An empirical study. *International Journal of Management, 20*(1), 101-108.

Sproull, L.S. (1981). Managing education programs: A micro-behavioral analysis. *Human Organization, 40*(2), 113-122.

Stephens, C.S. (1993). Five CIOs at work: Folklore and facts revisited. *Journal of Systems Management, 44*(3), 34-42.

Tsoukas, H. (1994). What is management? An outline of a metatheory. *British Journal of Management, 5*, 289-301.

Chapter XXIV

Final CIO Comments

Introduction

This chapter presents an overview of the final comments made by the CIOs. At the end of each interview the CIO was asked to provide an overall comment from a general perspective about how they interpret their role within the context of their company. The CIO also provided their perspective about their management experiences. These interpretive comments are divided into three main categories. The first category presented here includes comments about the internal operations of the CIO's business unit. The second category relates to the CIO's interpretation of how the information systems business unit should relate to the corporate user community. The third category discusses how the CIOs view their role in relation to senior management. A brief conclusion section ends this chapter.

Capella (2006) found that CIOs have only 100 days to prove their worth to an organization, and that the CIO position experiences an annual turnover rate double that of CFOs and CEOs. The following list might not be critical to the success of a CIO performing their assigned roles, but the items, as explained in the rest of this chapter, will most certainly contribute to performing the role in the most advantageous way for the overall benefit of the company.

- Information Systems Department
  - Staff
  - Work environment
  - Training
  - Retention
  - Communication

- User Relations
  - Change Management
  - Understand the business
  - Speak the user's language
  - Be patient

- Senior Management
  - Relationships
  - Manage expectations
  - Alignment with CEO
  - Understand the business
  - Communicate

Information Systems Department

For the most part, the CIOs had, early in their tenure, responded to such aspects as organization structure and the establishment of standards. In light of these aspects the CIOs either inherited an existing structure or previously implemented standards, or were presented with the opportunity to establish both organization structures and standards as part of their initial initiatives as CIO. Within the information systems department, the CIOs thought their major contribution would be made to support their staff to facilitate them in responding to user requests and to carry out their tasks related to responding to the users.

So, the emphasis was on staff. One aspect of this issue was work environment. While some CIOs commented that they wanted their staff to have fun, others settled for creating an enjoyable atmosphere at the workplace. Beyond the specific required work tasks, many CIOs encouraged social or sporting interaction among staff members. These events were meant to relieve stress and to create a sense of team which would facilitate work efforts.

Another staff focus was on training. It is incumbent upon everyone involved in information technology to ensure their skill sets remain current. In order to employ current state-of-the-art technology, it is necessary to possess the knowledge and skills about the use of the technology. Further, as companies evolve, so also do the necessary skill sets required to adopt technology to support this evolution. It is not enough to have a current skill set. Indeed, it is necessary to have the appropriate skill set which is aligned with the current information technology needs of the company.

Staff retention was also an issue that several CIOs were attempting to deal with. While financial rewards were one consideration for responding to this issue, it seemed that other aspects were considered more important. These other aspects were related to the environment and training, as discussed above. It was also incumbent upon the CIO to develop in individuals a sense of commitment. As individuals and their respective level of commitment are unique, the CIO requires advanced interpersonal skills to address the staff retention issue.

The CIOs further identified that communication within their business unit was very important. The form of the communication could be either formal, such as a regular business unit newsletter, or informal, such as e-mail or even frequent hallway chats. The CIOs felt their staff should be fully aware of any corporate level plans in order not only to know the future direction of the company but also how this future direction may be facilitated by the efforts of those individuals within the information systems unit. Further, the CIOs interviewed wanted to stimulate communication among their staff members. Thus, regular staff or project-related meetings were arranged to promote discussion of the aspects of various active development projects.

User Relations

The CIOs were cognizant that their involvement with users usually meant that a change would result in the users' environment or processes. This requires the CIO and staff to fully understand the aspects of change management and how individuals may react differently to change. If the information systems professionals were going to be involved in the revision of business processes, it would be beneficial if they were regarded by the users' community as relative experts in both the specific business as well as how information technology may be employed to facilitate change. So, in dealing with users, it was considered important to speak the user-oriented business language. If there was to be a discussion of technology, it must be kept relevant to the business and the language of the users. Overall, it was incumbent upon the CIO and the information systems staff to be patient with the users. Change takes time, especially for those who are unfamiliar with information technology and how it will change their tasks and environment.

Senior Management

Perhaps the most important comment garnered from the interviews from a general overall perspective was the relationship between the CIO and senior management. The CIO must be able to manage the expectations of other senior managers regarding the capability of information technology and the services available from the CIO's work unit. Tai and Phelps (2000) investigated the relationship between the perceptions held by CEOs and CIOs of the information systems strategy. One of their findings suggests the necessity for the convergence of perceptions in order for the company to obtain the most benefit from the application of information technology resources.

Another aspect of the relationship between the CIO and senior management related to the alignment (Reich & Benbasat, 2000; Seddon, Graeser, & Willcocks, 2002) of the interpretation of the individual role and the corporate expectations, as expressed by the chief executive officer (CEO). This alignment may be expressed as follows. The management of the corporate information technology resource may be viewed from two perspectives. These perspectives may, in general, be referred to using the titles chief technology officer (CTO) and chief information officer (CIO). The CTO will focus on the management of current operations with an emphasis on efficiency. That is, given the existing information technology resources, how can these resources best be employed to support the company in the near term? The other perspective is represented by the CIO, whose focus will be more on effectiveness. The CIO will look beyond the present information technology resource base with a view to employing information technology in an innovative way to facilitate future initiatives of the company. Thus, the CTO involves the management of programs within an established vision and evaluating performance of staff relative to established metrics. The CIO will display leadership by being involved with senior management in creating the vision and inspiring staff.

Both of these functions, CIO and CTO, are important. What is more important is the alignment or agreement between the CEO and the CIO that the role will involve those aspects associated with a CIO role or a CTO role. Interpretations by both the CIO and the CEO must be clear and explicit. Oren (1995) suggests that successful managers must ensure they accurately interpret the perception of their role. Further, Potter (2003) suggests that CIOs must be able to manage the expectations of their supervisors. With regard to the relationship between the CIO and CEO, Potter (2003) suggests that trust between the two individuals is the most important aspect of the relationship. The establishment of trust takes a long time. If the CEO is not familiar with the capabilities of information technology, it is incumbent upon the CIO to provide the necessary education. While this process will go a long way toward providing enlightenment and reduce the probability of the CEO having overoptimistic expectations, it will also contribute to the development of trust between the two individuals.

The CIO has to demonstrate a very good understanding of the business. Indeed, it seems more important than the CIO possess stronger business knowledge that information technology knowledge. That does not mean that information technology is considered unimportant at the senior management level. The CIO must be able to clearly demonstrate how the application of information technology can support the goals and objectives of the company.

Finally, the CIO must be a good communicator with senior management. As presented above, the CIO must possess advanced interpersonal skills and be able to interact with each individual in the appropriate manner. They have to be able to explain how the business and senior management will obtain what they expect from information technology.

Conclusion

This chapter presented a review of the categories which emerged from the final comments made by each CIO at the end of their respective interviews. The categories which emerged relate to the CIO management experiences relative to internal operations, relationships with the corporate user community, and interacting with senior management. In all of these cases, it was recognized that it was important for the CIO to present a positive image in the establishment of an agreed upon role. It was also important to establish as early as possible a reputation for meeting with success in the application of information technology in support of the overall company goals and objectives.

Each CIO seemed to really enjoy what they were doing. There was excitement in their voice when they described how their role was unfolding and how recognition was emerging for their contribution to the company goals and objectives. They are the types of individuals who like the challenge of identifying and understanding an issue, and overseeing its resolution. Finally, ever the optimists, they look forward with anticipation to a future where new technology may be employed in a novel way to benefit their company.

References

Capella, J. (2006). The CIOs first 100 days. *Optimize*, *5*(3), 46-51.

Oren, H. (1995). The successful manager in the new business world. *Management Review*, *84*(4), 10-12.

Potter, R.E. (2003). How CIOs manage their superiors' expectations. *Communications of the ACM*, *46*(8), 75-79.

Reich, B.H., & Benbasat, I. (2000). Factors that influence the social dimensions of alignment between business and information technology objectives. *24*(1), 81-113.

Seddon, P.B., Graeser, V., & Willcocks, L.P. (2002). Measuring organizational IS effectiveness: An overview and update of senior management perspectives. *33*(2), 11-28.

Tai, L.A., & Phelps, R. (2000). CEO and CIO perceptions of information systems strategy: Evidence from Hong Kong. *European Journal of Information Systems*, *9*, 163-172.

About the Author

M. Gordon Hunter is a professor of information systems in the Faculty of Management at The University of Lethbridge, Alberta, Canada. Hunter has previously held academic positions at universities in Canada, Singapore, and Hong Kong. He has held visiting positions at universities in Australia, Monaco, Germany, New Zealand, and the U.S. In July and August of 2005, Hunter was a visiting Erskine fellow at the University of Canterbury, Christchurch, New Zealand. He has a Bachelor of Commerce from the University of Saskatchewan in Saskatoon, Saskatchewan, Canada and a doctorate from Strathclyde Business School, University of Strathclyde in Glasgow, Scotland. He has also earned a Certified Management Accountant (CMA) designation from the Society of Management Accountants of Canada. He is a member of the British Computer Society and the Canadian Information Processing Society (CIPS), where he has obtained an Information Systems Professional (ISP) designation. Hunter chairs the executive board of The Information Institute, an information policy research organization. He has extensive experience as a systems analyst and manager in industry and government organizations in Canada. Hunter is an associate editor of the *Journal of Global Information Management*. He is the Canadian World Representative for the Information Resource Management Association. He serves on the editorial board of *Information and Management, International Journal of e-Collaboration, Journal of Global Information Technology Management*, and *Journal of Information Technology Cases and Applications*. Hunter is also a member of the advisory board for *The Journal of Information, Information Technology, and Organizations*. He has published articles in *MIS Quarterly, Information Systems Research, The Journal of Strategic Information Systems, The Journal of Global Information Management, Information Systems Journal,* and *Information, Technology and People*. He has conducted seminar presentations in Canada, the U.S., Europe, Hong Kong, Singapore, Taiwan, New Zealand, and Australia. Hunter's current research interests relate to the productivity of systems analysts with emphasis upon the personnel component including cross-cultural aspects, the use of information systems by small business, the role of chief information officers, and the effective development and implementation of cross functional information systems.

Index